The Good Ship

The Good Ship

SHIPS, SHIPBUILDING AND TECHNOLOGY IN ENGLAND
1200–1520

IAN FRIEL

British Museum Press

© 1995 Ian Friel

Published by British Museum Press
A division of British Museum Publications
46 Bloomsbury Street, London WC1B 3QQ

British Library Cataloguing in Publication Data
A catalogue record for this book is available from
the British Library

ISBN 0 7141 0574 0

Line drawings by Lynne Friel
Designed by Behram Kapadia
Typeset by Create Publishing Services, Avon
Printed in Great Britain by The Bath Press, Avon

Front jacket: Two ships in combat, from an English manuscript
of *c.* 1271. See Fig. 8.1.
Back jacket: A gun-armed four-master of *c.* 1485,
in the Warwick Roll. See Fig. 8.7.
Frontispiece: Three-masted carrack in an Italian engraving, *c.* 1470–80.
See Fig. 9.7.

Contents

For Lynne, Helen and David

Your great ship the Grace Dieu is ever as ready and is the fairest that ever men saw ...

Humphrey, Duke of Gloucester, to Henry v, 1420
(Public Record Office, London)

Hale how and rumbylowe,
Steer well the good ship and let the wind blow

Red Book of Bristol, 15th century

O see how well our good ship sails

The Pilgrims' Sea Voyage, 15th century

Preface and acknowledgements

My involvement with the study of medieval ships began in 1977 with what was supposed to be a one-year appointment on a special project at the National Maritime Museum in Greewich. The post eventually became permanent, as did my interest in the maritime history of the Middle Ages. My work in the field was greatly furthered by the help and encouragement of my colleagues Alan Pearsall and Pieter van der Merwe, who made my introduction to the study of maritime history both interesting and enjoyable. I must also record my thanks to the then Director, Dr Basil Greenhill, who originated the project, and to Professor Sean McGrail, who fostered further research into medieval maritime history when I later transferred to the museum's Archaeological Research Centre, and to the Director and Trustees of the National Maritime Museum for allowing me continued access to in-house research materials in the years 1988–90.

This book has grown in part out of the doctoral thesis, completed in 1990, and I wish to thank my supervisor, Professor Colin Richmond, for his support in what proved to be a rather longer 'voyage' than even a medieval mariner would have contemplated.

Thanks are also due to my editor at British Museum Press, Carolyn Jones, for her help and encouragement in seeing this project through to publication.

It is common for the married writer of an academic work to offer thanks to his or her spouse for their invaluable help, and this writer is no exception. My wife, Lynne Friel, has drawn the maps and other line illustrations, and has helped with the book in a thousand other ways. More than that, she and our children have had to live with the waters of ancient seas lapping at our front door for longer than any of us would care to remember! For that, and other reasons, this book is dedicated to them.

Ian Friel
Littlehampton, West Sussex
January 1994

Introduction

The history of maritime technology is sometimes considered as a separate field from the history of other human technological developments. For example, one study of ancient technology has much to say about the inventiveness of medieval people in areas such as wind- and water-power, but fails even to mention ships. Other historians have attempted to cross the cultural divide and consider the technology of ships in the context of other technological achievements, but, for the medieval period at least, the evidence is seldom easy to interpret and has not always been well understood. A further obstacle is the often confusing terminology associated with maritime matters; anyone who has heard a maritime scholar use the expression 'I hadn't quite hoisted that in' to mean 'I hadn't quite understood that' will be aware of this problem! Yet maritime societies and ships have always existed to serve the interests of land-based peoples, whether in trade, warfare, exploration, colonisation or some other field, and changes in maritime technology are affected by more general economic, technological and other changes.

The history of the medieval ship is often presented as no more than a prologue to the European voyages of exploration and colonisation from the fifteenth century onwards, and in one sense this is appropriate. The three-masted, skeleton-built ship that developed in the fifteenth century was the product of changes in maritime technology during the preceding two centuries and more, and it was this type of ship, grandly described as 'the space capsule of the Renaissance', that became the vehicle of overseas expansion. Unlike twentieth-century space projects, however, the development of this new type of ship was apparently never fostered by any state or other agency with the aim of exploring and conquering the world. It evolved because it was more manoeuvrable and durable than other kinds, and subsequently proved to be of use on oceanic voyages.

It is debatable whether or not those voyages would have taken place without the new type of ship. The Vikings were able to establish a presence in Greenland and North America in the tenth and eleventh centuries, using single-masted, square-sailed ships with clinker-built hulls. The small Greenland colonies maintained links with the Scandinavian homelands until the fifteenth century, with ships that were probably little different from those of the Vikings. The general poverty of the northern lands in the Middle Ages meant that no great fleets were available to re-supply the Greenland settlements with people and goods in the way that Spain and Portugal were later able to maintain their overseas colonies. Nevertheless it would not have been impossible for Columbus and his successors to cross the Atlantic using single-masted, square-rigged, clinker-built ships. The mixture of curiosity, adventurism, greed, religious fervour and other impulses that drove the early oceanic voyages was stronger than technology, and the impact of not having a better type of ship would have been felt not so much in terms of getting 'there and back again', to explore and to establish small settlements, as in terms of how many ships survived the voyages that followed. The casualty rate on oceanic voyages was high, and if Spain, Portugal and other European countries had been able to support and exploit their overseas possessions only on the level of the Scandinavian Greenland settlements, the history of the world since the fifteenth century would have been very different.

This study examines the development of shipbuilding in medieval England, placing it in the contexts of northern Europe and also the Mediterranean. It begins at the nominal date of 1200 because it was the early thirteenth century that saw King John's loss of Normandy (1204) and the sundering of the Anglo-Norman 'cross-Channel' state. The Norman coastline became a hostile frontier, a fact that had a considerable effect on English maritime history. John had to create a new navy to meet the threat of war from France, and also to enable the English to fight the French. The point at which this work ends, 1520, had just seen another naval 'revival', by Henry VIII, and was within a couple of years of witnessing yet another war with France – a series of cross-Channel conflicts that would later be brought to a temporary end by the rise of Spanish power. In 1200, the typical English ship was clinker-built (see p. 69) and had a single mast, a distinctively medieval form. By 1520, the average seagoing English vessel was skeleton-built and multi-masted, a true 'post-medieval' type. This book attempts to chart how, and why, these changes came about.

The English shipbuilding and shipping industries of the period 1200 to 1520 do not seem to have been strong in terms of the numbers of ships that they produced or used, but there is no sign that they were technologically inferior to the industries of other northern European countries. Developments in English shipping were generally part-and-parcel of developments in northern European shipping, and one reason for studying the English evidence is that it throws more light on the wider picture. The maritime industries, by their very nature, were more subject to changing international trends than many other areas of life. English shipwrights and mariners proved themselves able to build and rig some of the largest and most powerful ships north of the Mediterranean, and they may even have been responsible for such inventions of the period as the square-rigged foremast, the shipboard suction-pump and the dry-dock.

England often had a strong navy between the thirteenth and sixteenth centuries, able to project English military force on to the Continent and to defend the English coast. It is significant that throughout the Hundred Years War, the French were never able to invade England, despite many devastating raids, and the same was to prove true in the time of Henry VIII. The English merchant marine was weaker, in numerical terms, than those of some other states, and the shipbuilding industry does not seem to have been large. Both the shipping and shipbuilding industries, however, remained strong in terms of their technical abilities, providing a firm basis for the expansion of English maritime power that began in the late sixteenth century.

In medieval sources the phrase 'the good ship' signifies a number of things. Often it was merely a conventional statement, intended to show that a ship was in good condition, or well built, but in some circumstances it carried a special sense of approbation, suggesting that a certain ship embodied some quality of goodness by reason of its design, size or sailing abilities. The 'good ship' could bring wealth to some, by means of trade, but used in war or piracy it could bring death and disaster. Despite technological improvements that made ships more efficient, life for mariners of the sixteenth century remained as hard and dangerous as it had been for their forebears of the thirteenth century. The development of the oceanic sailing ship in the fifteenth century, however, meant that, for European seafarers, the 'good ship' took on a new form and the evolution of this new form is part of the wider picture illuminated by the study of changes in English shipping and shipbuilding technology over the course of the medieval period.

CHAPTER 1

Evidence

In September 1474 the Milanese ambassador in Paris sent a letter to his master, the Duke of Milan. He reported on information received by the French king about the threatened invasion by the King of England, Edward IV. The English naval build-up included the preparation of an old ship, to which the English 'in their superstition ... attach great importance and esteem, saying or pretending that it is the ship upon which St Thomas of Canterbury crossed to England, and for this it has I know not what charm'. Thomas à Becket's famous return to England had taken place just over 300 years earlier, in 1170 (see Figs 1.1 and 1.5), but even in an age of religious relics, to say that this was the same ship was clearly stretching credulity a bit far. The ship in question was probably the king's great ship *Grace Dieu*, which in fifteenth-century terms was an old vessel, built about thirty-five years earlier.[1]

Maritime history in the Middle Ages was little more than a string of chronicle accounts of battles evincing royal or national prowess. In fact, the 'famous battles' school of maritime history persisted well into the nineteenth century, and still has its adherents today. It was in the mid-1800s that scholars first began to pay serious attention to the documentary sources for medieval shipping. Pre-eminent among these was the French historian Auguste Jal (1795–1875), with his two works *Archeologie navale* (1840) and his remarkable international maritime dictionary *Glossaire nautique* (1848).[2] Jal's British contemporary, Sir Nicholas Harris Nicolas, published two medieval volumes of what was projected to be a much longer *History of the Royal Navy* in 1847, but the series was cut short by his death. Nicolas's work was heavily based on chronicles and public records, and gave the first scholarly account of English naval history to 1422. Both scholars' pioneering efforts remain of value.

Later nineteenth-century work tended to concentrate on naval history, the history of merchant shipping often only featuring when it had

1.1 A 'hulk-type' vessel, redrawn from an early thirteenth-century English manuscript (after Warren 1977), depicting Thomas a Becket's return from France in 1170.

some connection with the activities of royal fleets. Some historians, however, such as Michael Oppenheim, began to attempt to place medieval naval history within its economic and technological context.[3] The historical development of ships was one of the major concerns of the British Society for Nautical Research, which first published its journal, *Mariner's Mirror*, in 1911; its run of seventy-nine volumes (to date) is a major source for world maritime history.

The sources relating to medieval and early sixteenth-century ships can be divided into three broad categories: documentary material, pictorial representations and archaeological finds. This book will concentrate on the first two areas of study, with reference to archaeological material where appropriate. Each type of evidence has its own special strengths and weaknesses. The aim of this chapter is to try to outline some of the possibilities and problems in using the various sources, as these underpin the interpretation of the evidence in the succeeding chapters.

DOCUMENTARY EVIDENCE

The best written sources for the technological history of ships in medieval England are inventories and financial accounts. Few shipbuilding treatises survive from the Middle Ages; all date from the fifteenth century, and all of them are Italian (specifically Venetian). The earliest detailed English treatise on ship design is by the Elizabethan master shipwright Matthew Baker, compiled in about 1586.[4] Similarly, while some detailed shipbuilding specifications are known from medieval Italy and Spain, they are rare in English sources: only two examples are so far known for the period 1200–1520.[5]

An added complication is that most of these records relate to vessels owned and operated by the Crown. Most medieval English monarchs, from William the Conqueror onwards, possessed small numbers of ships that were really no more than the maritime equivalents of the horses kept in their stables. They were used for the transportation of people and goods, and sometimes for war. A few kings, in particular John, Edward III and Henry V, built up strong royal war fleets, but such fleets seldom lasted long. Medieval English kings simply did not have the financial resources to maintain a permanent navy or major dock-yards. There was no English equivalent of the great French galley-base at Rouen, the Clos des Galées, which existed from 1294 until 1418.[6] But on the whole, English kings did not need large royal fleets or shore-bases. The Crown could compel the owners of private ships to take part in expeditions, or grant letters of marque to others to act as privateers against an enemy. Many ordinary merchant ships could serve as both warships and transports, and purpose-built fighting ships also existed in private hands, for use in privateering and piracy. Henry V (reg 1413–22) used several of his vessels for both trade and war, and at least one of his ships, the oared balinger *Craccher*, was a gift from a notorious pirate (see p. 147). Moreover, the technology required for building, rigging and equipping royal ships for war was little different from that used for merchant vessels. The English medieval kings, and their early Tudor successors, relied on essentially civilian shipbuilding and ship-ping industries to supply their maritime requirements. This makes the inventories and financial accounts of the royal ships a valuable source for the general development of ships and ship construction in medieval England.

The data on wages and materials costs contained in these records are vital to an understanding of the economic factors which influenced medieval ship design and construction. One factor, however, that could undermine the usefulness of this information is the system of purvey-ance, which allowed the royal household to buy goods at an appraised value, in preference to other buyers. The system did not operate in cases where municipalities or other organisations built or repaired ships for the Crown, but it did function when the work was carried out by the clerk of the king's ships, the official charged (from the mid-fourteenth century) with the construction and upkeep of the royal fleet. Purveyors could be highly active. For example, between November 1399 and November 1402, two purveyors were employed for 764 days (some 70 per cent of the time) 'riding and labouring' in finding workmen and materials for the king's ships. It is necessary, therefore, to ask if the accounts reflected true market prices or 'special' lower rates that Crown officials were able to extract. If the latter, the accounts are of less value from the economic point of view.

Although we have relatively few accounts for non-royal ships that can be compared with the official records, the way in which purveyance operated may mean that these accounts are broadly valid. A statute of 1362 laid down that purveyors were to pay the common market rate for goods, as agreed between themselves and the seller, perhaps with other appraisers helping to determine the price. Payment was to be prompt. The system was unpopular and clearly open to abuse, but most Parliamentary complaints about purveyance in the early fifteenth century relate more to non-payment by the Crown than to unfair pricing. With regard to wages, the Crown also seems to have paid the 'going rate': payments to shipwrights in the early fifteenth century often carried the significant rider that the rates were paid, 'the Statute of Labourers notwithstanding' (this statute attempted to peg wages at certain levels).[7]

No substantial English shipbuilding accounts or inventories are known from before the late thirteenth century. References to expenditure on ships in the twelfth-century Pipe Rolls seldom have any detail (for an exception, see Chapters 4 and 7). The earliest significant set of royal shipbuilding accounts, dating from the mid-1290s, relates to the construction of eight galleys for Edward I in 1294–6, at Lyme in Dorset, Southampton, London, Dunwich and Ipswich in Suffolk, York and Newcastle upon Tyne. Most contain a great deal of information as to how, and on what, money was spent, and are all the more illuminating for their geographical spread. All told, there are detailed building accounts for twenty-three English vessels from the period 1294–1497, together with summary accounts for the building of a further nineteen ships. There are also detailed repair accounts for some seventy-three vessels, and inventories for a hundred and twenty-three craft of different types. The sixteenth-century material is more extensive, with building and repair records for Henry VIII's ships and naval dockyards, and new forms of documentation for non-royal vessels (see Chapters 3 and 10).

These medieval accounts do include some vessels built for the Crown by different towns (such as the 1295 galleys), but most were constructed under the supervision of royal officials, particularly the clerk of the king's ships. England lacked any permanent body for overseeing the construction and maintenance of the royal fleet until the first, faltering development of the Navy Board in the reign of Henry VIII.[8]

A difficulty with medieval work accounts, whether for shipbuilding or other activities, lies in deducing how much information has been left out. The aim of the official or officials in charge was to provide a record and justification of the expenditure for which they had been responsible, not to provide a technical record. It is fortunate, however, that so many of these clerks found that the best way to record expenditure on particular items was to use the terminology of the artisans that they employed, and sometimes to state exactly what uses those items were put to.

Some of these accounts are therefore highly informative, a good example being that compiled for the galley built in Ipswich in 1294–5 (see also Chapter 4). This names several hull components, showing that the galley's keel was made of at least two pieces, and that the stem- and sternposts were each made of more than one piece. Dimensions are rare in such accounts, but in this case we can work out that in excess of 7600 ft of boards were used in the hull, and 1600 ft of boards in the galley's 'hurdis' or defence upperworks. This planking was supplemented by sixty 'Estlond boards' (imported from the eastern Baltic or Scandinavia), and by thirty-two timbers from which boards and planks (the text distinguishes between the two terms) were manufactured on site. The account mentions the purchase of timber to make floor-timbers ('wronges'), futtocks, beams and 'scheldbemes' (slabbed beams?) for the internal framing, as well as other named components, probably also part of the framing. The planking was fastened by nails of Spanish iron and the floor timbers were secured by wooden nails 'wrangnayls', and the vessel had two iron-bound rudders. The building-team comprised a master carpenter, about thirty-three other carpenters and two boys. The galley was coated with pitch, tallow and rosin, a 'greaser' (*unguentarius*) being employed for some of this smelly work. The galley was a one-master, and was equipped with a hundred oars, four anchors, eleven flags and a variety of other gear. Work commenced at the beginning of December 1294, and finished in late April 1295. A small, thirty-oar barge was built to accompany the galley, and the construction of this is described in only slightly less detail.[9] Accounts for other vessels describe the work on a more detailed, week-by-week basis, for example the Southampton galley of 1294–5 (see Table 5).

The fourteenth- and fifteenth-century particular accounts are also informative, although often organised differently from those of the 1290s; they seldom give a week-by-week account of operations, but group the purchase of timber, ironwork, wage records and so on in separate sections. The later fifteenth- and early sixteenth-century accounts return to something akin to thirteenth-century practice, and the best are extremely detailed. For example, the account for re-caulking the *Mary Rose* in October 1517 shows that twenty-three carpenters and caulkers (most named) were employed for the work and states how many days each man worked. It also shows that they were supplied with 249 stones (1584.5 kg) of oakum for the work, and three 'potells' of oil.[10]

Until at least the 1450s, accounts were written in Latin, although some were set down in Norman French. There is a hiatus in the royal fleet accounts between the 1450s and the 1480s, but the earliest records of Henry VII's navy in 1485 are all in English. From the earliest ship-building records, however, technical terms are almost invariably rendered in English, with a few French terms thrown in.

Another major type of written record is the ship inventory, a listing of all the movables (including masts and rigging) found on a ship on a given day. An inventory does not say what should have been there, only what happened to be there at the time of the inventory. Some accounts give the inventories, acquisitions and disposals of gear for a group of ships over a period of time, allowing one to check the accuracy of the inventories. The king's ships accounts for 1413–22 are such a collection of documents, and their evidence suggests that the inventories were, on the whole, accurate. By comparing numerous inventories one can get an idea of what was typical for different types of ship at different times.

Unfortunately, the inventory-makers seldom seem to have started at one end of the ship and worked through in a systematic manner, and it is usually difficult to deduce the relative positions of items listed. Royal ship inventories between 1372 and 1422 indicate that the record-takers worked to a formula, listing the most significant items of gear first, then going on to lesser pieces. The things listed usually included the mast (or masts), spars, rigging, navigational equipment, armament, ground tackle (anchors, cables, etc.) and miscellaneous gear.[11] References to particular parts of a ship, or the decks, are not common. Nevertheless, with the evidence of the accounts and other sources, the inventories allow us to build up a reasonably clear mental image of the rig and equipment of ships of the time.

PICTORIAL EVIDENCE

There are thousands of images of medieval and sixteenth-century ships, some very striking, but are they reliable evidence of the appearance of contemporary ships? The answer here, as with the documents, is to avoid over-reliance on any single source, and to look at representational trends. Most medieval artists, whether painters, manuscript illuminators, goldsmiths or others, worked in traditions that had little concern with realism as we would understand it, and little knowledge (before the fifteenth century) of perspective. Some fifteenth-century and many sixteenth-century painters and engravers of marine scenes depicted ships with some attention to technical detail, but even these images are not without their contentious aspects.

An added complication is the tendency of artists to copy illustrations from other sources. For example, there is a marked similarity between ships depicted on ten English town seals of the thirteenth and early fourteenth centuries, and those on the contemporary seals of the northern Spanish ports of San Sebastian and Santander, pointing to important contacts between the two areas. Most show the same type of one-masted ship getting under way (see Fig. 1.2). The two earliest are those of Santander (1228) and Pevensey (c. 1230), but the detailed chronology of most of the others is uncertain, meaning that we cannot be sure whether the Spanish or the English versions came first, or if the theme was copied from some lost original. The Winchelsea seal is illustrated as the best example of the type.[12]

Some medieval depictions of ships appear well-proportioned and

1.2 Drawing (after Ewe 1972) of the town seal of Winchelsea, c. 1300, one of the finest of medieval English ship seals. The clinker construction of the double-ended hull is very clear, as is the 'Gothic' woodwork of the ship's castles. The seal shows the ship getting under way. Two sailors pull on the anchor cable in the fore part of the ship, assisting the efforts of the two men heaving at the bars of the windlass in the stern. A sailor shins up the backstays, to unfurl the sail, and two trumpeters in the aftercastle announce the ship's departure.

1.3 Common seal of Haverfordwest, *c.* 1291. This is the matrix (mould) for the obverse side of the seal. It depicts a one-masted, clinker-built ship with fore- and aftercastles and a starboard-mounted side rudder. The actual seal impression is about 90mm in diameter, and the 'hull' is only about 58mm in length. Seal matrices were often the work of goldsmiths, and this matrix gives some idea of their workmanship.

have an air of technical accuracy, the best examples being some images on town seals (see Figs 1.2 and 1.3). Seal impressions in wax were used to authenticate official documents; the seal (or seal matrix) itself was kept secure to avoid fraud. It is thought that the matrices were often made by goldsmiths, men used to small-scale, precision work. Many port and naval seals carried ship images: the German scholar Herbert Ewe lists 249, ranging in date from the twelfth century to the seventeenth, and even this list is not complete (e.g. the Haverfordwest seal, shown in Fig. 1.3, is not included).[13]

The type of ship image desired by the authorities commissioning a seal can only be guessed. There is an assumption that the hard-nosed merchants running a town would have wanted a representation of a real ship, rather than a purely heraldic vessel. In that case, however, one has to explain why for over 170 years the merchants of Paris retained the stylised image of a ship of about 1400.[14] Seal images could clearly become 'fossilised' for centuries before they were updated.

Town seals were almost always circular. Some distortion of the ship image to fit this format was inevitable, but it must be said that the majority of seal ships do not appear radically ill-proportioned. Many include credible technical detail, such as the accurate rendering of overlapping clinker planking or the right fixings for a stern rudder. They are usually rather sketchy, however, when it comes to rigging (too many ropes would have obscured the central image of a ship), and attempts to scale up ship designs from seals are fraught with difficulties. As with other forms of medieval pictorial evidence, the best approach is to review a range of images, from different periods, rather than to fasten on one image as the 'definitive' example of one particular ship type.

It is clear that in most areas of medieval art, ship images changed over time, and can be shown to reflect actual technical change. For example, a study of some 200 images depicting features of 'hulk' construction reveal a number of simple, but distinct, changes in the ships depicted. The double-ended hull of the 'Viking-type' ship is a familiar medieval image, but in the Viking ship the plank runs were attached to the stem- and sternposts. In 'hulk construction' the plank-ends curved sharply upwards and were fastened to each other, perhaps

1.4 A ship in a different medium. A lead ampulla (hollow badge able to contain holy water) made for the Feast of the Return of St. Thomas as a pilgrimage souvenir, probably in the fourteenth century. The ship appears to be a cog-type, although the upper strake does not terminate on the stempost.

1.5 Copying into another medium: 'Master W's Kraeck' (see Fig. 4.5) appears here in a tapestry, probably of the late fifteenth century. As in many earlier medieval illustrations, the human figures are on a larger scale than the ships.

with an internal wooden collar or an external rope collar (see Figs 1.1 and 2.2). 'Hulk construction' in fact takes its name from the ship image on the seal of New Shoreham (see pp. 35–6). In 'hulk construction' images before the mid-fourteenth century, the double-ended, 'Viking-type' hull form predominated; from the second half of the fourteenth century, most such images show distinct differences between a 'sharp end' and a 'blunt end'. The bow remained curved, with relatively fine lines, and the stern became more rounded and blunt. This can be related to the development of the stern rudder in the twelfth century (see pp. 81–3), since it was easier to fit a stern rudder to a straight sternpost than to a curved one. Documentary evidence shows that in the first half of the fourteenth century the side rudder all but disappeared and, given that the side-rudder was linked with the double-ended hull form, it is

apparent that the 'hulk' image changes reflected reality, although perhaps lagging behind it by some decades.[15]

Ships were also represented in other media; they are found scratched in plaster or stone, carved in stone or wood, woven in tapestry (see Fig. 1.5), cast in metal or shaped in stained glass (see Figs 1.6, 3.1, 4.5). A version of St Thomas à Becket's ship (see p. 21) even occurs as a pilgrimage souvenir in the form of a lead *ampulla* (hollow badge able to contain a drop of holy water), probably of fourteenth-century date. This relic of a Canterbury pilgrimage was found in Norfolk (see Fig. 1.4).[16]

1.6 A maritime monument: a chapel erected in 1517 at St. Peter's Church, Tiverton in Devon by the merchant John Greenway. Greenway was also a ship-owner, and the chapel has many carvings of ships, anchors and other maritime motifs, as well as liberal use of Greenway's monogram. (Photographed in 1981, before restoration).

ARCHAEOLOGICAL EVIDENCE

The third major source of information for medieval maritime history is archaeology. One might think that the investigation of actual remains

1.7 The Bremen cog, *c.* 1380. Recovered from the river Weser near Bremen in 1962, the almost-intact hull parts of this cog of about 130 tons burden took many years to re-assemble.

of medieval vessels would supply all the answers, but this is not quite the case. For a start, complete ship remains are rare. Viking ship-burials, such as those found at Oseberg and Gokstad in the nineteenth century, have provided unparalleled evidence of what Viking ships were like, but medieval Christians did not bury their dead in ships, and vessels left derelict on the shore either rotted away or were broken up for scrap. Wreck remains, whether fully immersed or covered by shore-line mud, offer the best chance of finding the remains of ships and their contents intact; a sunken vessel rapidly buried in mud and silt is preserved from the oxygen-using bacteria and sea creatures that would normally eat away wood and other organic remains. The Bremen cog of *c.* 1380, the *Mary Rose*, lost in 1545 (see Figs 1.7 and 1.8) and the Swedish warship *Vasa* (sunk in 1628) are all celebrated examples of well-preserved wrecks, but most ship remains are much more fragmentary, in many cases consisting only of the bottom of a ship, preserved by the mound formed by its ballast-stones.

Such remains give us information about hull form, construction and equipment not available from written or pictorial sources, for example the detail of shipwrights' tool-marks on individual pieces of wood. Experimental archaeology, in the form of building complete replicas of vessels, can yield much important data about their construction and performance, although knowing how fast a particular type of vessel could travel does not necessarily reflect its performance when in regular use (see Chapter 5). Information of this kind will grow in extent as more sites are excavated, thanks to the ingenuity, courage and determination of maritime archaeologists. Underwater archaeology has been around for less than fifty years, and scholars will certainly have to adjust their thinking in the light of the new discoveries that it will, quite literally, bring up.

1.8 The recovered section of the Tudor warship *Mary Rose* in the Mary Rose Trust Ship Hall, Portsmouth. The *Mary Rose* was built at Portsmouth in 1510, as a warship of 600 tons, and may have been rebuilt in the 1530s. The ship belonged to the first 'generation' of broadside-firing warships, and was lost in action against the French off Spithead on 19 July 1545. The excavation and recovery of the ship became the most famous project in the history of underwater archaeology.

The recent excavation of a fifteenth-century wreck off the Breton coast exemplifies both the virtues and the limitations of archaeological evidence. The remains consist largely of a section of the port side of the ship, measuring some 17×4 m, preserved up to a point above the waterline. No cargo was found on the site, but the excavators believe that the ship may have been built originally in Gascony or northern Spain. The wreck will undoubtedly yield a great deal of information about constructional techniques and materials used, as well as giving some idea of the hull shape. The only survival of the rigging of the vessel, however, seems to be a fragment of what may have been the mainmast-step, so it is impossible to know if the ship had more than one mast. The ship may have been lost *en route* to Bordeaux to lade wine (see Chapter 7); the voyage could be dangerous, and Henry v lost his 220-ton *Cog John* off the Breton coast in 1414. The excavated remains do not reveal where the ship was going or where it had come from, what sort of rig it had, whether or not the ship had castles (superstructures) or how many crew there were.[17] Some of this information could be supplied by documentary and pictorial sources, at least in general terms.

CHAPTER 2

Ships and Shipmen

THE NATURE OF SHIP-OWNING

Throughout history, vessels have been built for specific owners to serve particular purposes, be it trade, warfare or fishing. Even the construction of a dugout canoe involves some expertise, and a small medieval vessel was considerably more complex than that.[1] In medieval England, ships and boats were owned by people from a wide range of social levels. At the lower end were boat-owners like the fishermen of Dunwich in the early fifteenth century, who owned and skippered their own small boats, with crews of perhaps up to six men. These boat-owners were admittedly a step up in terms of wealth and position from the skippers who worked other men's boats, but even in a small place like Dunwich they seldom rose very far up the social scale. For example, in 1406–7, a certain Robert Fraunce skippered a boat owned by Edmund Sparhauk. A proportion of the catch of each boat was paid to the town as a 'dole', and the boat captained by Fraunce turned in a reasonable dole of 12s. 9d. In the following year, Fraunce fished in his own boat, probably a smaller vessel, and turned in doles of 2s. 4d and 4s. 6d, low figures even in the context of what seems to have been a poor year for the Dunwich fleet. Typical of better-off fishing-boat owners was John Moreff, the town's Member of Parliament and one of its bailiffs; in the 1420s he had at least three boats or 'farkosts', all skippered by hired men. In his case, fishing may have been only one part of his trade (see Fig. 2.1).[2]

Larger vessels sometimes belonged to single owners, although it was not uncommon for them to be in multiple ownership (ship-owning has been described as one of the oldest forms of business association; see Scammell, 1962). The wealthier people in a port, as in some of the Devon ports and at Southampton, were often also important ship-owners, with several ships each. At the other end of the scale were ships

rbm c xbi kl Dutū Ualentini ẽpt 1 inr. m.lc.
vīī d xb kl
c xïīī kl cē iuliane uirg̃ ꝛ m̃ns. .m.lc.
rb f īīī kl

2.1 A small fishing boat, English MS, early 14th century.

divided between several people – as many as nine in the case of one Dartmouth ship.[3] Ships might also belong to an institution, such as a town government or a religious house: in 1400 New Romney in Kent had a barge built to serve as the town's 'common ship', and in about 1430 Lydd had its own ship. Two centuries earlier, in 1234, Margam Abbey in South Wales owned a ship, and a year later nearby Neath Abbey was licensed to trade with England using its 'ship … called *Hulc'*. Women ship-owners, while far less common than male owners, did exist: in 1250 Ellen Lambard of Bristol obtained a safe conduct for her two ships *Lambord* and *La Sauvee* to trade to Bordeaux. It seems that specialist ship-owners (ie people who made a living by hiring out their ships) were extremely rare. The term 'ship-owner' does not occur until about 1540, and a man such as William Canynges of Bristol, who in the 1460s owned ten ships (some very large) and his own shipyard facilities, was an exception. The usual pattern was probably for merchants and others to own or have a share in ships as just one part of their business. Not all owners were merchants; between the 1460s and the 1480s the East Anglian gentleman Sir John Howard (later the first Duke of Norfolk) owned at different times some ten or twelve ships, of which at least six were used in foreign trade.[4]

One of the earliest merchant ships that can be traced in more than one instance in English sources is an unnamed Cardiff vessel, seized by the English authorities at Pembroke in about 1216 carrying 'wine and chattels' of Dublin and Drogheda men. In May 1216 King John gave the ship to William Marshall, Earl of Pembroke; the merchants were able to get their goods back but had to pay Marshall for freighting the cargo to them. By February 1218, Marshall is recorded as having sold to Peter Blunt, a Drogheda merchant, a ship which he had been given by King John. Thus, in two years or less, this ship was in Welsh, English and then Irish ownership, the transfers having been achieved by seizure, gift and, finally, sale.[5] This incidentally shows that material found inside a medieval wreck on the sea-bed does not necessarily tell us much about its origin, still less its complete history.

The most important single ship-owner in medieval England was the king. The 'king's ships', however, are often seen as no more than a part of naval history, and their occasional use for trading expeditions by great 'sea kings' such as Henry V and Henry VIII tends to be dismissed as a sideline, rather as if a modern British aircraft carrier were to be used to import cars from Japan. Certainly the importance of the medieval royal ships in warfare and in 'keeping the seas' clear of pirates and foreign enemies, was recognised by contemporaries; but to see the royal fleets of the Middle Ages as the straightforward predecessors of the modern Royal Navy is to misunderstand the medieval context. Royal ships were used for many purposes, as the 'service career' of Henry IV's barge *Holigost* demonstrates. In the summer of 1400 it participated in a naval expedition against the Scots; the following year it took Richard II's widow back to France; and in 1402 it conveyed Henry's daughter Blanche to Dordrecht, later forming part of the fleet that brought his new wife from Brittany. In 1405 the *Holigost* was granted to one of the king's shipmasters. Arguably this was typical of royal shipping in a time largely without open warfare, but analysis of the activities of some of Henry V's ships shows that, even in wartime, the royal fleet did not always operate as a modern 'royal navy'.[6]

The pattern of use of Henry V's ships between September 1413 and June 1416 can be analysed in terms of 'ship-days', because their complete crew wage records survive in summary form, indicating when the ships were in harbour, when they were at sea, and in what types of voyage they were employed. This, it must be remembered, was the period that saw the renewal of the Hundred Years War with France, and Henry's first great expedition across the Channel, in 1415. It emerges that only 17.8 per cent of the time was spent in naval operations, with 32.9 per cent on trading voyages, 41.3 per cent in harbour and 8.3 per cent in other ways, including trading voyages aborted because of bad weather or wreck, and a voyage to Calais with soldiers' pay.[7] Evidently, even a great warrior-king like Henry V used royal ships during wartime almost twice as much for trading voyages as for warlike activities. Most of the trading voyages were to Bordeaux, freighting wine for merchants, with a couple from Newcastle to London with sea-coal, and even one to Prussia for timber, pitch and other materials.

The nature of medieval ship-owning illuminates the process of technological change in shipbuilding. Shipwrights built vessels in response to orders from owners who wanted a ship or ships for particular purposes, and, although shipbuilding specifications for the period before 1600 are largely lost, it is possible to speculate as to how different forms of ship-owning affected technological developments. Most ship-owners were probably merchants and seamen, and a significant proportion may have been master/owners. For example, of 63 English ships mustered at Plymouth in 1450 and 1451 to take part in an expedition to Gascony, 61 had single owners and two were of unknown ownership.[8] Thirteen were skippered by their owners, and not all of these were small ships: one was the 300-ton *Barry* of Fowey, owned and captained by a Julian Hicke. At least ten vessels belonged to small private merchant fleets (see Table 1).

Most of the ships in this force were drawn from Devon and Cornwall; recent research shows that the ownership of more than one ship was fairly common in Devon between the mid-fourteenth and early fifteenth centuries (see n. 6). One of the 145 fleet owners, John Clerk of Dartmouth (with three ships, of 400, 200 and 100 tons) may have owned another ship, the *New Trinity*, at around this time and had shares in at least four others. A slightly later example of part-ownership was Thomasia Hill, the widow of a Bridgwater (Somerset) merchant, John Hill, who in 1482 sold to Thomas Phelipe Esquire a quarter-share in the ships *Margaret* and *John* of Bridgwater, and an eighth share (or 'half quarter' as the document puts it) in the *Nicholas* of Bridgwater. This would of course have been division by value rather than by physical objects, although the sale document noted that Thomasia had also handed over an oar and an anchor that belonged to the ships.[9]

Did one particular form of ownership favour technical innovation more than another? The evidence of the 1451 Plymouth fleet is significant, because it was in the mid-fifteenth century that some of the largest English ships of the Middle Ages were built. Vessels in the 300–400 ton range were not so common again until the early 1600s.[10] The bigger the ship, the bigger both the potential rewards and risks. However, though one would expect to find prudent ship-owners spreading the risks inherent in large vessels (see Fig. 2.2) between several owners, the evidence of the 1450–51 list suggests that large ships were owned, and often also captained, by single individuals. Men such as John Clark and Jenyn Troivuse were tying up large amounts of capital in hundreds of tons of timber and nails which could go to the bottom and take their owner's fortune with them. The single ship- or fleet-owner thus

2.2 Three-masted ship on a church bench-end of *c.* 1485, St. Winnow, near Fowey, Cornwall. The carving shows the crew of a ship praying for salvation from a storm, portrayed as a demon (top left). This may well have been a votive offering, presented to the church by the master or owner of a ship that had survived a storm.

emerges as the main source of demand for technological change, in this case the construction of larger vessels.

By contrast, multiple ship-owning partnerships were probably less likely to take risks with new designs or with technological development, for changes of any significance would presumably have required the consent of all the partners involved. We do not know if Thomasia Hill, with what was probably her late husband's 'portfolio' of shares in the three Bridgwater ships, was a 'sleeping partner' or not, but it seems unlikely that these vessels, divided between perhaps four to eight owners, represented the cutting edge of maritime technology in 1482.

Ultimately the question of the relationship between ship-owning and technological change in the period before 1600 may be too ill-documented to be clearly answered. However, there are strong indications that it was the single owner who was the most receptive to new ideas that could increase the profits to be made from his or her ships, or increase the certainty of those ships reaching home.

THE NUMBERS OF SHIPS

There is no way of knowing the absolute numbers of English ships before the national shipping lists of the Elizabethan era (see Chapter 10), but it is possible to estimate minimum numbers. While a project on medieval Devon shipping has yielded some impressive results,[11] the principal sources remain medieval ship lists compiled at specific dates. Chronicle evidence of the size of fleets is unreliable, and often uncheckable; assertions that Henry v took between 1400 and 1600 ships with him to Normandy in 1415 are difficult to credit,[12] and the actual lists made of ships in fleets or other groupings seldom record more than about 200 vessels (see Table 2).[13]

Most figures derived from shipping lists relate to larger vessels, of 100 tons or more. Figures for 1359 come from a survey of shipping in East Anglia numbering 151 vessels from ten tons upwards with a combined tonnage of 5498. One hundred and thirty-four of these craft (88.7 per cent) were of less than 100 tons burden. If this is any guide for the national figure, it suggests that vessels of 100 tons and more made up no more than about 10–20 per cent of the total of English shipping. Using the data in Table 2, this would make the national shipping total in the second half of the fourteenth century around 1000–2000 vessels, with a possible decline in numbers (although not in sizes) in the first half of the fifteenth century. While no more than a guess, these figures are not outlandish; some 200 years later, in 1582, the most extensive of the Elizabethan national shipping surveys listed 1630 vessels of 20 tons and upwards.[14]

THE SIZES OF SHIPS

The earliest group of English ships for which there is any substantial dimensional information is Queen Elizabeth's navy, and even the earliest Elizabethan listing dates only from about 1591.[15] Before this date, the historian's main source for making comparisons between different sizes of ships is tonnage data. Unfortunately, tonnage statistics are the most uncertain form of evidence in early maritime history. The word 'ton' derives from the Old and Middle English word *tunne*, meaning a cask of liquid (OED). In medieval English commercial and legal usage, this usually meant a wine container of 252 gallons (554.4

litres) capacity. Ships measured in 'tuns' are first mentioned in English sources in the thirteenth century. Medieval tonnage measurement seems most often to relate to the carrying capacity of a ship (how much a vessel could carry was the most important measure of its economic value); but such measurements are often uncheckable. For example, in the case of vessels hired or arrested for government use, part of the payment due to the owners was calculated on the basis of 3s 4d per ton; it was thus in the Crown's interest to rate a ship's tonnage on the low side, and the owner's to rate it higher. However, the records of tonnage and crew sizes for ships in English royal service between 1399 and 1422 show a fairly direct correlation between tonnage and crew size, suggesting that the tonnage figures were fairly reliable. In the 1320s the English Crown was using a ratio of approximately one man per four tons of ship as a way of reckoning the number of men required to crew vessels of more than 100 tons in royal service. There is also evidence that in the fifteenth century there was a developing notion of 'dead-weight tonnage' measurement, which included the accommodation, cooking and other spaces not used for cargo. This 'tons and tonnage' measure was used in connection with Elizabethan royal ships, but it was always distinguished from 'portage' or 'tons burden', which were measures of notional carrying capacity.[16]

Exactly how tonnage was measured is very difficult to say. In some cases it may have been reckoned by the partial or full loading of a ship. An English ship was seized at Bordeaux in 1459 because her cargo capacity was found to be 200 or 300 tons more than the 400 tons stated in the ship's letter of safe conduct. The owner successfully fought the seizure on the grounds that as this was the ship's first voyage, he did not know the hull's actual capacity (see Burwash, 1969, p. 90). This situation may not have been unusual.[17]

Where medieval sources refer to a ship's tonnage as estimated (*per estimacionem*), they do not say what process was used, although it was probably largely empirical. The earliest recorded English formula for calculating burden was known as 'Baker's Old Rule', having been set down (though perhaps not invented) by the Elizabethan master ship-wright Matthew Baker in 1582. It is a simple formula which continued in use for centuries. It used a few key dimensions as the means of establishing a measure of capacity.[18]

$$\frac{\text{Keel length} \times \text{Beam} \times \text{Depth in hold}}{100} = \text{tons burden}$$

Probably the most accurate guide to the real carrying capacities of ships is to be found in the detailed customs records of what they actually loaded (see Table 3).[19] The evidence is fairly clear-cut: even on a dangerous long-distance route like that to Bordeaux, the larger, more capacious (and more defensible) ships were almost always outnumbered by vessels of less than 100 tons burden. The 1359 listing of 151 ships arrested for royal service in eastern ports from King's Lynn to Harwich revealed 107 vessels of less than 30 tons, some as small as ten tons burden. For comparison, a study of the tonnages of 75 vessels mentioned in the *Close Rolls* between 1400 and 1412 shows that three-quarters were below the 100-ton mark. It is clear that small ships predominated throughout the fourteenth, fifteenth and early sixteenth centuries. Whatever the total number of seagoing vessels in England at any one time, vessels of more than 200 tons were not common. Their brief heyday seems to have come between the 1430s and 1450s.

The documentary evidence of ships' sizes includes the specifications issued for royal galleys. These usually only stated the number of oars that the vessel was to have; the galleys ordered by Edward I in 1294 were to have 120 oars each, and a barge ordered by the king in 1304 from the city of Newcastle was to have 24 oars and a crew of 26. A rare exception to this convention was the order to the City of London in 1373 to build 'two good and strong barges (oared warships), each one eighty feet on the ground (i.e. along the keel, or at least along the flat of the keel) and twenty feet in width'. At least one of these barges was built, the 80-oar *Paul*.[20]

The one reasonably detailed ship specification to survive from before the sixteenth century is for a 42-oar balinger (another oared warship type) that the citizens of Cambridge were having built in London in 1378 for the Crown. This document was more concerned with ensuring that broad areas of construction were to be well performed, with good materials, than with the actual size of the vessel. The balinger was to cost £142. It was to be built of *Englisshboard* (oak), 'well clenched' with good iron nails and 'well-drilled', with *ribbes* measuring 12 feet inside the vessel. The caulking was to be made from pitch and hair, and the balinger was to be equipped with a mast, a yard, a sail, three anchors, three cables and a windlass. The agreement was concluded with a London shipwright on 10 February 1378, and the balinger was due to be ready and in the water within forty days. The assumption seems to have been that the shipwrights would understand what was required to make a good vessel, as long as they knew how many oars it was to have: the number of oars was obviously a key to the size of an oared craft because it determined the length of the keel (see Chapter 5).[21]

A letter written to Henry V in 1419, trying to induce him to buy a large ship being built at Bayonne, gives tantalisingly precise, though incomplete, data on the size of a large sailing ship of the period. It had a keel of 112 ft (34.1 m), a main beam of 46 ft (14.0 m) a stempost 96 ft (29.3 m) in height (this was probably measured on the curvature of the stem, rather than from the top of the stem to the ground), and a sternpost of 48 ft (14.6 m). This vessel (which Henry did not buy) must have been of more than 1000 tons burden, almost comparable with the king's 1400-ton *Grace Dieu* of 1418, the remains of which lie in the River Hamble in Hampshire. Only the bottom of the *Grace Dieu* survives, but this has a keel length of at least 125 ft (38.1 m), and a breadth of some 37.5 ft (11.4 m): the original maximum beam may have been as much as 50 ft.[22]

Specifications survive from the early sixteenth century for a vessel called the *Mary Gonson*, probably built between 1510 and 1530. They detail the dimensions of the proposed vessel. For example, the keel of the ship was to be 80 ft (24.4 m) long and the keel and the rakes of stem and sternpost would have given the ship a length from stem to stern of 115 ft (35.1 m). The maximum beam was to be 32 feet (9.8 m), and the total height of the hull would have exceeded 33 ft (10.1 m). The *Mary Gonson* would have had two decks below the weather deck in the waist, as did the contemporary 600-ton warship *Mary Rose*. Study of the hull remains of the latter have shown that the *Mary Rose* had a keel of about 105 ft (32 m), a breadth of about 37 ft (11.4 m), and a draught just under 15 ft (4.5 m). English shipwrights from at least the early fifteenth century were clearly able to build very large vessels, and the tonnage figures given for the greater ships were evidently not just fantasy.[23]

THE TYPES OF SHIPS

More than sixty names of ship-types can be found in English records between 1200 and 1520. While it is possible to get some idea of the relative sizes and functions of most of these, only a minority can be identified in pictorial or archaeological sources (the same is true of other parts of Europe). They include the cog, the *cocha* or carrack, and the hulk.

Cogs have been identified both in pictorial images and in wreck-finds (see Figs 2.3 and 1.7). The cog was a flat-bottomed cargo ship with high sides, and distinctive straight, angled stem- and sternposts. It was one of the most important and capacious types of merchantman in northern Europe during the thirteenth and fourteenth centuries and, when 'exported' to the Mediterranean in about 1300, gave rise to a new type, the *cocha* or carrack (see Fig. 4.5 and Chapter 9).[24]

The 'hulk' type is referred to in English written sources from the thirteenth century onwards (cf. the Neath *hulc* of 1235 – this was not 'hulk' in the later sense of a laid-up vessel). Identifications of hulks in medieval art and in archaeological finds are based on a single source, the seal of New Shoreham in Sussex (see Figs 2.4 and 2.5). The earliest-known use of this seal was in 1295, and on the reverse side it bears the image of a ship and the Latin legend HOC HULCI SINGNO VOCOR OS SIC NOMINE DINGNO ('by this sign (image) of a hulk I am called mouth, which is a worthy name'; 'Hulkesmouth' was an alternative name for the port of Shoreham). The vessel is one-masted, with a side-rudder,

2.3 A cog on the seal of Stralsund, Germany, 1329.

and the hull form is excessively curved, following the circular shape of the seal. Its unusual feature is that the plank runs do not terminate at stem and sternposts, but instead they run up at stem and stern to end in horizontal lines under the castles. In other words, the vessel type represented appears to have lacked stem- and sternposts. This form of structure, not unlike that of a banana, has been compared with a type of keel-less vessel of the eighth or ninth century found at Utrecht in Holland. Vessels of the 'hulk' type occur in many other medieval illustrations (see Figs 1.1 and 2.4) but so do vessels that had, say, a 'hulk' stem and a 'conventional' sternpost (see Fig. 2.6), and problems arise

2.4 A 'hulk-type' vessel in an English manuscript of c. 1118–40. This vessel does have certain credible features. For example, the realistic positions of the nail-heads indicate a 'reverse-clinker' hull, and the plank runs terminate at horizontal, nailed wooden 'bands', rather than at stem- or stern-posts (which are absent).

when one attempts to use the New Shoreham seal as the basis for describing the hulks recorded in medieval and sixteenth-century documents, since there is no evidence as to what these vessels looked like, or how they were built.

It is sometimes asserted that the cog and hulk merged into a composite design by about 1400, but this is to ignore earlier evidence, such as the thirteenth-century Southampton seal, that shows both 'post' and 'hulk' construction in the same vessel. Hulks were evidently important trading vessels in the thirteenth and fourteenth centuries, but we do not know if what was termed a hulk in thirteenth-century Sussex was the

37

2.5 Hulk on the town seal of New Shoreham, Sussex ('Hulkesmouth'), *c.* 1295.

2.6 A vessel with elements of 'cog' and 'hulk' construction, depicted on the second town seal of Southampton, thirteenth century.

same thing as, say, a Baltic hulk of the fourteenth century. 'Hulk construction', for want of a better term, existed: but it may not have defined a single vessel type.[25] It is not easy, therefore, to differentiate vessel types on the basis of name alone, and one has always to be aware of the context in which the name was used. For example, two royal 'cogs', the *Cog Thomas* and the *Rodecog*, were supplied with over 50 oars apiece in the mid-fourteenth century, and so were almost certainly oared ships. Sail-powered cogs, however, were the wrong size and shape to use oars.[26] Another problem is that type-names change over time. The term 'galley' in thirteenth-century England denoted a clinker-built, north European oared ship, but by the fifteenth century it tended to be applied only to vessels of Mediterranean origin (for a discussion of oared ship types, see Chapters 5 and 8).

CHAPTER 3

Building a ship

WHO WERE THE SHIPWRIGHTS?

Noah was the only biblical shipbuilder, so it is not surprising that he became a symbol for medieval European shipwrights. The majority of shipbuilding scenes in medieval art are representations of the Ark under construction, with Noah either pausing to listen to God or hard at work with his sons (see Fig. 3.13). This theme was inevitably picked up by the shipwrights themselves. At York from 1376, and at Newcastle upon Tyne from 1427, the cycles of Corpus Christi plays included the Noah story, put on by the local shipwrights' gilds. Both plays were performed until well into the sixteenth century.[1] Nevertheless, the Noah story was not the full extent of the medieval English shipwright's 'repertoire'. In 1486 the city of Bristol staged a lavish pageant to welcome the new king, Henry VII. One of the speeches lamented 'That Bristow is fallen into decaye' through losses of ships and other troubles, and called on Henry to restore the local shipping and cloth industries. The pageant also included 'the Shipwrights' pageaunt, with praty conceyts playing in the same withoute any speche'. Henry promised to encourage Bristol's trade and shipping.[2]

Beyond these isolated references, however, we know little of the 'culture' of English shipwrights in the Middle Ages. Shipwrights' gilds existed at Newcastle, York, London and elsewhere, but shipbuilding was a relatively poor and ill-organised trade, lacking the economic clout of some others. The London gild was a fraternity of St Simon and St Jude (both saints sometimes appear in medieval English art holding boats – see Fig. 3.1) and was certainly in existence by the late 1360s. The earliest surviving set of ordinances for the gild date from 1426, with amendments of 1483. They deal with internal organisation, apprenticeship and, to some degree, the need to ensure a good standard of workmanship. Between 1428 and 1433, six London shipwrights are

3.1 St. Simon or St. Jude, depicted on a late-medieval rood screen in a Norfolk church.

noted in the city records being sworn in as masters of *the mistery of shipwryghtis*, but there are few other clues regarding the history of the London gild (all its other early records seem to have been lost in a fire).[3]

The only substantial body of information on shipwrights' activities is to be found in the accounts and other records dealing with the construction of royal ships, although, since there was no separate 'naval' industry, these also reflect the 'civilian' shipbuilding industry. Despite King John's short-lived galley-base at Portsmouth in the early thirteenth century, the royal ship maintenance facilities at Ratcliffe on the Thames in the fourteenth century, and on the River Hamble in Hampshire in the reign of Henry v, the Crown did not have any permanent dockyards. The foundation of what was to become Portsmouth royal dockyard did not take place until 1495. Brian Dietz has argued that the siting of new dockyards and naval stores at Deptford, Woolwich and Erith in the reign of Henry VIII led to the growth of the London shipbuilding industry in the sixteenth century; even in the late 1500s most of the royal master shipwrights were heavily involved in private ship construction.[4]

The size of the shipbuilding labour force was one of the crucial factors in determining the capabilities of the industry in the period 1200–1520, but it can only be guessed at. Only two sets of figures, over two centuries apart in date, give anything approaching a 'national' picture (see Fig. 3.2).[5] Six of the accounts for building royal galleys in 1294–6, and a repair account from Portsmouth in 1294, indicate the numbers of shipwrights involved. The London and York accounts name the shipwrights employed, numbering 50 and 69 respectively at the two sites. The other accounts only give numbers of unnamed men, but unless the turnover of the workforces was very high a total figure of 270 men employed at the seven sites seems plausible. This gives an average of just under 39 shipwrights at each site. Considering that most of these places were major towns, and that the English population was approaching its pre-Black Death peak, these figures are not very impressive. By contrast, the manpower involved in the great castle-building projects of the time makes the shipbuilding effort look puny – in the summer of 1295, for example, the building of Edward I's castle at Beaumaris is thought to have employed an average of 1800 men.[6]

The second set of figures comes from a great round-up of shipwrights, caulkers and other ship construction specialists to work on the construction of Henry VIII's massive 1000-ton *Henri Grâce à Dieu* and three galleys at Woolwich in 1512. A total of 252 men were conscripted, from as far afield as Cornwall and Yorkshire. We know where they came from because the government paid travelling expenses ('conduct money') based on the distance. There are no figures for any London men, who were perhaps deemed to live too close to require expenses. The highest figure for a single place (Smallhythe, 38) scarcely equalled the average for the mid-1290s. This may be partly explained by population decline following plague and famine in the fourteenth century (England in 1512 had from one half to two-thirds fewer people than in 1295). Only four places – Smallhythe, Ipswich, Dartmouth and the ports of the Exe estuary – could muster twenty or more men each to send to Woolwich.[7]

The fact the government had to scour the country for shipbuilders does not suggest that they were numerous in London in 1512. A similar

3.2 Comparative numbers of shipwrights in various English ports, 1294–6 and 1512.
[ ] = 1294–6;
( ) = 1512.

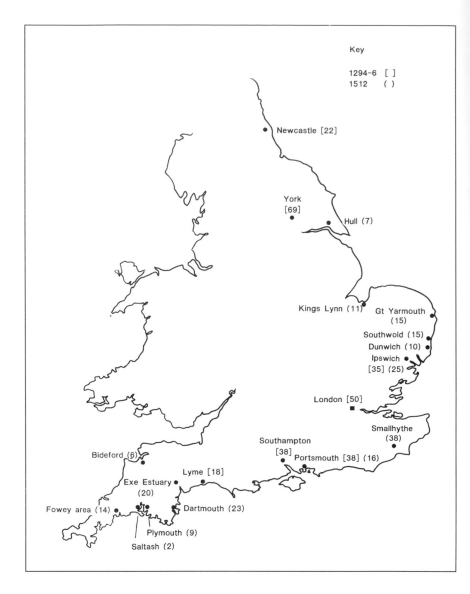

Key

1294–6 [ ]
1512   ( )

Newcastle [22]

York [69]

Hull (7)

Kings Lynn (11)

Gt Yarmouth (15)

Southwold (15)

Dunwich (10)

Ipswich [35] (25)

London [50]

Smallhythe (38)

Southampton [38]

Portsmouth [38] (16)

Bideford (6)

Lyme [18]

Exe Estuary (20)

Fowey area (14)

Dartmouth (23)

Plymouth (9)

Saltash (2)

'call-up' had been ordered in 1356, when officials were sent to East Anglia to raise shipwrights to build vessels at Ratcliffe, a few miles east of London.[8] Similarly, when the 1400-ton *Grace Dieu* was built at Southampton between 1416 and 1418, orders had to be sent out to fetch shipwrights from the West Country.[9] The overall impression is that the shipbuilding labour force was never very large, even when England was relatively heavily populated, and that after the catastrophes of the fourteenth century its size declined sharply.

The names of shipwrights are given in some accounts, though the evidence is too fragmentary to allow us to say much about even the most important individuals. John Hoggekyn, the master shipwright engaged in 1416 for the construction of the *Grace Dieu* at Southampton, must have been considered a man of great skill and competence, but nothing is known of his career before he began work on this ship. In 1421 he was given a pension of 4d per day for physical deterioration suffered as a result of working on the king's ships, and was still receiving it as late as 1439.[10] Hoggekyn, however, was an exception, as most shipwrights were employed on a casual basis.

The names of other master shipwrights occasionally surface in the records. Henry Hellewarde, the master shipwright of the 1295 York galley, apparently reappears among the thirty-six people listed in the 1297 lay subsidy (tax) return for the long-lost port of Ravenserod which stood at the mouth of the Humber. He was a man of some wealth in his community, assessed as able to pay 5s – only six people in the port paid more. In 1298–9 he was the master carpenter for the repair of a royal barge at nearby Ravenser, but little more is known of him. Welsh shipwrights are even less well-recorded than their English counterparts. English shipwrights were used for some royal shipbuilding in Wales and, when a small ship was built at Conwy in 1301, the participation of Welsh workmen was restricted to the felling of trees. There are some signs, however, of native Welsh craftsmen who worked in the clinker construction tradition: in 1302, for example, the Menai ferryboat at Llanfaes was repaired by two Welsh carpenters, Iorwerth and his assistant Madoc.[11]

If it is difficult to trace the careers of individual shipwrights, can we at least identify families or even 'dynasties' of craftsmen? The construction account for a second galley built at London in 1295 suggests the presence of family groups. Nineteen out of the total of fifty shipwrights employed had one of six surnames: Ballard (four), ?Hetfend (three), Smart (three), le Palmer (four), Stone (three) and Tidy (two).[12]

Family groups might be expected in a craft industry such as shipbuilding, but the trade was not necessarily dominated by them. The six London 'families' in 1295 were, after all, outnumbered by some thirty-one other men with different surnames, and the twenty-six man team that re-built the balinger *Petit Jesus* at Bursledon on the River Hamble in Hampshire in 1435–6 included only five men with shared surnames – three named Bull, and two called Came.[13]

Shipwrights probably learnt their trade through the apprenticeship system, but (with the exception of the London gild) there is little sign of formal shipwright apprenticeships in the Middle Ages and the early sixteenth century. The names of different types of shipwrights, and their respective rates of pay, suggest that the trade had a distinctive craft structure between the thirteenth and early fifteenth centuries. The master shipwright was responsible for the overall design of a vessel and the conduct of the work. The berder (also termed boarder, bircher or hewer) was apparently concerned with fitting and shaping timbers, boards and spars, and probably also oversaw the work of clenchers and holders. The clencher (or clincher) clenched over the nail-points on the inside of a clinker-built hull. The holder (also helder, hoyller) held in the nail-heads on the outside of a hull as the points were clenched over on the inside; as their work was complementary to that of the clenchers, these men were often employed in equal numbers. Boys, servants or general workers were occasionally employed to help the shipwrights.

This arrangement is reflected in the pay structure found in most accounts. When the Newcastle galley was built in 1295, the master was paid 4d per day, the carpenters below him were paid 3d per day, the *clynckers* 2½d, the holders 2d and workers 'serving the carpenters and clenchers' 1¾d. A similar arrangement existed over a century later. The workforce for the construction of Henry v's *Trinity Royal* at Greenwich between 1413 and 1416 included master shipwrights paid 8d each per day, shipwright berders at 6d, clenchers at 5d and holders at 4d (these wage-levels were higher than those specified in the restrictive Statute of Labourers, a fact often stated in the royal accounts, and perhaps another indication of the shortage of shipwrights). Government directives attempted to set the wage-rates of these craftsmen, and used these terms, as late as 1559.[14]

There is no explicit evidence of a man progressing from servant to holder, then clencher, berder and, finally, master. Nevertheless, the congruence of wage- and skill-levels means that this was probably the normal career-path for English shipwrights.

The structure of their trade was dictated by the technology of clinker construction (see Fig. 3.3). The shell of overlapping planks was the main load-bearing element in a clinker-built hull. The planks were fastened together at the edges by thousands of clench-nails, and the insertion and clenching of these was the main feature of the monotonous work of clenchers and holders. The shaping of planks, frames and other parts of the structure required more skill, and was the concern of the berders. Overall design and direction was supplied by the master shipwright. The fact that clinker technology changed little in its essential features between the early Middle Ages and the fifteenth century may indicate that the four- or five-level organisation of the shipwright's trade was very ancient. Evidence for the impact of the introduction of the radically different skeleton construction on the trade, will be discussed later (see pp. 66–7).

The organisation and direction of work on a ship construction site may not always have been straightforward. Some projects clearly had more than one master shipwright. The Southampton galley of 1295 had four English masters and one Bayonnese, and the contemporary Lyme galley had four masters. In other accounts, there are no identifiable master shipwrights: barges were repaired or built at Great Yarmouth and Newcastle in 1303–4, apparently without master shipwrights. Thirty-three or more shipwrights worked on a great boat at Newhithe

in 1400 without an obvious overseer, and the same was true of the building of the balinger *Godegrace* by forty-six or so men at Ratcliffe in the following year.[15] These instances of multiple masters – or none at all – on complex projects suggest that shipwrights took some decisions in common, and that the trade was not rigidly hierarchical.

English shipwrights thus appear to have been relatively few in number and poorly-organised. It would also seem that the trade was not held in very high esteem. John Hoggekyn, the master builder of the *Grace Dieu*, received 8d per day; the master joiners on the same project, practitioners of a 'higher class' of woodwork, received 12d per day. Shipwrights at the top of their trade did not receive the social recognition accorded them in, say, the reign of Elizabeth I, when royal master

3.3 Dutch shipwrights at work on a small, clinker-built boat. Note the lack of frames at this stage of construction. Painting by a Master of Gouda, 1565 (detail).

45

shipwrights such as Matthew Baker were men of importance. There is one reference to a 'king's master shipwright' in the medieval period, dating from 1401. A certain William Ussher is described in this way, but almost nothing else is known about him, and his name does not even feature in the royal accounts as the constructer or repairer of the king's ships.[16] For much of the medieval period, however, shipbuilding had a fairly consistent internal organisation at the level of the worksite: shipwrights in the north-east worked in much the same way as those in the West Country, and the 'work culture' of the English shipwright was a national one.

MATERIALS

Timber was the single most important raw material in European ship and boat construction from prehistory to the nineteenth century. Boats made of skin or other materials were used in certain areas, but most seagoing craft, and all vessels of any size, were made of wood.[17] The maritime primacy of Britain in the eighteenth and nineteenth centuries, and its ever-growing numbers of naval and merchant ships, led to a belief that the demands of shipping ate up the country's woods and forests.[18] Recent research, however, has cast doubt on this idea, and it has been suggested by Oliver Rackham that, 'as a major consumer of timber, the shipbuilding industry was short-lived', the main period of consumption being restricted to the early industrial period.[19]

Medieval England does not seem to have suffered from any serious shortages of timber, despite the fact that so many of the things in daily use, ranging from houses to carts, and from boats to food bowls, were made of wood. There is little evidence of a medieval English 'timber problem' in the sense of a lack of trees, although vessels were not necessarily built with timber from the nearest wood. According to Rackham, the trade 'followed no obvious pattern of supply and demand; it reflected also the requirements, ownerships, habits, whims of the individuals involved. Timber was often used from distant rather than nearby sources, and many journeys seem to us unnecessary'.[20]

As so much of the medieval evidence for ship construction comes from governmental sources, the picture of timber supply is even more complicated. The Crown could call on resources not available to other ship-owners. The royal parks and forests were good sources of timber, which could be supplied *gratis*, and the system of purveyance conferred other advantages (see Chapter 1). Timber might also come to the Crown as a gift, although it is impossible to ascertain just how freely it was given. The supply of 349 oaks for timbers for Henry v's new 'great ship' *Trinity Royal*, built at Greenwich between 1413 and 1416, illustrates both the gift-giving process and the potential variety of the sources of supply. Almost half of the oaks came from royal parks or woods at Eltham in Kent (125) or Langley Park in Hertfordshire (40), but the remaining 184 came from eight religious houses in Kent, Essex and Hertfordshire.[21]

Such free supplies, seldom available to the non-royal shipbuilder, mean that in some royal shipbuilding accounts the recorded expenses of timber under-represent the actual amount consumed. Distortions of this sort can usually be identified. Either the amount of timber recorded is clearly insufficient for building a vessel, or the use of large amounts of free timber is indicated by transportation costs. A good example of this is the account for rebuilding the king's ship *Grand Marie* at Southampton in 1422–3, which records only a modest £8 4s 8d being spent on timber for this major undertaking. The true amount of timber used is suggested by the payments for its carriage: 140 cartloads of wood were brought from the royal New Forest and another wood.[22]

However, the weight of the evidence in royal shipbuilding accounts – whether built directly by the Crown, or for the government by local authorities – suggest that it was rare to build ships with timber from a single source; for most projects, timber seems to have come from a multiplicity of suppliers, often in small amounts. Three of the 1295 galleys had over forty named timber suppliers apiece: forty-four for the second London galley, sixty-four for the York galley and a staggering eighty-nine or more for the Newcastle galley. In each of these cases, three-quarters or more of the suppliers sold timber and boards in lots worth less than £1. The pattern is repeated in later accounts. The twenty-six-oar Newcastle barge of 1304 had over thirty-one suppliers, the eighty-oar galley *Philippe*, built at King's Lynn in 1337, had thirty-two. In both cases most suppliers sold goods worth less than £1. Even as late as 1519, the *Katerine Pleasaunce*, a ship built for Henry VIII, had over twenty-four suppliers, eleven of whom made less than £1 each out of the deal.[23]

As a large user of shipbuilding materials, the Crown would presumably have been able to attract the interest of any large timber merchants, had they existed. The accounts of the king's ships between 1399 and 1411, however, reveal that over this period (there is a gap for 1402–4) at least 102 people supplied the clerk of the king's ships with timber, but only forty of them sold timber in amounts that exceeded £1 in total value. There was also a high turnover of suppliers: out of forty-three in 1399–1400, only nine supplied timber in the following accounting year, which also saw the appearance of thirty-two new suppliers. By 1410–11 only one of the suppliers of 1399–1400 was still selling timber to the Crown.[24]

The fact that the Crown had to buy so much timber in a piecemeal fashion suggests that timber supply may have been a problem for English shipbuilding in general. Building accounts for vessels constructed by municipalities tend to confirm this. The reason for a 'timber problem' probably lay in the lack of an organised system of supply. The multiplicity of small-scale (and probably, in most cases, non-specialist) suppliers seems to have created a situation in which the shipbuilding industry had to acquire its essential material on an *ad hoc* basis. Contemporaries would not have seen this as a problem, but it must have acted as a powerful brake on the development of the industry.

The supply situation for some other materials was different. Iron, whether worked or unworked, was usually bought from smiths, occasionally in large quantities. Two examples serve to illustrate this. In 1337, 3.45 tons of Spanish iron was supplied for the construction of the galley *Philippe* at King's Lynn. The iron came from five men, the smallest individual quantity being 280 lb (127.3 kg). The total cost of each hundredweight (112 lb; 50.9 kg) was 11s., of which half was taken up with the cost of the material and half with its working into nails, anchors and other items. Just over half the iron was supplied by one man, and a similar pattern is observable in the royal accounts of the years 1399–1402. Fourteen individuals sold iron for the king's ships in this period, at a total value of £86 9s, but £67 3s of this (77.7 per cent) came from a London smith named John Esgaston.[25]

Iron was only mined and processed in a few areas in medieval England, such as the Weald and the Forest of Dean. Imported iron, from the Baltic and particularly from Spain, was reputed to be of higher quality than the native product (Spanish iron was also used for shipbuilding in other parts of northern Europe). Recent research has challenged the view that Wealden iron was quite so poor in quality as some scholars have thought, but England seems nevertheless to have been heavily dependent on imports. In the year 1449–50, more than 1380 tons were imported – enough for millions of nails – and between 1487 and 1494 there were three years when recorded imports ranged between 2000 and 2900 tons. The bulk of imported iron came from the Basque provinces of Spain, although most of the small amounts of steel (seldom used in shipbuilding) brought into the country came from the Baltic.[26]

There was also a tendency for a small number of suppliers to predominate, where expensive items such as cordage and sailcloth were concerned. In at least one case there may have been a special relationship between the Crown and a particular merchant family. The clerk of the king's ships bought some £334 10s worth of canvas and cordage in the years 1399–1402 and 1404–6. Three men supplied materials worth more than £40 each, and a fourth, William Reynwell, was paid £140 13s for his goods (42.0 per cent of the total). Reynwell was a prominent London ironmonger (having moved from the Girdler's gild in 1399), who died *c.* 1403–4. In 1415 his son John, a fishmonger and later alderman of the City, sold sailcloth and canvas to the value of £285 to the Crown, for use in the first of Henry V's great ships, the *Trinity Royal* (for evidence of the manufacture of cordage in England, see Chapter 5).[27] The handling of higher-value goods such as iron, cordage and canvas would have required the possession of capital, and it was perhaps inevitable that their supply tended to be in fewer hands than that of timber.

THE SHIPBUILDING SITE

Carriage of materials

Once acquired, the construction materials had to be moved to the place where the ship was to be built. Carts and boats were used extensively for transportation. The actual state of the road network in medieval England is not easy to determine. B. P. Hindle has concluded that many Roman roads were still in use, particularly in central and southern England, in addition to routes which had been opened up since the Roman period. Individual studies have highlighted the importance of road traffic in the medieval economy. For instance, the Southampton Brokage Books of the fifteenth century show that in about 1440, wine was travelling by road up to sixty miles from the port, and dyestuffs were transported over a hundred miles, as far west as Exeter, and as far north as Leicester.[28]

The distances over which shipbuilding materials were transported were less spectacular, but vessels rarely seem to have been built with timber from an adjacent wood. The Ipswich galley of 1295 drew

3.4 Sources of some materials for the 1295 London galleys.

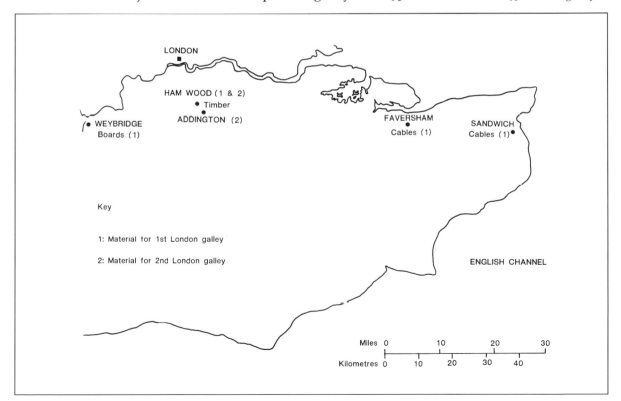

3.5 Sources of some workmen and materials for the 1295 Southampton galley.

3.6 BELOW Sources of some materials for building the 'great boat' of the *Trinity* at Newhithe, Kent, 1400.

materials from Stoke, just the other side of the River Orwell, but timber also came from Nacton Park, some four miles away, and 507 boards were bought at Bawdsey and carried the ten miles to the town. Timber for the London galleys of 1295 was carted at least ten miles from two woods in Surrey, but as can be seen from Figure 3.4, boards bought at Weybridge (over twenty miles distant), and cables from Faversham and Sandwich, were all moved by boat. The timber sources for the contemporary Southampton galley were within ten miles of the port (see Fig. 3.5), but as with the London galleys, specialised items such as the mast, yard and sail were brought some distance by water.

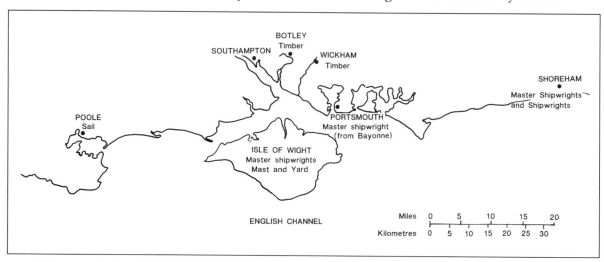

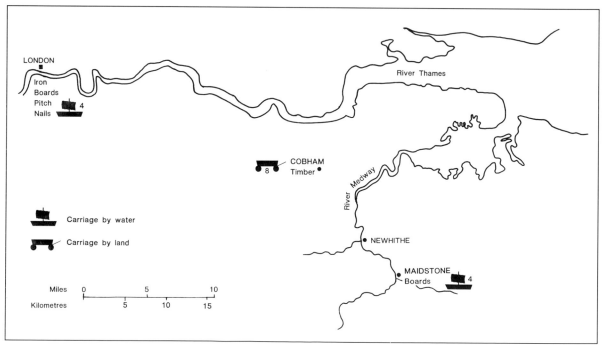

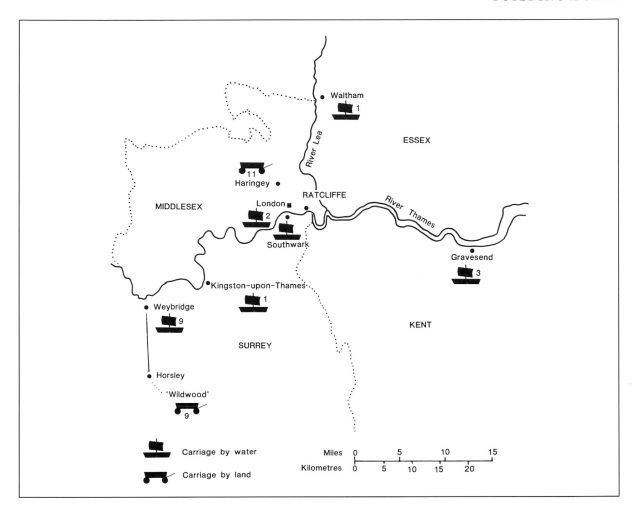

Waltham
1

ESSEX

River Lea

11
Haringey

RATCLIFFE

River Thames

MIDDLESEX

London
2

Southwark

Gravesend
3

Kingston-upon-Thames
1

Weybridge
9

KENT

Horsley

SURREY

"Wildwood"
9

Carriage by water

Carriage by land

Miles   0   5   10   15
Kilometres 0   5   10   15   20

3.7 Sources of timber for building the balinger *Godegrace*, at Ratcliffe, 1401.

Distances of ten to twenty miles may have been the practical limit for the carriage of timber by road, but it is clear that water transport made much longer journeys possible. When the 'great boat' of 40 oars for the *Trinity* was built at Newhithe in 1400, iron, pitch and some other materials made the long journey down the Thames, out into the Thames estuary, and then down the Medway (see Fig. 3.6). In the following year the builders of the *Godegrace* at Ratcliffe obtained timbers from as far west as Horsley in Surrey (taken by cart to Weybridge and then on by boat), and as far east as Gravesend (see Fig. 3.7).[29]

There was no shortage of heavy road vehicles, even in the later thirteenth century. For example, in the eleventh week of the construction of the second London galley, thirty carts were at work moving timber from Adington Wood in Surrey. Most of these had two-horse teams, but two had three horses apiece, and one even had six, being used to carry the galley's heavy mast-step to Greenwich (presumably for transhipment). Just over two centuries later, the building of the

Katerine Pleasaunce required the movement of over 500 cart-loads of timber, besides considerable river traffic.[30]

Type and organisation of sites

Medieval records seldom specify the locations of shipbuilding sites, although it was quite common for vessels to be built on rivers: riverine locations were less exposed than coastal sites, and some great ports, such as London, Newcastle and Hull, were situated on rivers. There is less evidence of ships being built on the sea-shore. Of the vessels studied here, only the Dunwich galley and barge of 1295, the contemporary Lyme galley and the ship *Margaret* of 1415–16 (a royal ship from Beaumaris in Wales) seem to have been constructed by the sea, for all of these places lacked deep rivers.[31]

Ships were built at all major ports, and many minor ones, but it is hard to identify actual shipbuilding 'quarters'. One exception was the tiny Kentish port of Smallhythe, situated on the north bank of the Reding Creek, a few miles from Rye, Winchelsea and the sea (see Figs 3.8 and 3.9). The area seems to have had its heyday between about 1400 and 1550. The New Romney town ship was built at Smallhythe in 1401, and in the decade 1410–20 the port constructed the barge *Marie*, the balinger *George* (120 tons) and the great ship *Jesus* (1000 tons) for the Crown. The 40-ton royal balinger *Gabriel Harfleur* was also rebuilt there,

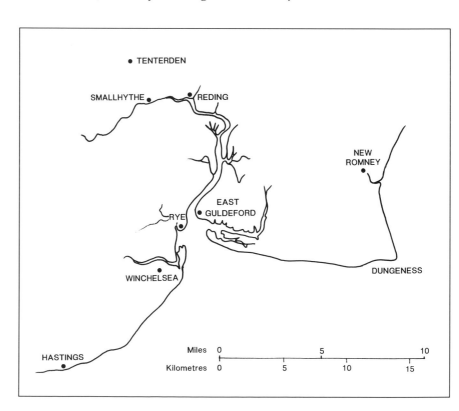

3.8 The area around Smallhythe, Kent, in the later Middle Ages (after Mayhew 1987).

3.9 Modern photograph of what appears to have been a medieval shipbuilding dock, at the former shipbuilding centre of Smallhythe in Kent. Although it is now used as a garden pond, this unusual straight-sided feature was drained some years ago and a number of ship's clench-nails were found at the bottom.

giving a total of more than 1160 tons of shipping in ten years. In the later 1480s the nearby settlement of Reding built Henry VII's 1000-ton *Regent*, and Smallhythe itself was still supplying the Tudor monarchy with warships as late as the 1540s.[32]

Another small Kent port, at Newhithe on the river Medway, was also a shipbuilding centre, though on a humbler scale than Smallhythe. In addition to the 'great boat' built about 1400 for the *Trinity*, Newhithe shipwrights built and maintained the boats used for repairing Rochester bridge. In 1450–1 two shipwrights from the port were paid over £15 for building a 26-ton lighter for the Bridge Wardens.[33] Both these sites in Kent show the virtue of sheltered riverside locations for shipbuilding; and Smallhythe in particular demonstrates that it was possible to build even the largest medieval ships far from major ports.

It was, however, the great ports, with their concentrations of ship-owning merchants, that provided shipwrights with most of their work. Particular areas around these ports may have functioned as shipbuilding quarters, but, even in London and its environs, evidence for this is not strong. In the sixteenth century, such places as Wapping, Shadwell, Ratcliffe, Limehouse and Blackwall on the north bank of the Thames were important centres for shipbuilding and repair, but, despite the existence of a royal ship maintenance store at Ratcliffe in the mid-fourteenth century, there is little indication of a flourishing maritime industry in these areas in the Middle Ages. A royal vessel, the 100-ton balinger *Godegrace*, was built at Ratcliffe in 1401, but the fact that a dock had to be dug specially suggests that there may have been no suitable local docks.[34]

In fact, with the exception of places such as Smallhythe and the handful of temporary royal bases, the general impression is that, since medieval ship construction did not require expensive fixed installations or equipment, the selection of a site was rather arbitrary. Vacant plots were hired for the construction of the Southampton galley in 1294 and for building the galley *Philippe* at King's Lynn in 1337. In 1497, 6s. 8d was paid to hire a site and 'Workehouse' for construction of the bark *Mary Fortune*, 'the grounde wher the said Ship was made'. The building area for the 1295 Newcastle galley had to be cleared before work commenced, suggesting a virgin site.[35]

The haphazard digging of building docks seems to have caused problems in some places. In 1475–6 the city of Bristol forbade anyone without licence 'to break any ground in and about Bristol to make any ship'. Some shipwrights failed to fill in the docks they had dug, and at Southampton in the sixteenth century this was a recurrent public nuisance: in 1573, unfilled docks by the West Quay and the watergate were becoming navigational hazards.[36] Some shipwrights built ships wherever was convenient to them, without regard to the interests of other users of the river-bank or shoreline. This further suggests that established yards were rare. While some great merchants, such as the fifteenth-century Bristol magnate William Canynges,[37] could afford to run yards to maintain their own ships, building 'on spec' or waiting for orders would have been too risky for most shipwrights, given their low social and economic position in the Middle Ages. It is unlikely that there were many shipwright 'entrepreneurs', and without such craftsmen/businessmen established yards could not exist.

Even temporary sites required a basic infrastructure, usually in the form of store buildings, a workshop, access to a smithy and a site enclosure to prevent theft. The site for building the first London galley in 1294–5 was enclosed with a fence consisting of 140 pieces of timber and 33 empty tuns, the latter presumably broken up into barrel-staves to serve as fence planks. A carpenters' workshop (*domo carpentariorum*) was made from wattle and daub, and thatched with reeds. Fences were also used to protect the Southampton, York and Newcastle galley sites, and that of the galley *Philippe* at King's Lynn in 1337. In the case of the Newcastle galley, a fenced garden was used for storing timber, and it had a locked gate. The builders of the York galley had at least two huts, one of which was a forge. This was another wattle-and-daub building, roofed with turf, and tiles were used to make a hearth and chimney. Some form of smithy was erected for the work on the balinger *Godegrace* at Ratcliffe in 1401, although here the chimney was made from eight pieces of elm. The fifteenth-century accounts are generally less informative about site structures, but we know that the dock for building the *Grace Dieu* at Southampton between 1416 and 1418 was enclosed with a 'hedge' of thorns and stakes. The site for rebuilding the balinger

Petit Jesus at nearby Bursledon in 1435–6 was also enclosed.[38]

In the mid-fourteenth century, the Crown had some workshops and stores for its ships at the Tower of London and Ratcliffe. The inventories of their gear show that there was some rope-making machinery on site (see Chapter 5), but also a large number of wood- and metalworking tools, including a lathe, hammers, axes, saws, chisels, anvils, bellows, pincers and other items. A *fforgehouse* (smithy) was established at Southampton in the reign of Henry v for use by the royal fleet based there and in the River Hamble, and a couple of storehouses were built at the village of Hamble itself (a 'hovel-store' measuring 160 feet by 14 feet was also erected at Southampton in the 1420s for the storage of masts).[39] Semi-permanent installations of this type were a rarity. It was more common either to build temporary huts or to hire premises. Most shipbuilding sites were makeshift and cheap.[40]

The only real technological changes in shipbuilding procedures (aside from the major change from clinker to skeleton construction) took place in the ways ships were moved from the building site to the water, or vice versa (see Fig. 3.10). Launching ships down a slipway has long been the usual method, but the documentary evidence suggests that matters were not always that simple for medieval vessels. The Ipswich, Lyme, Newcastle, Southampton and York galleys of 1295, and the King's Lynn galley *Philippe* of 1337, were all built above water-level and launched by pulling them to the water. The *Philippe* seems to have been simply pulled to the river, but in the other cases the method was more elaborate: a launching channel was dug from the galley to the waterside, and the vessel was pulled down it on rollers. The launching channels do not appear to have been intended as anything more than temporary aids to launching: they cannot have been building docks, as most were dug towards the end of each construction period.[41]

Early medieval ships were probably run ashore into mud berths ('wet docks') for repairs below the waterline, but such repairs were only possible at low tide. A new technique appears in the sources from the 1330s onwards, a development which could be called the 'tidal dock'. When the royal ship *All Hallow's Cog* was repaired on the River Itchen near Southampton in 1337, a dock (*fossum*) was dug to accommodate the ship, with a wall which stood between the ship and the water.[42] The ship must have been floated in at high tide, and allowed to settle on the bottom at low tide. Once the dock was empty of water, a wall could be hastily thrown up to prevent it refilling at high tide. With repairs completed, the wall could simply be broken down and the vessel allowed to float out as the water rose.

A variation would have been needed for the construction of ships, with a dock dug at the waterside, but separated from the water by a bank or wall which would only be breached when the ship was capable of floating. Two small oared vessels, the *Cog Johan* and the *Jonette*, may

3.10 Different types of shipbuilding, launching and docking facilities known to have been in use in England between *c.* 1295 and *c.* 1500 (with the dates by which they are known to have been used):

A Launching channel (by 1295)
B Wet dock at high tide, with the dock flooded (by 1295)
C Wet dock at low tide, with the dock drained
D 'Tidal dock' at high tide, with the wall or dam in place (by 1330s)
E 'Tidal dock' at low tide, with the wall or dam in place
F Dry dock at high tide, with the gates closed and the water pumped out. The pump is shown on the left-hand side (by 1495)
G Dry dock at high tide, with the gates removed and the dock flooded, ready for the ship to be floated out.

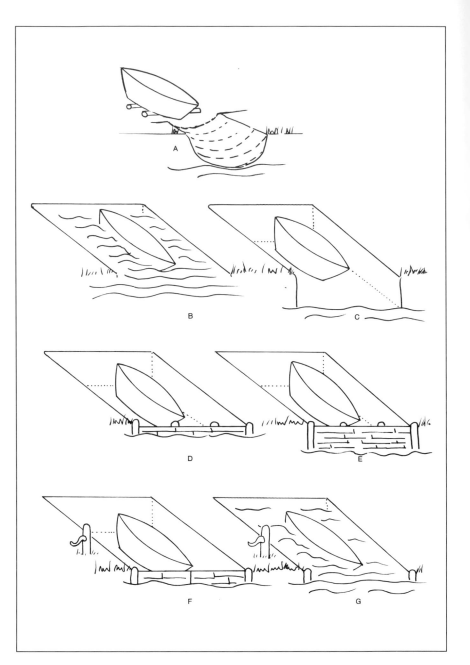

have been built by this method at Winchelsea in 1348. Forty man-days were spent by diggers making *delfs* ('diggings') for the construction of each of these craft. As construction was specified here rather than launching, the two *delfs* may well have been building docks. Some type of dockhead wall or 'weir' (*ware*) seems to have been erected in 1373 at the entrance to a covered dock, or 'galley house', built for a royal galley at Fordwich in Kent in 1373.[43]

By the beginning of the sixteenth century, tidal docks seem to have been in common use: between 1401 and 1423, eight royal ships were either built or rebuilt in docks. These were used for work on vessels ranging in size from the 40-ton balinger *Gabriel Harfleur* to the 1400-ton *Grace Dieu*.[44] The channel-launching method may have sufficed for shallow-draught vessels such as galleys, but sailing vessels with deeper hulls would have been much easier to 'launch' if they could simply be floated off the bottom of a dock.

Tidal docks were the predecessors of the great dry-dock constructed at Portsmouth in 1495. Built for the maintenance of Henry VII's two great ships the *Regent* and the *Sovereign*, the dock cost just over £194, and at that date was probably the most expensive waterfront installation in English history. The dock was emptied by means of an 'Injyn [engine] to drawe water owte of the seid dokke', evidently some type of pump, assisted by four iron-bound buckets. There were wood-and-iron gates, but these had to be partially sealed up with clay, and were difficult to open: the 'gates' may have in fact been a removable dam rather than a pair of hinged openings. Nevertheless, the dry-dock was a great advance, for it meant that water could now be emptied from a dock without having to rely on the tide. Furthermore, it was now possible to build docks with floors below the low-tide mark, making it easier to dock very large ships. Despite such advances, dry-docks were never very common in the sixteenth-century, and many vessels clearly continued to be built on level ground adjacent to water. When Henry VIII's new ship *Katerine Pleasaunce* was launched at Deptford in 1519, a stable had to be partially demolished to allow the vessel to reach the river! This must have been a surface-launching, for no dock would have been dug behind a waterside structure.[45]

Henry VII's dry-dock was not the only innovation in its field. In 1517 the construction of a new dock was ordered at Deptford dockyard. It was to be large enough to hold five of the king's great ships (including the *Mary Rose*), but unlike the dry-dock it was to remain filled with water at all times. The dock was to be equipped·with a gate and a system of sluices, used to keep the dock filled, even when the Thames was at low tide.[46] By 1520, English skills in dock engineering seem to have been in advance of those to be found elsewhere in Europe.

Tools and gear

Each shipwright, like any other medieval craftsman, would have owned a set of the tools of his trade. There are occasional references to the transport of shipwrights' tools to the building site (in North Wales in 1282, or at Southampton in 1295), showing the existence of personal tool-kits, but the strongest evidence is of the negative kind: with the exception of certain types, tools are seldom listed in shipbuilding accounts in any quantity. It is possible, however, to build up a picture of the sorts of gear to be found on a late medieval shipbuilding site; none

was very expensive, and few items could be considered as specialised 'maritime' equipment.

The hand-tools most commonly listed are augers. They are mentioned, for instance, in the accounts for the York galley and barge (1295), the *Grace Dieu* (c. 1418), the *Grand Marie* (1422–3) and *Petit Jesus* (1435–6). Augers were used to drill holes into planks or frames for trenails or iron bolts (see Figs 3.11 and 3.12). This arduous work wore the tools out very quickly; more than ten replacement augers had to be bought for work on the York galley.[47]

A mid-1360s inventory of shipwrights' gear in royal ownership includes two bolsters (a type of chisel), two other chisels, four hand-hammers, a lathe with wooden stocks, two pynsons (pincers?), one saw and two sledge-hammers (see Figs 3.12 and 3.13). The side-axe and adze were used for squaring, shaping and trimming timbers and planks (see Fig. 3.13), but there is little written record of their use in England. They had been the basic tools of European shipwrights from at least the early Middle Ages: in medieval France and Italy, master shipwrights were known as 'masters of the axe'. The reason for their non-appearance in English records is probably because they were commonplace items in the personal tool-kits of individual shipwrights.[48]

Miscellaneous ancillary equipment on a site could range from rope for dragging timber, to wheelbarrows (the latter used in at least one case to carry earth from a dock). Clay pots were a common purchase, for heating pitch, tar and tallow used in caulking (filling the spaces between the planks with waterproofing materials). For instance, thirteen such pots were bought for carrying and heating pitch used in caulking the 'great boat' of the *Trinity* at Newhithe in 1400. These materials were applied to a hull in a number of ways. The 'greaser' (*unguentarius*) of the Newcastle galley used an old net for tallowing the hull, and a net was used to apply pitch and tar to the York galley. Mops (*mappoldes*) for pitching and tallowing were made from a range of materials including sheepskin and canvas. References to other tools of the caulker's trade are very sparse, although two *kalkyngireyns* ('caulking irons') were used in the repair of the balinger *Gabriel Harfleur* in 1415 (these were probably chisel-like implements used to drive the caulking materials – old rope or moss – between the planks: see Fig. 3.14).[49]

Laying the keel was the first step in building a vessel, and for most craft of any size, timber blocks or stocks would have to be set into the ground to provide a level platform. The *Godegrace* account of 1401 mentions the purchase of timber for blocks, and those for the *Thomas* (1418–20) and the *Petit Jesus* (1435–6) show that both vessels were laid upon stocks for rebuilding. Some of the pieces of timber of unspecified purpose, mentioned in some accounts, probably served this function.[50]

As a hull progressed, it needed to be shored up to prevent collapse. A

3.11 A breast-auger being used to drill holes for clench-nails in the hull of a clinker-built vessel. English manuscript, thirteenth century.

Coment uře seigꝫ comenda a noel faire vne arch et y metre vne paire de touf les besr pour le deluge

3.13 Noah building the Ark. French manuscript, early fifteenth century. The 'Ark' is actually a flat-bottomed punt-like craft. The carpenter on the right is using a side-axe, the traditional medieval shipwright's tool, to trim a plank pegged to some trestles.

large number of shoring spars were bought for the Newcastle galley of 1295, and 32 alder spars were used to prop up the Lyme galley. At least 280 oaken and alder spars were needed to support the 600-ton *Sovereign* when it was placed in the new dry-dock at Portsmouth in 1496.[51]

Shipbuilding scaffolds are only mentioned in the Newcastle galley and the *Godegrace* accounts (see Fig. 3.15 for an illustration of a scaffold). This is somewhat surprising, as one would imagine that scaffolding

3.14 A caulker working with a caulking-iron on the plank-seams of a ship (after a Flemish manuscript of *c.* 1470–80, now in the British Library).

would have been required to allow the shipwrights easy access to a hull as it rose higher. Two ladders used for this purpose are referred to in the *Mary Fortune* account of 1497, but the apparent lack of this type of structure is difficult to explain.[52]

Workers and operations

The time taken to build a vessel varied from site to site. The York galley was ready after twenty-six weeks to be sent down the Ouse to Swinefleet, where it needed four weeks' further work. The contemporary 120-oar Newcastle galley rolled into the water after twenty-three weeks, but final fitting-out was only achieved by about the forty-first week. Smaller vessels could be built much faster. A 26-oar barge was built at Newcastle (perhaps from a pre-existing hull) in five weeks in 1304, and a 30-oar barge was completed at King's Lynn in 1337 in a speedy three weeks. Later accounts are less informative about building times. An exception is the account for constructing the *Katerine Pleas-*

aunce at Deptford. The shipwrights began work on this vessel on 22 February 1519, and seem to have finished most of their work by late October.[53]

Shipwrights were, of course, the main part of the labour force on a shipbuilding site, but they were by no means the only people employed. Often carpenters (apparently not always shipwrights) were sent to a particular wood or park to select and fell timber for a vessel: a skilled eye was required to choose the right pieces of timber to make curved frames or the wooden brackets or 'knees' (in the eighteenth century this was called 'compass timber'; in the sixteenth century, 'crooked timber'). In the York galley account, the first payments to carpenters are not to shipwrights, but to 25 men felling trees in Scalm wood between 23 and 25 February 1295. The first week of the actual construction of the galley did not begin until 27 March. The practice of tree-felling for particular ships went on into the sixteenth century, and could involve a considerable amount of labour. The total number of shipwright man-days spent in building the *Katerine Pleasaunce* in 1518–19 was 3811, but the man-days for felling timber amounted to 471, equivalent to over 12 per cent of the shipwright effort.[54]

Shipwrights were capable of producing boards and frames out of timbers using their axes or adzes alone (it was a commonplace image in medieval shipbuilding scenes; see Fig. 3.13), but sawing was perhaps a faster method. Sawyers assisted with shipbuilding work from at least the late thirteenth century and probably much earlier. They worked on the Lyme and Southampton galleys, and were employed on many sites (usually in teams of two) throughout the medieval period (see Fig. 3.15). The work could be very arduous: for example, 3500 ft (1067 m) of timber was sawn for the *Mary Fortune* in 1497.[55]

There were two other major classes of specialist workers employed in shipbuilding: smiths and caulkers. Smiths produced the many thousands of clench-nails, spikes, bolts and ordinary nails required for a hull as well as other pieces of ironwork, such as chains and rigging- or rudder-fittings. These men sometimes worked on site, in purpose-built smithies, or used their own nearby workshops. Ships of any size required ironwork in enormous quantities. For example, 14,715 iron clench-nails and other fasteners were supplied for the 54-oar Lyme galley of 1295; over a century later, labourers grubbing around in the charred wreckage of Henry v's *Grace Dieu* in the River Hamble were able to recover over 7.5 tons (7636 kg) of clench-nails, bolts and chains.[56] For its size, the shipbuilding industry must have been a prodigious consumer of ironwork.

The only new shipbuilding trade to appear in the later medieval records was that of the caulker or *calfatour*. The caulker was a workman employed to waterproof the seams of the hull planks (see Fig. 3.14). The term 'caulking' is first noted in the account for building the galley

3.15 OPPOSITE Detail from a painting of the Martyrdom of St. Catherine, Antwerp School, *c.* 1540, showing shipbuilding and ship repair on a beach. Two small boats are being worked on in the foreground, and two ships are being careened for caulking. The vessel in the middle ground is being hauled over by means of a beach-windlass, with a cable attached to the mainmast. The one in the background is being re-caulked from a raft (see Chapter 9). Another large ship is under construction, with a scaffold built around it to give the shipwrights access to the hull as it rises higher. Nearby, two sawyers are at work on a timber set up on trestles.

Philippe at King's Lynn in 1337, where 450 Norwegian boards were purchased *pro calefattacione et dennagio* ('for the caulking and dunnage/ceiling') of the galley. The existence of the trade is also indicated by a 1348 reference to the tallowing and caulking (*la netter suer & calfat*) of the castle of the *Cog Thomas*, and in 1364–5 twelve barrels of pitch and tar were used *super calfating* the ships *Philippe* and *Seinte Marie Cog*. Caulkers were employed with some regularity in the fifteenth century, as in the maintenance of the ship *Trinity* in about 1401, its rebuilding as the *Trinity Royal* between 1413 and 1416, and in the construction and maintenance of other major vessels belonging to Henry v.[57]

Wooden vessels needed caulking, however, long before the term was coined. It seems likely that this work was done either by shipwrights, or by the type of men described in the Ipswich, Lyme and Newcastle galley accounts: *unguentarii* ('greasers'). These were men who greased the hull with a preservative coating of tallow, a task which was linked with the waterproofing function of caulking. As caulkers were not employed on every building project (in the *Trinity*'s 'great boat' – large oared boat – of 1400, or the balinger *Godegrace* of 1401, for example) it seems that the caulking may still sometimes have been carried out by the shipwrights themselves. Nevertheless, caulking emerged as a distinct trade in England, perhaps towards the mid-fourteenth century.[58]

Craftsmen from the house-building industry were employed on a number of ship construction projects. Ordinary carpenters sometimes worked on the superstructures of vessels. In 1348 seven 'castle-wrights' were paid to make a castle for the vessel *Cog Johan* and to work on the defensive bulwarks of the same vessel, and in about 1416 a number of house-carpenters worked on the great ship *Jesus*. Joiners were occasionally also used in shipbuilding for lighter and more decorative work, such as the making of rails.[59] Painters were employed on some vessels, but they are not so common in the accounts as to suggest that many medieval vessels were a blaze of colour. Elaborate decoration – including woodcarving – was probably reserved for a few special royal ships, such as Henry v's *Trinity Royal*. In 1416 the decorations of this great ship included a gilded copper crown for the topcastle, a painted wooden leopard wearing a crown, and even a gilded copper sceptre to go on top of the capstan, worked in the form of three fleur-de-lis. Masons, bricklayers and plumbers worked on the installation of brick cooking hearths in ships, for example the *Trinity Royal* or Henry viii's *Mary Rose*, but we do not know how much they were used in the construction of ordinary merchantmen (for a further discussion of cooking facilities, see Chapter 6).[60]

A range of other workers were employed in shipbuilding, but, like the building craftsmen mentioned above, none could be described as shipbuilding specialists. They performed the truly menial tasks and included porters to shift wood and gear about the site, boys to act as servants to the shipwrights, or to keep watch on the site at night, and the labourers who dug ditches or docks. Women are rarely mentioned as workers in connection with ship construction. The sail of the galley *Philippe* at King's Lynn in 1337 was sewn together by a group of women (a job, it would seem, more usually undertaken by sailors) and a maidservant was employed for the three painters who painted the Newcastle galley in 1295, but these are isolated references.[61] Shipbuilding in the Middle Ages, as in later periods, was a man's world.

Between the late thirteenth century and the latter part of the fifteenth the English shipbuilding trade apparently experienced little significant change. The development of the building dock and the appearance of the caulking trade were important steps, but they were changes of technique within an established tradition of clinker ship construction. The advent of the Mediterranean technique of skeleton construction in the mid-fifteenth century (see Chapter 9) presented this traditional industry with both a different form of technology and the possibility of radical changes in craft organisation. The potential for resistance to new methods could have been considerable, and the explanation for the introduction, and later triumph, of skeleton ship construction in England may lie in the economics of the trade.

THE ECONOMICS OF SHIPBUILDING

This discussion is based on the analysis of accounts for building some thirty-three vessels, ranging in date from Edward I's galleys of 1295 to a Newcastle municipal barge of 1510 and the *Henri Grace a Dieu* of 1512. Seventeen of the accounts date from the period 1295–1348, and the remaining twelve from the years 1400–1514 (some accounts cover more than one vessel), so they can be studied as two chronological groups. The majority of these were royal ships, but for reasons set out in Chapter 1, I believe that the information on costs contained in these accounts is valid as evidence of more general trends in shipbuilding economics. Table 4 gives the average percentage costs of some materials and wages recorded in these sources. The proportional costs (1295–1348 percentage figure followed by that for 1400–1514) of the shipbuilding sites themselves (1.44; 0.86) were minimal, and may even have declined in the fifteenth century. Also, the relative costs of waterproofing materials (4.44; 4.24) and rig (12.01; 14.17) altered very little over the period. The lack of change in the 1400–1514 accounts is all the more remarkable when one considers that at least four of these accounts were for vessels with three or more masts; the earlier ships were all one-masters. The development of the multi-masted vessel, the other great shipping revolution of the fifteenth century (see Chapters 5 and 9), does not seem to have cost much more, in proportional terms, than the old one-masted rig.

The most dramatic shifts in relative costs occurred with respect to timber, boards, iron nails and shipwrights's wages. Boards and timber became rather less costly (boards: 15.49; 11.51; timber: 14.08; 5.58) but the average proportional cost of iron nails almost doubled (7.39; 14.04). Out of all these vessels, only the *Henri Grâce à Dieu* was skeleton-built; the rest were clinker-built. Iron nails, particularly heavy clench-nails, were a major component in clinker construction, whereas skeleton-built ships made much greater use of the cheaper wooden fasteners (trenails), evidently an incentive for switching to skeleton construction.

Another incentive was in the form of the rising wage costs. The 1295–1348 figures (23.33 per cent) pre-dates the Black Death and a succession of other plagues, which induced a catastrophic drop in population. This decline levelled off in the fifteenth century, but there was no significant rise in population levels until the 1520s. The resulting labour shortage meant that workers now had an advantage when it came to wage demands: the real purchasing power of wages, both of skilled and unskilled men, began to rise in the second half of the fourteenth century, and continued to do so until the early sixteenth century.[62] While it is not surprising to find this reflected in the shipbuilding industry, clinker and skeleton construction required different types of labour. Quite a large proportion of the workforce for clinker construction, in which the hull was shaped from a shell of planks, had to be fairly skilled men, such as the berders. A skeleton-built hull, on the other hand, was formed from a skeleton of frames on to which the planks were then nailed. The shaping and erection of frames could be done by a few skilled men; nailing on the planks was labour-intensive, but did not call for great skill.

It is believed that skeleton construction originated in the Mediterranean between about the seventh and eleventh centuries AD. Hull construction in the Roman period was a complex process, and, after the collapse of the Western Roman Empire in the fifth century, the skills required were probably in short supply. It has been plausibly suggested that skeleton construction developed out of a search for a cheaper alternative.[63] An analogous situation seems to have existed in fifteenth-century England, where clinker construction was becoming much more expensive, in terms of wage costs and the relative cost of iron nails. Skeleton construction seemingly offered an alternative requiring fewer skilled men and used a cheaper method for holding a hull together. The traditional names of craftsmen – berder, clencher and holder – are conspicuously absent from the accounts for the construction and maintenance of the mostly skeleton-built royal ships in the reign of Henry VIII (although the terminology remained in legislation for decades). The old three- or four-level wage structure also seems to have broken down, not surprisingly, for it was tied to the old craft structure, which in turn was based on clinker construction. When the

Katerine Pleasaunce was built at Deptford in 1519, the shipwrights and caulkers employed were paid at eleven different wage-rates, ranging from 1d to 8d per day. What the royal accounts do not reveal is a sudden tumbling of the proportional wages costs in shipbuilding. Just under 61 per cent of the total amount spent on building the *Henri Grâce à Dieu* and three galleys at Woolwich in 1512–14 went out in wages and associated expenses. About 60 per cent of the total work required to build the *Katerine Pleasaunce* was carried out by the shipwrights who received the top wages, a proportion actually greater than on some early fifteenth-century construction projects. This means either that potential savings in wages was not one of the factors which promoted the adoption of skeleton construction, or that contemporaries *believed* it was cheaper because it dispensed with the old, fixed wage structure. Other possible reasons for the triumph of skeleton construction are discussed in Chapter 9, but one thing is clear: clinker construction, which had been the predominant shipbuilding technique in England since at least the seventh century, was gradually 'dethroned' by skeleton construction in the second half of the fifteenth century.[64]

An overview

In the period 1200–1520 a certain number of general trends are evident. The shipbuilding industry may have been lacking in numbers, had low status and little corporate organisation, but its organisation at the level of the work-site remained fairly tight and consistent for at least 150 years, and probably for much longer. English shipwrights produced many different types of vessels, from small oared boats and barges to galleys and balingers of 100 oars or more, and from tiny merchantmen to the four 'great ships' of Henry V. One of these great ships, the *Grace Dieu* of 1418, ranked among the largest European ships before 1600, a remarkable achievement for a small industry. The skills of English shipwrights do not appear to have been inferior to those of their northern European counterparts.

Despite the technical achievements of the industry, English shipbuilding in the medieval period had a somewhat makeshift, casual air. The average construction site probably soon degenerated into muddy squalor, littered with wood fragments and reeking of smoke, pitch and tallow. Some sites left unsightly and dangerous holes in the ground, to plague local inhabitants and water-users alike. This casualness perhaps reflected the trade's overall lack of organisation, but such structural weakness may have had its advantages. A well-organised industry, with stronger gilds, might have been able to mount fierce resistance to the introduction of a new and potentially destabilising technique such as skeleton construction. Instead, English shipwrights seem to have adopted the new technology with relative ease.

CHAPTER 4

Hulls and castles: the parts of a medieval ship

The ship has been described as one of the most complex machines of pre-industrial times, and as 'the supreme technical achievement' of some early societies.[1] Cathedrals, castles and other great buildings may have been able to outdo the average ship in terms of sheer numbers of 'parts', but few human artefacts were called upon repeatedly to move people and goods over long distances in the teeth of very changeable, and sometimes hostile, elements. The ship combined technical complexity and versatility in ways that were not matched until the advent of steam-powered transportation.

CONSTRUCTION AND MATERIALS

Timber and boards

The documentary sources provide little evidence of the actual shapes of vessels, and while the pictorial material is better at showing what ships looked like, it is of limited use in trying to understand internal technical detail. Archaeological data provide the key to understanding just how ships were put together, but wreck evidence is seldom complete. One way in which shipbuilding accounts can help is in giving us an idea of the numbers of parts required to make a ship. The accounts do not always name the timber components used in building a vessel, but even a bald list of pieces of timber bought can contribute towards an estimate of the minimum numbers of timbers and boards used.

Sometimes the accounts list only a handful of pieces of timber. A mere seven separate timbers were listed in the brief construction account for the barge of the 1295 Ipswich galley: this was a clear under-counting, for over 600 ft (182.9 m) of boards were used in building this 30-oar vessel. Others show a similar disparity. The 1295 Southampton galley account records at least 160 timbers, a more respectable figure, but probably far from the total number of timber components used, as in excess of 12,444 ft (3793.9 m) of boards were used in the galley's hull and decking. Other accounts probably get closer to the truth. The construction of the second London galley, a huge craft of some 100 or more oars, required 2545 boards and 1111 separate pieces of timber. Neither figure gives the actual total of separate parts in the finished hull, because no count is now possible of the pieces of timber cut or sawn to make frame components or other boards on site. A century later the 100-oar balinger *Godegrace* had a hull made up of over 116 timbers, and castles with over 112 frame-parts, with more than 1655 boards used. Even quite small vessels had complicated structures. The royal escomers *Cog Johan* and *Jonette*, built at Winchelsea in 1348, were small ships with 18 and 16 oars respectively, but their hulls needed over 480 timbers and 1274 boards between them. Tudor ships were no less complex. Repairs to the warship *Mary and John* after a fire in 1512 absorbed at least 147 'loads' of timber (each probably equivalent to a ton in weight) and well over 6700 ft (2042.7 m) of boards. Some 800 timbers were removed from the wreck of the 700-ton Tudor warship *Mary Rose* before it was raised, leaving many more planks and timbers in the surviving third or so of the hull that was lifted to the surface in 1982.

It is clear that the framing and planking of even quite small medieval and sixteenth-century vessels could be very complex: each of the hundreds or thousands of separate pieces of timber or planking had to be shaped to fit an overall design, fitted into position, adjusted if needed, and then fastened in place as part of a structure that would have to withstand many stresses and strains.[2]

Clinker construction, which predominated in England until at least the mid-fifteenth century,[3] is a form of 'shell construction' (i.e. the main load-bearing part of a shell-built ship's hull is the shell of planking, with the frames playing a subsidiary role). The planking is built up from the keel and stem- and sternposts, with most of the frames inserted at a relatively late stage (see Fig. 4.1). This process is the reverse of skeleton construction, in which the skeleton of frames is constructed first, and the planking is then nailed to the frames. In skeleton construction, it is the framing which is the main load-bearing element (see Fig. 4.2). While these descriptions do not do full justice to the complexity of the processes involved, the general lines of development are fairly clear.[4] In clinker construction, the shell of boards consisted of strakes of overlapping planks, fastened together at the edges by nails that were clenched over on the inside faces of the inner planks, a sequence that can be followed in some medieval shipbuilding accounts. Table 5 (see Appendix) summarises evidence from the Southampton galley account of 1295, in terms of the order in which items were purchased or made over a period of seventeen weeks.

Although the exact meanings of some of the terms in the account are

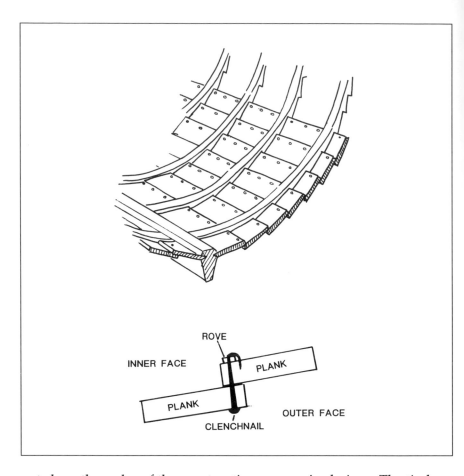

ROVE

INNER FACE

PLANK

PLANK

OUTER FACE

CLENCHNAIL

not clear, the order of the construction process is obvious. The timbers for the keel, stems (both stem- and sternposts) were purchased along with several hundred boards (totalling 7420 ft, or about 60 per cent of the total recorded length of planking used in the vessel) before construction even started. The first reference to other frame-elements does not come until the fifth week, with the purchase of floor-timber nails (floor-timbers, as the name implies, were the lowest frame members, usually attached to the keel: futtocks were attached to the floor-timbers). Actual floor-timbers are not mentioned until the ninth week. Work on the decking and defensive breastworks does not seem to have commenced until the twelfth week, with the castles, mast and yard following in the sixteenth week. Other timbers for the frame were still being bought as late as the fourteenth week. This is a shell-building sequence, with the keel, stems and a large amount of planking coming first (along with the clench-nails that fastened the planking), and the bulk of the frames being made and inserted later.

The lengths of the boards used in construction are not usually specified in the accounts, and even those few records that give an idea of board length never record the total length of planking used. Substantial

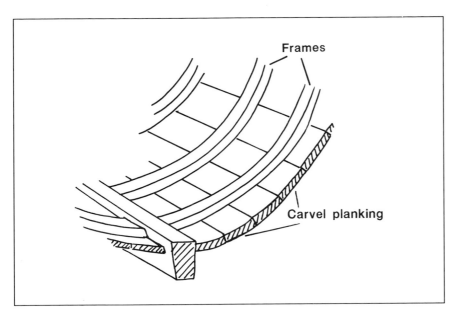

Frames

Carvel planking

minimum figures are available, however, for three of the 1295 galleys, those built at Southampton (60 oars; 12,444+ ft/3794+ m), Ipswich (100 oars; 7600+ ft/2317+ m) and Lyme (54 oars; 6200+ ft/ 1890+ m). Some idea of what this meant in terms of the vessels' sizes and construction can be gained by a comparison with a hypothetical reconstruction of the remains of the tenth-century Graveney boat. This was a small Anglo-Saxon trading vessel, able to carry some 6–7 tons of cargo, and with an estimated overall length of 44–45 ft (c. 13.7 m). The planking expansion diagram for the boat gives eleven strakes per side, with a total of about 830 ft (253 m) of board. The smallest of the 1295 galleys used at least seven times as much planking as the Graveney boat. Even allowing for extra decking, and the probability that the galleys were at least twice the size of the earlier vessel, the difference is considerable. The three galleys used more planking than one would expect to find in a single-skin clinker hull, suggesting that some or all of these vessels had double or even triple layers of planking, like that found in the wreck of the *Grace Dieu* of 1418.

The majority of the boards used in English shipbuilding, like most of the timbers, were of oak. In accounts from the fourteenth century onwards these were denoted as English-board, or sometimes Weald-ish-board (board from the Weald of Sussex and Kent). Boards used for some of the 1295 galleys ranged in length from 6 to 28 ft (1.8 8.5 m). In the Middle Ages and the sixteenth century the planking used in ships was manufactured both by sawing and cleaving or splitting tree trunks. Imported boards, also used in considerable quantities, included wain-scot (perhaps oak, in this context) and other boards from Scandinavia and the Baltic. Known initially as Eastland- or Estriche-board, some boards later acquired more specific names, such as Righolt (board from Riga), Pruce- or Spruce-board (from Prussia) and deal-board. Apart from the wainscot, most of these boards seem to have been softwood planks. As the majority of English hulls were almost certainly planked with oak, it is not easy to say where the expensive imported boards were used, although it should be noted that the early seventeenth-century authority Captain John Smith stated that 'spruce Deale' boarding was used for making the upper deck of a ship because 'it is better than any other'.[5]

Fastenings

A wide range of fastenings has been used in the history of wooden boat and ship construction. The great authority on wooden vessel construction, the late Commander Eric McKee, distinguished at least forty historical and modern methods of fastening planks, using a remarkable variety of nails, battens, tenons and even rope. More than fifty names for nail-types can be found in late and medieval English shipbuilding and repair accounts, although some may have been synonyms for the same kind of fastening. The commonest types of iron nails were the clench-nails and roves, used in clinker construction, and a range of ordinary nails, perhaps not unlike modern sash nails in shape, that were simply listed by their price per hundred. There seem to have been other, more specialised, types, such as 'calfat-nails' for caulking and 'hatch-nails' for decks, although these may have been ordinary nails being named from the uses to which they were put rather than from any peculiarity of design.[6] Wooden nails, or 'trenails', were among the most common types of fastener. These were long wooden pegs, often made on site, used to help secure the frames and sometimes, apparently, the planks themselves. Trenails were hammered into holes drilled by augers (see Chapter 3) and they could provide very strong fixings. Trenails were among the cheaper types of nail; the most expensive fasteners were large iron bolts, of up to 14 lb (6.4 kg) in weight. These never seem to have been used in large quantities, at least before the sixteenth century, and the most costly metal fastenings in regular use were the clench-nails and spikes, or 'spikings'.

The clench-nail consisted of two pieces, the main nail part and a metal washer called a rove. Clench-nails had to be fairly large, in order to penetrate at least two layers of planking, and this, with their separate rove, made them quite expensive. The biggest clench-nails known were probably those used in the hull of the *Grace Dieu* of 1418. Some of the nails that fastened the triple-skin planking of this massive hull were over 0.22 m (8.6 ins) in length, with 20 mm (0.8 in.) square-section shanks and domed heads 60–70 mm (*c.* 2.5 ins) in diameter. The rectangular roves over which these nails were clenched measured about 50 × 70 mm (2.0 × 2.75 ins). A study of clench-nail costs in accounts between 1294 and 1497 shows them costing about 21d per 100 on average between 1294 and 1380, and 30d per 100 on average between 1399 and 1497. The average cost in the period 1294–1313 was actually only about 15d, the major hike in prices coming in the mid-fourteenth century. Even 15d was a large figure however: 100 clench-nails might have been enough to secure two strakes or lines of planking on one side of a vessel, but it was the equivalent of several days' wages for a master shipwright. By comparison, the average cost of spikes was about 13d per 100 between 1294 and 1380, and about 26d between 1399 and 1497. The exact uses for spikes are not clear, but they were used in large numbers and may have helped to fasten frame elements together.

These figures are based on a fairly small range of examples, and the averages conceal some considerable variations in individual prices. The general trend is clear, however: the costs of the commonest metal fasteners rose sharply in the second half of the fourteenth century. Trenails were cheaper, and in relative terms became cheaper still, at about 9d per 100 between 1294 and 1380, and about 15d from 1399 to 1497. The introduction of skeleton construction into England in the second half of the fifteenth century probably did not require the development of any new types of nail. Although 'carvel nails' are mentioned in some accounts, and skeleton construction did not use clench-nails, it is probable that the iron spikes and trenails already in use would have been sufficient for skeleton construction (furthermore, trenails did not degrade as fast as iron nails). Although it may appear a minor concern, the cost of fastenings may well have had an influence on the pace of technological change in shipbuilding (see Chapter 9).[7]

Hull structures

The framing of clinker-built hulls may have been subsidiary to the plank shell, but it was still important, and both the planking and the frames relied on the keel as the 'backbone' of the hull, giving it structural integrity. The building accounts suggest that single-piece keels were common: out of eighteen examples (all from oared craft) recorded between 1295 and 1497, thirteen were made from a single timber, four from two timbers each, and one from three timbers. The actual lengths of most of these keels are unknown, although the keel of the 1295 Newcastle galley (of about 120 oars) was composed of one timber of 56 ft (17.1 m) and another of 52 ft (15.9 m); the balinger *Godegrace* of 1401 (100 oars) had a three-part keel made of two pieces each 40 feet in length, and one other timber of unknown length; the 68-oar balinger *Anne* of 1416 had a single-piece keel of 68 ft. One cannot estimate the lengths of the two multi-part keels just by adding the lengths of the individual parts together, because these had to be overlapped to form secure scarf joints. This evidence does, however, suggest a correlation between keel length and the number of oars in oared fighting vessels:

the 80-oar barge *Paul* of 1373 had an 80-ft keel. R. C. Anderson's suggestion that at least some English oared ships had an allowance of 2 ft of keel length to every pair of oars seems likely to be true (the implications of this for rowing technology will be discussed in Chapter 5). Data regarding the keels of sailing ships are lacking, but, if the formula 2 ft of keel = 2 oars was generally true, it suggests that single-piece keels of up to 80 ft were possible; at least one 80-oar vessel, the royal bark *Mary Fortune* of 1497, had a keel made of a single timber.[8]

Our understanding of many medieval shipbuilding records is made more difficult by the obscurity of some of the Middle English or Norman-French sea terms to be found in them. The interpretation of some of these is problematical, and in the first instance must be the concern of the etymologist. Thus the study of English medieval ships is indebted to the researches of the Swedish scholar Bertil Sandahl.[9] Although the problem of terminology can be particularly acute when it comes to words relating to hull framing, it does not mean that the documents have nothing to tell us about medieval ship structures.

It is clear that stem and stern assemblies of vessels could be quite complex. These assemblies might include a veritable menagerie of parts called stems, grounds, eches, underlouts, pike-wrongs, fowl-hooks, breasthooks, stem-locks, halse-knees, skegs and fore-skegs. 'Grunds' and 'underlouts' appear to have been the same thing, a separate section between the stempost proper and the keel: the New-castle galley of 1295 had an 'underlout' made of two timbers, while the Ipswich galley of the same date had two 'grunds' (probably one for each end of what may well have been a double-ended vessel). The 'brond' or 'brand' seems to have been the topmost of part of a stempost, while the 'eche' may have been a middle part. These four terms fell out of use during the fourteenth century, while most of the others seem to have remained current well into the fifteenth century, and some are still used by modern wooden boatbuilders.[10]

The main frames of vessels were much simpler, consisting of two main parts, the wrangs (floor timbers), in the bottom of the hull, and the futtocks, which were usually attached to the floor timbers and helped to support the sides. References to both types of timber are common in the medieval accounts, but one is seldom able to estimate how many such pieces were in the hull of a particular vessel. One possible exception was the royal ship *Mighell*, repaired between 1378 and 1380. The 'repair' may actually have been a rebuilding, for a new keel was fitted, along with two stems, twenty-six pieces of timber for wrangs and futtocks, twenty-three wrangs and twenty-seven futtocks. Assuming one futtock attached to each end of a wrang, the vessel may have had twenty-five floor-timbers and about fifty futtocks.[11]

The frames inside a hull were strengthened by a number of longitudinal timbers, ceiling planking and transverse beams. One of the widest

4.3 Town seal of Dunwich, c. 1199; drawing after Ewe 1972. Double-ended, clinker-built vessel with simple 'watchtower'-type fore- and aftercastles, and a topcastle. Four projecting beam-heads are visible, along with a large, starboard-mounted side rudder.

beams was the mast-beam, which seems to have been positioned just in front of the mast, to reinforce it. When in 1348 the mast of the escomer *Jonette* had to be moved further back (*plus arer*), two beams were bought for the purpose. Pictorial evidence (see Fig. 4.3) indicates that the beam-heads often projected through the planking, and in some cases, as in the *All Hallow's Cog* of 1337, had to be caulked with canvas to prevent them from shipping too much water.[12]

Caulking

Preventing water from entering the hull was a constant preoccupation of makers of wooden ships, and various methods were used in the attempt to make hulls watertight. Shipwrights or specialist caulkers (see Chapter 3) either laid an organic 'stopper' material between the planks as they were assembled, or drove the material into the seams between the planks after assembly, using a caulking iron (a tool like a broad chisel) and a mallet. Caulking material might consist of unpicked rope (oakum or tow), wool or other animal hair, moss or canvas. Sometimes it was already mixed with pitch, tar or bitumen before use. The hull remains of the 1418 *Grace Dieu* were caulked with moss and tar. Pitch and tar were imported from the Baltic, part of the great trade in timber, planking and other 'naval stores' that was evidently in full swing by the fifteenth century, and probably much earlier. The tar was a residue distilled from the gum of pine trees, and the pitch was a mixture of tar with resin or rosin (rosin was a solid residue left after turpentine oil had been distilled from crude turpentine). Once the caulking material was between the planks it was sealed in place with hot tar or pitch. It is possible that the underwater parts of hulls were normally coated with pitch: some pictures suggest a marked colour difference between the hull above the waterline and that below. After caulking, and perhaps after painting and varnishing, the hull was usually given a coating of tallow (animal fat), designed to help the vessel move faster through the water. In some cases this was applied by a man called a 'greaser' (*unguentarius*). Whether or not the tallow actually did have the intended effect, it would certainly have contributed to the vessel's smell.[13]

Embellishment

Although highly decorated ships occur in paintings and manuscript illuminations, the meagre documentary evidence regarding the painting and embellishment of ships mostly relates to large, prestigious royal warships. The Newcastle galley of 1295 was brightly painted: a glue or size called *cole* was mixed and boiled with eggs and applied to the surfaces of the galley's castles and breastworks to 'whiten' them before painting, and tin foil was used to cover nail heads before paint was applied. The painting materials included azure blue, vermilion, ochre, brown, red and white lead pigments, varnish, verdigris, orpiment (a bright yellow pigment), oil and cynopre (red or green dye). One hundred pieces of silver foil were bought to decorate the 'brands' (probably the tops of the stems) of the galley, along with painted tilts (cloth covers, like a canvas tilt on a lorry) to cover the hull, and banners. The painting was carried out by a certain Master John, assisted by two other painters and a maidservant. A similar galaxy of colours was used in decorating Henry v's *Trinity Royal* of 1415, and a century after that a London painter named John Wolfe received 10s for painting and gilding of 'the Collere' of Henry viii's new bark *Katerine Pleasaunce*. These vessels, and others which are documented, must have presented remarkable sights, but we still do not know how ordinary merchantmen looked. Brightly painted manuscript illustrations are perhaps not very reliable here, and most vessels probably had a nondescript appearance, sometimes enlivened by flags or painted wooden pavises (shields hung along the side).[14]

Internal features

Written information on medieval ships' internal features is sketchy. Ships had had some form of decking since Viking times, and by the thirteenth century the Middle English word 'hatch' or 'hatching' was being used for decking. It is often impossible to know whether this describes a simple working platform in a shallow-draught vessel or the covering of a deep hold. English ships supplying the royal armies in Ireland in 1171 and 1172 were issued with tilts and 'granaries' to cover the wheat they were carrying, which suggests that they may have lacked substantial decking. As remarked above, archaeological finds show that Scandinavian merchant ships of the period from before 1000 until at least the thirteenth century had only small half-decks at stem and stern, with open holds in the middle (e.g. the two merchant ship finds of *c.*1000 at Roskilde in Denmark, the twelfth-century Ellingaa ship, and the small thirteenth-century coaster found in the former harbour of Kalmar Castle in Sweden). The introduction of the full deck, with hatched access, would clearly have been a considerable advance from the point of view of the carriage of cargo. In the Mediterranean, large sailing ships with two or even three decks were being built as early as the thirteenth century, but it is not known for certain if northern European ships of any size had more than one deck before the fifteenth century. Repairs to the 330-ton royal ship *Nicholas* in about 1415 involved work on the ship's *overloppe* and *hacches* (decking or decks). It has been suggested that until the late fifteenth century, 'overlop' meant a platform running between the fore and aft superstructures of a ship, rather than an 'orlop' deck in the sense of a ship's lowest deck. Whatever its exact meaning here, the distinction between 'orlop' and 'decking' indicates that there were at least two separate deck-platforms in the ship. By the first half of the sixteenth century, larger vessels such as the *Mary Gonson* and the *Mary Rose* had at least two decks below the open weather deck (see Chapter 2).[15]

The form of a vessel's hold and superstructure naturally affected its internal features. Cabins were in use in some English ships from at least the late thirteenth century, and possibly earlier. In 1296–7 carpenters were employed at Harwich making cabins in two vessels for a voyage by the Duchess of Brabant. It is not known how many cabins were made, but they were evidently elaborate structures; 50 timber stanchions were used, along with 476 expensive planks, including poplar, Eastland and Irish boards. The cabins appear to have been below decks, or at least underneath the superstructures, for the carpenters were supplied with six pounds of candles to light their work (assuming that they were not forced to work at night!). Cabins aboard medieval ships were generally for the use of the rich and powerful and their entourages, and they must have been very restricted in number.

'Scaffolds' or platforms were erected under the deck or decks of the great 300-ton royal ship *Trinity* in 1401–2 to accommodate the knights, harbingers, squires and other members of the household of King Henry IV's new queen on their voyage from Brittany. Five lockable storage 'offices' were provided for the butlers, pantlers, spicers, ewerers and chandlers. Some cabins are known to have been made in the castles of vessels, presumably in the space under the castle deck. In 1337 the royal ship *Cog Edward* had some in its castle, with some curiously-named (and otherwise unparalleled) items called *lalkahs* or *alkahs*. The latter had hasps and staples, so were presumably hinged, and may have been doors or ventilation scuttles of some sort. The *All Hallow's Cog*, repaired about the same date, had at least two cabins in its castle, with two hinged and lockable doors. The most sumptuous cabins of the period before 1520 may have been those built for Henry VIII and Katherine of Aragon in the *Katerine Pleasaunce*, constructed in 1519 and perhaps one of the closest things to an English royal yacht before the time of Charles II. The construction of 'serten Cabans & Chambres' (at least three in number) for the king and queen in the vessel included the use of a hundred wainscot boards, one dozen 'Joyned scotes [boards] for the quene is Caban [*sic*]' and, in what may well be the first reference to the use of window glass in a ship, 112 ft (34.1 m) of glass for 'Glasynge the seyd Chambres' with two 'panes of the kings armes and the quenes for the seyd cabans', with eighteen window bars.[16]

Most medieval and sixteenth-century ships probably had only one cabin, for the master or owner, with the rest of the crew bedding down either on the deck or under it. The 700-ton Tudor warship *Mary Rose*, lost in 1545, had cabins for some of the ship's officers on the main deck. The cabins of the ship's barber-surgeon and carpenter were recovered with much of their contents, along with what may have been the pilot's (navigator's) cabin. The latter may simply have been a sleeping-place, for it contained a hay-stuffed mattress as well as personal possessions and navigational instruments; the other two contained instruments and tools, but no sign of beds. There is little evidence of officers' cabins before this date, although any ship's carpenter could probably have hammered together a few planks and timbers to make a cabin if required. One of the few medieval English poems about sea travel, known as *The Pilgrim's Sea-voyage*, describes a voyage on a ship carrying pilgrims to the shrine of Santiago de Compostella in northern Spain from the point of view of the seasick passenger. At one point, the ship's owner is checking that all is well:

> Anone he calleth a carpentere
> And byddyth hym bryng hym hys gere
> To make the cabans here and there
> With many a febyll cell.

'A feeble cell' is probably as much as most passengers (or even ships' officers) could expect in terms of cabin accommodation.[17] For some information about kitchens see Chapter 6.

Superstructure

The superstructures in medieval and sixteenth-century ships were essentially military features, although latterly they were used for other purposes, such as accommodation (see Chapter 8). The primary evidence for their construction and appearance is to be found in pictorial material, and the earliest closely dated image of a northern European ship with 'castles' is on the town seal of Dunwich in Suffolk, c. 1199 (see Fig. 4.3). This vessel has a forecastle, an aftercastle, and a topcastle set at the mast-head. The fore- and aftercastles resemble simple watch-towers, standing on stilts. The platforms have crenellations and appear to have latticework sides. The topcastle platform has a similar configuration, although it would have sat atop the mast, with the mast-head in the centre. An analysis of sixty-six town and other seals depicting ships from the period c. 1150–c. 1300 from northern Europe (including northern Spain) reveals thirty-two (48.5 per cent) with castles, of which four fall within the period c. 1199–c. 1250, fifteen between c. 1250 and c. 1300, (dated to within fifty years or less), and thirteen are of known thirteenth-century date.[18]

These figures suggest that castle structures became increasingly common on ships in the thirteenth century, common enough for the merchant communities that commissioned the seals to want these symbols of dominance and security included in their designs. Most of these castles were of the 'watch-tower' type, free-standing structures mounted entirely on stilt legs (see Figs 1.2 and 4.3). Some eight seals depict castles partially supported by the stem- or sternpost; and four – the Ipswich seal of c. 1200 (Fig. 4.4), the New Shoreham seal of c. 1250–1300 (Fig. 2.4), and the Hull and Nieuport seals of c. 1300 – show castles fully integrated into the hull structures. Analysis of thirty-five images of castle-equipped vessels of the period c. 1300–c. 1500 reveals twenty-nine instances of the 'integrated' castles (including three with 'semi-integrated' castles), five with 'semi-integrated' castles alone, and one 'watch-tower' type, the c. 1350 seal of the Danish port of Stubbekøbing. It is not difficult to see a technological progression, from the simplest type, the watch-tower, to that which fixed part of the castle to a stem- or sternpost, to the 'fully integrated' type, which made the fore- and aftercastles much more a part of the hull structure. The Bremen cog, built c. 1380 (see Figs 1.7 and 6.1), had an aftercastle structure secured to the sides of the vessel, and in outward appearance resembles the 'integrated' type of castle found on the later seals.

In tracing the early history of superstructures, documentary sources add some information to the pictorial record. For example, the Newcastle galley of 1295 had three castles, described as a *castrum anterius* (forecastle), *castrum* (which must have been the aftercastle) and the *castrum capitale* or topcastle. The aftercastle was supported by six posts (and had at least seven other timbers), with twelve or more timbers

4.4 Town seal of Ipswich, *c.* 1200. Drawing after Ewe, 1972. Although of similar date to the Dunwich seal (fig. 4.1), this seems to depict a vessel with much higher sides, and more complex castles. The hull is clinker-built, and although the stem is rather curved, the vessel in other respects resembles a cog. The aftercastle appears to be fastened directly to the hull, rather than sitting on independent stilts, and the forecastle seems at least partially attached to the top of the stempost. This is also an early depiction of a vessel with a stern rudder, an innovation apparently introduced in the twelfth century. As with ships carrying side-rudders, the steering position was underneath the aftercastle.

used in the forecastle, while the structure of the topcastle included sixteen boards. The castles, however, were not the only part of the galley's superstructure. Like some other war vessels of the time, the Newcastle galley had defensive breastworks called *hurdis*, which were probably erected along the sides of the galley and were supported by a number of fork-shaped timbers. They also had sixty hasps, suggesting that part of the breastworks may have been hinged. The contemporary Ipswich galley also had breastworks, made out of 1600 ft (487.8 m) of boards and fastened by 5000 nails. Although the term *hurdis* seldom occurs after the first half of the fourteenth century, this type of structure may well have continued in use, as large, removable 'blindages', for sheltering archers, were found in the waist of the *Mary Rose*.[19]

Both documentary and pictorial sources indicate that some vessels had multi-stage castles. Two-stage aftercastles are shown on the seal ships of Faversham (thirteenth century), Ipswich (*c.* 1400–50) and Kil-cleth, Ireland (*c.* 1500),and the famous engraving of a *Kraeck* (carrack) of *c.* 1470 (see Fig. 4.5) shows a vessel with two-stage fore- and aftercastles. In the early fifteenth century, these were called 'summer-hutches', and in 1416 two were built in Henry v's 'great ships' *Holigost* (760 tons) and *Trinity Royal* (540 tons), for use in the Duke of Bedford's expedition to Harfleur. Nineteen pieces of timber and over a hundred boards were used to build the two structures. A summer-hutch built in the 1000-ton *Jesus* in the same year needed 27 pieces of timber and 140 boards, suggesting that it was of some size and complexity. The 1400-ton *Grace Dieu* of 1418 is known to have had an extra fighting-stage that was fitted on top of the forecastle for sea service. Summer-hutches probably looked much the same as the fighting platforms underneath them, as can be seen on the *c.* 1415 bench-end carving from King's Lynn (see

Fig. 9.2) or the *Kraeck* engraving. Some vessels may have had planked fighting-towers instead: the carving of *c.* 1449–51 from the Hôtel Jacques Coeur at Bourges in France shows such a structure (see Fig. 9.3). The increasing use of guns at sea in the fifteenth century was to lead to these temporary extra stages becoming permanent, as castles developed into multi-stage gun platforms (see Chapter 8). Henry VII's great warship *Sovereign* had a two-stage forecastle and a summer-castle (by then the word denoted a permanent structure) with three decks.[20]

STEERING GEAR

There were three basic types of steering gear in late medieval England. The first consisted of a large oar, sometimes called a scull, that was either held like an oar, or loosely tied to the hull (sometimes, it appears, at the bow as well as the stern). This was perhaps the most ancient type of rudder, but seems to have been used as late as the fifteenth century. In the mid-1460s the Hull north ferry boat was equipped with a scull, which was clad with iron, probably to protect it from damage against the river-bank or to enable it to be used as a punt-pole. The 'great boats' of Henry VII's ships in the 1490s each had a fore-scull and an after-scull, indicating that the boats could be steered at both bow and stern. The second type (now termed a 'steering-oar') was sometimes called a *sideroder* or 'side rudder' in Middle English, although more often just a 'rudder'. It consisted of an oversize oar fixed to the side of the ship at the stern, by means of a flexible iron or rope joint, resembling a 'universal joint' in operation (see Figs 1.1, 1.2 and 4.3). A tiller projected inboard at deck level to allow the rudder to be handled. In use since at least the early Middle Ages, rudders of this type are common in northern European ship iconography of the fourteenth century. The third type was the stern-rudder. This was attached to the sternpost of the ship by iron hooks called pintles which located into iron rings (gudgeons) fixed on the sternpost. A tiller was fixed to the top of the rudder, and projected inside the ship. The stern-rudder was in existence by 1200: it can be seen on a vessel carved on the font of Winchester Cathedral (dated *c.* 1170) and on the Ipswich seal (see Figs 4.4 and 4.5).[21]

Even a century or more after its introduction, mariners do not appear entirely to have trusted the stern-rudder, at least on certain types of vessel. Some of the 1295 galleys had combinations of side-rudder and stern-rudder. The Lyme galley, for example, had a *gubernaculum* (rudder) bound with iron, and a *culrother* or stern-rudder. The combination of the two types was probably intended as 'insurance' should one be lost at sea. By the 1330s, the side-rudder was starting to die out: the 80-oar galley *Philippe*, easily as big as some of the 1295 galleys, had only a stern-rudder, as did the barge *Paul* of 1373.

The reasons for the decline of the side-rudder were probably much

the same as those advanced many years ago by R. C. Anderson. He reasoned that the side-rudder was more vulnerable to collision or battle damage (a major consideration, given that many battles involved ships grappled side-by-side; see Chapter 8). The side-rudder could also be lifted clear of the water if the vessel heeled over too much to one side, causing it to lose steerage. The stern-rudder may have been less effective as a steering instrument, but it remained in the water all the time (if a vessel's stern was leaping clear of the water, the ship would have been in such trouble that the rudder type no longer mattered). The stern-rudder was less easy to damage, and could easily be fitted to a vessel with a straight sternpost (it may have actually encouraged the building of ships with straight sternposts). The northern European stern-rudder was introduced into the Mediterranean in about 1300 as part of the equipment of the cog, or *coche*, as the type became known there. The stern-rudder there was known, among other things, as the *timon bayones* or 'Bayonnese rudder', after the Basques who played a major part in introducing the cog into the Mediterranean. Although there are documented examples of *coche* with side-rudders, the stern-rudder was the normal type of steering gear on Genoese *coche* by the period 1350–70. The advantages of the stern-rudder must have been very strong in order to enable it to oust the highly developed southern European side-rudder.

Although the side-rudder may have become obsolete in the fourteenth century, it persisted in nautical terminology, having given its name to the side of the ship on which it was usually mounted, the 'steer-board' or 'starboard' side.[22]

4.5 Master W's Kraeck ('Carrack'), *c.* 1470. This is one of the best-known of medieval ship illustrations. Whilst not a 'scale' drawing, it shows considerable attention to detail and proportion. A recent study (Sleeswyk 1990) has suggested that the artist was a Flemish engraver named Willem a Cruce, and that the Kraeck engraving was prepared as a 'plan' to be followed by shipwrights making large model carracks for Burgundian ducal festivities in 1468.

The hull is evidently skeleton-built, as shown by the smooth planking and the large longitudinal wales that served to strengthen the structure. An open lading port is visible near the stern, at a level suggesting that the vessel has at least two decks.

The fore- and aftercastles each have two stages, and are topped by roof-like structures that could have supported canvas tilts (as shelters) or anti-boarding netting (some such netting can be seen on the foretop). The heavy rudder has two ropes fastened to it, to prevent it from being lost if it became unshipped from its pintles. The two 'sentry-box'-like features on either side of the stern are almost certainly toilets! The ship's armament includes four cannon in the aftercastle, pointing over the gunwale, and a swivel gun in the mizzen top. The main top has a 'craneline' with a winch and the bags which would have conveyed ammunition up from the deck. A huge grapnel and iron chain can be seen at the bow, used to secure the carrack to an enemy vessel.

The engraving shows a relatively early three-masted ship, although it is apparent that by *c.* 1470, the foremast was already being made larger than the mizzenmast in some ships. The mainmast is a 'made' (composite) mast bound with wooldings, and the main top is reached by means of a 'Jacob's ladder' rather than ratlines – a Mediterranean characteristic. The print gives a good impression of the large number of pulleys and deadeyes used by a large sailing ship, and shows the huge main parral, with its five rows of parral balls.

CHAPTER 5

Motive power

During the Middle Ages the only two means of moving a ship at sea in a controlled way were sail power or oar power, and in northern Europe before the fifteenth century the only sail type in common use was the so-called 'square' sail (in reality this was often rectangular in shape). It was attached to a yard or sailyard slung from the mast (at right angles to the line of the keel) and controlled by a variety of rigging ropes. The square sail is particularly well suited for sailing when the wind is blowing from behind or from one side of the ship, but it has a limited capacity for sailing into the wind. In southern Europe and the Mediterranean, the main sail type from the end of the Roman period to *c.* 1300 was the triangular lateen sail, slung from a yard set in the same line as the keel. Like the modern fore-and-aft rigged yacht sail, the lateen is particularly fitted for sailing into the wind, although it can become unstable in a following wind. The introduction of the lateen into northern Europe in the fifteenth century, and the development of multi-masted rig will be discussed in Chapter 9.

SPEED

Medieval administrative records generally give little information about exactly how long voyages took (for example, accounts of crews' wages record dates over which wages were paid, and not necessarily the starting and finishing dates of voyages). Mediterranean sources suggest that the big lateen-rigged ships of the twelfth or thirteenth centuries could reach up to three knots in favourable conditions, but that average speeds were lower. Indeed, the *cochas* and carracks of the fourteenth and fifteenth centuries seem to have been little faster than their lateen-rigged predecessors, with estimated average upwind speeds of 1 knot, and average downwind speeds of 1.85 knots.

An idea of average sailing speeds can be gained from the records of a series of voyages undertaken by some of Henry V's ships between 1413 and 1416. Most of these journeys were from London to Bordeaux and back, loading wine for London merchants. The round-trip distance between London and Bordeaux is approximately 1400 nautical miles (2594 km), according to modern nautical distance charts, but these are designed for motor vessels that are not dependent on the wind, and are a great deal more seaworthy than any medieval ship. In the Middle Ages, the standard route from London to Bordeaux was a 'coast-hugging' one, with either the Isle of Wight or Plymouth and the Cornish ports acting as jumping off points for the Channel crossing. St Matthieu in western Brittany was often the next port-of-call, followed by more coast-hugging down to the Garonne estuary and Bordeaux. As one historian pointed out, the fact that the use of this route persisted, despite the dangers posed by pirates and political instability, shows the degree to which medieval mariners feared storms on the high seas. The round-trip route from London, via Plymouth and St Mathieu, to Bordeaux is approximately 1980 nautical miles (3669 km), about 40 per cent longer than the modern motor-vessel route.

The London–Bordeaux voyages by Henry V's ships involved a total of ten vessels (ranging in size from some 80 to 330 tons) making sixteen voyages. Total voyage times (measured by crew payments) varied between 93 and 150 days, but these times incorporated stopovers of unknown length, including the time taken to load and unload wine. Counting the stopovers, the average rate of progress was 0.9 knots on the fastest voyage and 0.55 knots on the slowest. These speeds are of course meaningless in terms of the actual speeds of the vessels involved, which with the time spent in port, would have been faster (although, as the Bordeaux voyages were generally made in convoy, even the fastest vessel would have had to keep to the speed of the slowest ship). An uninterrupted run from London to Bordeaux, with a ship under way all the time, at an average speed of 1 knot, would have meant a journey of just over 41 days; it was later to take Columbus some 44 days' sailing time to cross from Spain to the Bahamas. In reality, of course, ships were able to sail at speeds greater than 1 knot. In 1488 the small merchantman *Margaret Cely* made a passage from London to Bordeaux that involved a 22-day run ('crawl' might be more appropriate) from London round to Plymouth at an average speed of just over 0.5 knots, and ended in a comparative dash from Fowey in Cornwall to Blaye near Bordeaux, averaging some 3.6 knots. Part of the ship's return journey, as far as southern Brittany, was made at the slower average speed of just over 1 knot, but this was made with a wine cargo.

One has to draw a distinction between the speeds that could be achieved by a vessel in certain circumstances, and the overall rate of advance on a voyage. Speed was of value in war, or in trying to make or evade a piratical attack, but it seems only to have been achievable by certain specific types of medieval vessel, such as the oared war and merchant galleys of the Mediterranean. Most merchant voyages probably followed the coast-hugging pattern of those on the Bordeaux route, putting into harbour along the way to re-victual or shelter.

Meterological conditions, of course, had an overriding effect on the operating capabilities of sailing ships. For example, around late December 1414 or early January 1415, five of Henry v's ships set out from London on a wine voyage to Bordeaux. A storm blew them back from the 'Foreland' of the Isle of Wight to the Camber by Winchelsea in Sussex, where they sheltered. Most eventually returned to London, arriving there about 20 February 1415, apart from one which had to put into Southampton for repairs. Some seven weeks' sailing time had been wasted because of bad weather. Each of the five vessels was a one-master, with only limited abilities to tack against the wind, although the conditions seem to have been so severe that it is doubtful if extra masts and sails would have helped. The times taken on the sixteen voyages discussed above do not permit neat conclusions about sailors being able to make easy use of the prevailing winds in timing their voyages to Bordeaux. Two of the shortest voyages of the sixteen (93 and 99 days) were made in the September–December period, but the three longest (150 days) were also made between a September and a January. The ability of a ship to be able to put on an extra turn of speed would always have been appreciated, but the physical and logistical realities of medieval and sixteenth-century seafaring meant that travelling and trading by sea was a slow business.[1]

MASTS AND SPARS

From the early Middle Ages to the early fifteenth century, the average English (and northern European) ship was single-masted, carrying one square sail. The mast was usually stepped in a hole in the keelson, above the keel, supported by beams and wooden blocks (mast-partners) at deck level, and by rigging ropes higher up (the standing rigging). Apart from the keel, the mast and yard were the largest timbers in a sailing vessel. The construction of a mast for a small vessel was relatively easy, requiring only a long, straight tree (a mast constructed from a single stick is known as a pole mast). The masts needed for larger vessels were more of a problem; the solution was to make a mast out of several different pieces of timber, scarfed together. It is not known when the 'made mast' was first introduced in northern Europe, although indirect indications occur in documents of the mid-fourteenth century, which refer to rope or iron bands placed around a mast at intervals to help hold the separate pieces together. Sometimes termed 'wooldings', these can often be seen in medieval ship illustrations (see

5.1 A made mast on an Italian carrack of *c*. 1445. The vertical lines on the mast represent the different mast components, and the horizontal bands the rope wooldings that held the mast together (after Howard 1987).

e.g. Figs 4.5 and 5.1). In 1348, iron bands were made to fasten the mast of Edward III's ship *Cog Thomas*, as part of a programme of work on the mast that kept six carpenters employed for twenty-one working days. In 1359, four hawsers made of white (i.e. untarred) Bridport rope were supplied for 'knotting about the mast' of the royal ship *Alice*. The hawsers were heavy, weighing 256 lb (116 kg) in total, suggesting that the mast was both 'made' and large. The mast wooldings (or 'knottings') were sometimes secured in place using cheap 'clout-nails' (probably broad-headed nails suitable for work with rope or canvas). Woolding work on the mast of the 300-ton *Trinity* in 1400 involved the use of 153 lb (69.5 kg) of cordage and 2000 clout-nails, an average of 13 nails for every pound of cordage (or 29 per kg).[2]

Little is known about the actual structures of made masts in the Middle Ages and the sixteenth-century. The only piece of an early made mast so far found was a 10 ft stump still *in situ* in a wreck unearthed at Woolwich in 1912, which may have been the remains of the *Sovereign*, a great royal ship of 600 tons, built in 1488, rebuilt in 1509 and finally laid up in 1521. The mast measured 52 in (132 cm) in diameter, and consisted of a central pine spindle surrounded by eight

5.2 The made mast of the Woolwich Ship, possibly Henry VII's 600-ton *Sovereign* of 1488 (after Salisbury 1961).

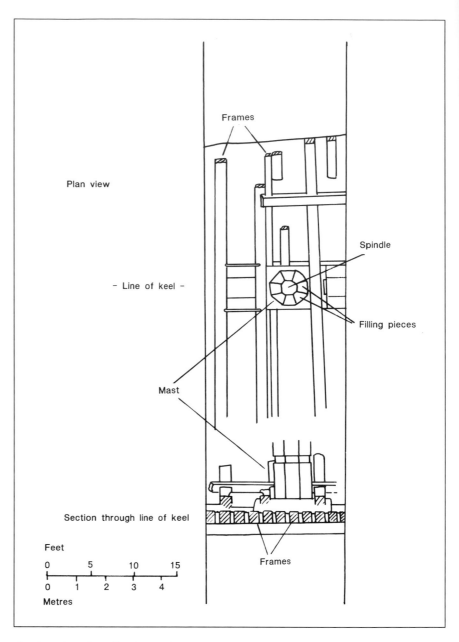

thick oaken baulks, bound together by iron bands (see Fig. 5.2). There is documentary evidence of such masts. When Henry VIII's 1500-ton *Henri Grâce à Dieu* was built at Woolwich in about 1512, £17 was paid for a great mast to act as the *spyndell* of the ship's mainmast. Complete masts were sometimes the component parts of other great masts. For example, the great mast of the 1000-ton *Jesus*, built in 1416, was made from seventeen other masts.[3]

Masts required one or two mast-head pulleys (see Fig. 5.3), which were used, with the ties, to raise or lower the yard. Documentary

[Medieval manuscript illumination with Old French text:]

Coment ihc vuint alamer de galilee 7 entrint de denz vne neef p̄ paller la meer en le re
nume q̄ est apelle Geralenon. 7 melteuuint cauint il eloist denz la neef il se euchoist
de lure vne cue 7 dormilt. 7 la mer cumencoit a tempelir li lindulement q̄ ceuus q̄ eloi
ent dedenz quidoient ben auoir ete perilt 7 auoient grant pour 7 vn del apolles dilre le
alnt velter 7 dilolt leinour nou l̄ati chca amene tei elte tiere 7 ihc euelriut 7 co
maudolt la meer q̄ ele le celolt de tempelter 7 illi le feloit ele

[Lower banderole:] Coment cuint ihc elolt la meer palle vuint en la tere de Geralenon il trouat deul q̄ elto

references to such pulleys are rare, probably because in inventories they were accounted as part of the mast structure. The great ship *Grace Dieu* of 1418 is known to have had a mast-head pulley, for it was removed, along with the topcastle, when the upper part of the main-mast was cut off in 1432. The structures actually securing the mast in place had to be strong. Aside from the keelson, mast-step and beams, down in the hold, at deck level there were the mast-partners (or 'lerings') and 'forelocks'. The partners went either side of the mast, providing transverse support; the forelocks, as the name suggests, seem to have given longitudinal support, probably on both the fore and aft faces of the mast. The forelocks may have been the first things to be taken out when a mast was being removed, allowing the mast to be tilted forwards or backwards. On some ships, the partners or lerings were very large, and contained much ironwork. Repairs to the lerings of the *All Hallow's Cog* in 1337–38 involved the use of seven special lering-nails (costing 2d each, and therefore expensive and large), twelve iron bolts (worth 2½d each) and 168 other iron nails – perhaps a hundredweight of iron in all. Just under seventy years later, in 1405, the replacement of the lerings and forelocks in the 260-ton ship *Katerine* was made using 4 cwt of iron for lering-nails, bolts and rings, and seven pieces of timber. These timbers alone cost one-and-a-half times as much

5.3 Sail, oar and stern rudder: Christ calming the storm in the Sea of Galilee, English manuscript, early fourteenth century (The Holkham Bible). The illustration indicates that the vessel has a masthead pulley, and possibly a rope (?) parral. The forestay is tied round the stem, and is used to keep some of the planking in place (the vessel combines 'hulk' construction and 'post-to-post' construction). The oar-ports in this reverse clinker vessel are in the top strake, and the ship is steered by a stern rudder which has a fork-like tiller which reaches round the sternpost.

as a mast bought to serve as the ship's bowsprit. When the *Katerine* was broken up, a year or two later, the removal of *les lyrynges* took three carpenters one-and-a-half days to complete. Repairs to the great made mast and the mast-partners of the 1000-ton *Jesus* in 1417 used 1387 lb of iron in lering-nails, bolts, bands and spikes, 110 wainscot boards and 45 pieces of timber. Medieval masts could be huge, heavy and complicated.[4]

Such complex masts required a good deal of skill on the part of carpenters and were costly. It is difficult to gauge the actual sizes of masts from their recorded prices, although these give some idea of the relative size and importance of different masts and spars in the same ship. The price of a mast was a function of its size, technical complexity, materials, availability and other factors, but it is difficult to discern any clear pattern in mast prices. For example, the Dunwich galley of 1295 and the *Godegrace* of 1401 were both vessels of 100 oars yet, though a century apart, their masts both cost £14. The masts of smaller vessels tended to be cheaper, and it is possible that masts in general became relatively cheaper in the fifteenth century.[5]

Medieval and early sixteenth-century English documents seldom specify mast length (see Table 6, which summarises the few references to actual or minimum sizes of masts).[6] The figure for the *Grace Dieu*'s mainmast (?190 ft) would seem excessive, were it not for the evidence of the wreck itself in the River Hamble. The keel of the wreck is at least 125 ft (38.1 m) in length, and on this basis, contemporary Mediterranean shipwrights would have given the ship a mainmast of at least 180 ft (54.9 m). Most of the other figures in Table 6 are estimates, based on the known actual or minimum sizes of sails or rigging, although the *Marie*'s mast length (72 ft) is stated directly in an account, and the *Grace Dieu* figure is estimated from measurements taken by an Italian galley captain who dined aboard the ship in 1430. The *Regent* figures are from a rare document specifying what was required for the ship (mainmast, 114 ft; mizzenmast, 93 ft), and also stating what was actually available at Bristol (mainmast 107.25 ft, mizzenmast 105 ft). A total of nine masts were specified for the *Regent*, of varying dimensions. The following list offers an interpretation of how the masts might have been intended to be used (specification figures):

> Bowsprit: 1×84 ft
> Foremast: 1×84 ft
> Mainmast: 1×114 ft $+ 4 \times 72$ ft
> Main topmast: 1×84 ft
> Mizzenmast: 1×93 ft
> Bonaventure mizzenmast: 1×84 ft.

The dimensions of both the specifications and the actual masts show that mastmakers were working, to some extent, to scales of proportions in making masts. For example, the four 72-foot and the four 84-foot had length: circumference ratios of 1:16, and the mizzenmast had a ratio of 1:15.5. The mainmast at Bristol had a ratio of 1:13, but some of the others do not work out as clear whole or fractional numbers. Several different proportional systems seem to have been in use.

A study of the relative costs of masts and yards and bowsprits in ships between 1295 and 1497 shows that, in proportional terms, the mainmast and main yard were far and away the most expensive of the masts and spars. Twelve examples from the accounts over this period show the cost of the main yard varying between 10 per cent and 50 per cent of the cost of the mainmast, with an average of 31 per cent for the period 1295–c. 1380 (eight examples) and 20 per cent (four examples) for the period 1406–97. The costs of only two bowsprits can be separated out, and these come out at between 1 per cent and 5 per cent of the mainmast, suggesting that the spars in question were fairly light. The mizzenmasts of the balinger *Anne* (1416) and Sir John Howard's carvel *Edward* (1466) seem to have been similarly light, at 5 per cent and less than 6 per cent of the costs of their respective mainmasts. The foremast of Howard's carvel was just 3 per cent of the mainmast cost (interestingly, contemporary pictures of ships with early foremasts show these as smaller than even the mizzenmast; see Fig. 9.3). The foremast of the oared bark *Mary Fortune* of 1497 was evidently somewhat larger in proportional terms, with its cost at 10 per cent of that of the mainmast. These figures cannot be translated into exact sizes, but they indicate that the mainmast and mainyard, even after the introduction of multi-masted ships, remained by a long way the most costly and complex of the masts and spars used.[7]

The pictorial evidence may seem easier to quantify. At first, foremasts appear as much smaller than the mizzenmasts, but by about 1470 (cf. the *Kraeck*, Fig. 4.5) the foremast was generally shown as higher than the mizzenmast. It is possible to work out proportional sizes from the heights of masts illustrated, and it is clear from the few surviving medieval shipbuilding texts that shipwrights worked to specific proportions in making masts. Nevertheless, the pictorial evidence remains no more than a rough indicator. For one thing, none of the pictures shows where the masts were stepped, a crucial factor in determining the actual length of a mast. The mainmast had to be stepped in the very bottom of the ship, but early mizzen- and foremasts may well have been stepped on decks above this point. For example, in small two- or three-masters the mizzenmast would have to be so positioned that it did not obstruct the tiller (see Fig. 10.3).

Determining the appropriate size of a mainmast may well have been relatively easy, for it seems to have been based on the length of keel, and therefore had some relation to the size of the ship. This sort of information would have been simple to codify. Determining the right size of mizzenmast, foremast and topmast for an early three-masted or 'full-rigged' ship must have been much more difficult, and more a matter of experiment. Given that even in the sixteenth century mariners apparently could not determine the actual tonnage of a new ship until it had been on its first voyage (see p. 33), it is doubtful that ideas about the proper proportions for masts were at all fixed until many years after the introduction of the multi-masted ship.

Both hardwoods such as oak and softwoods such as pine and spruce were used in mast-making. The mast of the Woolwich ship (see pp. 87–8) consisted of a pine spindle surrounded by oak baulks. In the mid-1490s a Southampton brewer supplied a spruce tree (which he is said to have grown) for use as a foremast in the *Regent*, and in 1531 Henry VIII's *Great Bark* had a 75-ft spruce mainmast. More unusually, in 1501 seven small alder trees were used in making bowsprits, masts and outliggers (horizontal poles projecting from the stern used for the mizzen sheet pulley) for the great boat and cock-boat of the *Regent*. Pine and spruce ('spruce' derives from the Middle English word for Prussia, from where the timber first came to England) tend to grow tall and straight, and have a good strength in relation to their weight. They have long been traditional mastmaking timbers, but we have no way of knowing how much they were used in English mastmaking in the Middle Ages. It is possible that oak was the most common timber used in England, simply because it was so easily available. There are occasional references to the movement of finished masts by sea (both as internal cargo and towed, attached to a great iron swivel) from such places as Dartmouth in Devon, an area in which pines and similar softwoods were probably rare, suggesting that these were English or Welsh oak masts. Although white oak can be hard to work, forest-grown white oak trees can reach up to 30 m in height and could have been used to make masts.[8]

By comparison with made masts, most yards or sailyards were probably simple structures. Single-piece yards are likely to have been the most common, although two-piece yards are known from documentary and pictorial evidence (particularly from the Mediterranean). There are references to the yards of English royal ships being strengthened or lengthened, and the specifications for the main yard of the *Regent* in about 1512 envisaged the use of two masts, each 81 ft (24.7 m) long and 4.5 ft (1.4 m) in circumference at their large ends. Of course, the actual yard would not have been 162 ft long, as the two masts would necessarily have overlapped for a considerable distance in order to form a strong scarf joint. The main yard actually on offer for the ship in Bristol at the time was 84 ft (25.6 m) long, just over three-quarters the length of the mainmast. Details of yard fittings are rare, although most yards probably had cleats (small pieces of wood fixed to the yard to stop ropes slipping). Some ships were equipped with shear-hooks,

5.4 OPPOSITE A ship from the Bodleian Apocalypse, English manuscript, thirteenth century. This one-master has a sail with reef-points, and a forestay which is tied to the stempost. The forestay and stem-binding also seems to secure the bowsprit, which is set on the post side of the stem. The bowsprit has an attachment-point for the bowlines. As one might expect with an early bowsprit, the feature looks as if it has been 'tacked on' to the double-ended hull, an adaptation of an earlier form. The 'horned' item on the sternpost is a 'mike' or yard-crutch.

The side-rudder has a very prominent projecting 'shoe', a feature often found in such illustrations: it was probably designed to give the rudder extra 'bite' in the water.

which were blades attached to the end of a yard-arm and used to tear or cut the sails and rigging of an enemy ship during a close action. The one-masted royal ship *Marie* of Weymouth of about 1410 had one shear-hook, but a four-master, also called *Grace Dieu*, of 1485 had six, four on the yards and two on one of the forestays.[9]

The bowsprit has long been a regular part of the equipment of sailing ships. Its original purpose was to provide an attachment-point for the bowlines. One bowline ran to either vertical edge of the sail; when the ship was sailing to windward (or 'close-hauled'), the bowline was pulled tight in order to keep the windward or weather edge of the sail tight, to prevent it from collapsing. The bowsprit, projecting out from the bow of the ship, enabled the crew to get a much greater purchase on the bowlines (see Fig. 5.4).

The bowsprit, however, was not the first device to be used for sailing close-hauled. The Vikings had an item of gear called a *beitiáss*, in use from at least the ninth century. This was a wooden pole which was latched behind the windward edge of the sail, with the heel of the pole placed in a hole cut in a wooden block (the ninth-century Gokstad

burial-ship had blocks on either side of the ship, abreast of the mast). The *beitiáss* was used to hold the windward edge of the sail taut when sailing on a tack, and modern experiments have suggested that it could also be used to help a vessel in a following wind. This spar was still in use in northern Europe in the thirteenth and fourteenth centuries, and was called a 'lof' or 'loof' in England. Details of the equipment used with lofs are uncertain, although some vessels had wooden structures called port-loofs that evidently helped to support the lof. The port-lof on the Newcastle galley of 1295 was composed of at least six timbers, suggesting something more complex than the wooden blocks used in early Viking times. Other vessels had rope tackles to assist the lof. Some idea of just how common lofs were can be gained from the summary inventories of twenty-one vessels arrested in north-east England in the mid-1290s, most of which came from Frisia and Holland, with one from Stralsund in Germany and another of unknown origin. They ranged in size from 30 to 100 tons, and while only thirteen had bowsprits, eighteen had lofs (in most cases vessels had both lofs and bowsprits). Lofs began to fall out of use in the fourteenth century: of seventeen recorded instances of lofs on English vessels between 1295 and 1436, fourteen date from before 1350.[10]

The lof was supplanted by the bowsprit and the bowlines. The earliest evidence of a bowsprit is pictorial, on the town seal of Ipswich of *c.* 1200 (see Fig. 4.4). While it is difficult to know the time-lag between the development of a medieval technical innovation and its first appearance in art, the bowsprit was possibly first introduced during the twelfth century. Between 1200 and 1250, bowsprits appeared on ship-seal illustrations in places as far apart as Ipswich, Elbing in Poland (seal first recorded 1242), Stavoren in the Netherlands (first recorded 1246) and Wismar (first recorded 1256). The combined presence of a lof and a bowsprit on a ship was perhaps initially a case of mariners' understandable reluctance to put their trust in one new item of gear, much in the way that stern- and side-rudders were both used in some vessels of the late thirteenth and early fourteenth centuries (see pp. 81–3). It seems to have been fairly common on both oared and sailing vessels. The 80-oar galley *Philippe* of 1337 had this combination, as did three of the 1295 galleys and twelve of the above-mentioned twenty-one foreign ships. Fifteen of the ships arrested in the north-east of England in the 1290s were described as cogs. The peculiar horn-like arrangement on the bows of the cogs illustrated on the early Stavoren, Wismar and other seals may have been a support for the lof, rather than an oddly positioned rest for the sailyard. The thirteenth-century vessel excavated in Kalmar harbour in Sweden may have had such an item. The lof clearly fell out of general use between the mid-fourteenth century and the early fifteenth, probably because of increasingly confident and efficient use of the bowlines and bowsprit.[11]

ROPE AND SAILS

The rigging and sails used by English ships in the Middle Ages generally derived from hemp (*cannabis sativa*). This was reflected in the medieval Latin terms for hempen cordage (*canabis*) and for canvas (*canevacium*). Analysis of pollen samples suggests that hemp and flax (which was also used to make canvas) were grown in England from at least Anglo-Saxon times, but there is no documentary evidence of their cultivation until the later Middle Ages. Hemp and flax were grown in many coastal and riverine parishes of Suffolk in the 1340s and, by the sixteenth century, nearly 15 per cent of the sown acreage in the Norfolk Fens was given over to hemp cultivation. Hemp and flax were also cultivated in the Lincolnshire Fenland and in Somerset in the thirteenth century.[12]

The most famous ropemaking centre in medieval England was the town of Bridport in Dorset. In 1211, King John bought 3000 'weighs' of hempen thread at Bridport for making ships' cables, with further purchases following in 1213. These are the first documentary references to the Bridport industry, but their very scale suggests that it was already mature by the early thirteenth century. Bridport had officials employed as 'searchers' of hemp and flax in the late fourteenth century, and there was a common weighing beam and weights by the sixteenth century, but much else in the industry's organisation remains obscure. What is clear is that Bridport thread was widely used and was transported considerable distances, even by road. For example, in the years 1348–51, just over 85 cwt (4327.3 kg) of 'white' (untarred), 'black' (tarred) and other thread was bought at Bridport and other places in Dorset and Somerset and transported to London for royal use. Several journeys were made, involving a total of ten carters each making round trips of 140 leagues (420 miles, or 676 km). The cordage was packed into large canvas bags called sarplers, but the costs of packing were far outweighed by the costs of transport and of the thread itself. This was an expensive operation, costing over £134, the thread making up 81.5 per cent of the cost and the transport coming to almost 15 per cent.[13]

Bridport, however, was not the only ropemaking centre. For example, in 1277 the Devon borough of Plympton Erle was said to have been receiving Bridport hemp and turning it into rope. In the fourteenth century, some Dartmouth deeds suggest the presence of a ropewalk (a place in which rope was made) and in the early fifteenth century, some cordage from Norfolk and Kent was being supplied to the king's ships. The accounts for the king's ships in the period 1413–16 show that imported cordage was also used. Cordage of named foreign origin (from Bordeaux, Holland and Normandy) made up just over 14 per cent of the total. This was not just cordage used in rigging ropes, but included cables, buoy-ropes and other similar items.[14]

The requirements for ropemaking were minimal: some hemp, a piece of winding machinery to twist the fibres together, and a long, straight building (or even a lane, as at Bridport and elsewhere). The ropemaking gear owned by the Crown in the 1350s and 1360s included winches, hooks ('cable-hooks'), 'whelps' (projections from the windlass drum which stopped the rope slipping when under strain) and 'tops' (conical pieces of wood through which the strands were fed when being made up into ropes). This terminology would have been familiar to ropemakers of more recent times, suggesting that medieval ropemaking equipment was essentially similar to that used in the eighteenth century.[15]

The most common types of cordage named in the sources are thread, lines, ropes, hawsers and cables. Thread and line were the lightest varieties. Thread tended to be more expensive than other cordage, and so may have been of a higher quality; it was often used for sewing sails. Lines were typically light ropes, such as the cranelines used to pull ammunition up to the topcastles of ships (see Fig. 4.5). Ropes, hawsers and cables are less easy to define: a modern definition of a rope is a piece of cordage of more than 1 in. diameter; a hawser can be a heavy rope or small cable of 5 in. circumference or more; while from the late eighteenth century the circumference of a cable was traditionally related to the width of the ship. A study of the known weight-ranges for 603 ropes, hawsers and cables used by the English royal ships in the period 1399–1420 is summarised in Table 7, which shows that ropes were generally of 1 cwt or less, hawsers were mostly in the 2–5 cwt range, and a significant proportion of cables (40 per cent) exceeded 6 cwt.[16] Documentary evidence shows a weight progression from rope to hawser to cable, and it may prove possible to identify these different types of cordage in wreck remains.

Just how much cordage medieval shipping consumed can be estimated from the accounts of the king's ships between 1413 and 1420, which show that the total of approximately 11039 tons of royal shipping consumed about 216 tons of cordage, of all types. This figure includes rigging, cables and lines supplied to new ships, as well as replacements for worn-out items, and works out at about 1 ton of cordage for every 51 tons of shipping. Interestingly, the standards set down for cordage and equipment supply to the royal ships in 1602 indicates that a proportion of 1 ton of cordage (rigging and cables) to every 33 tons of ship was used by then. The cordage requirements of English royal ships apparently increased by some 58 per cent between the early fifteenth century and the early seventeenth century. Even allowing for the fact that we are not quite comparing like with like (actual as opposed to estimated consumption), the disparity between the two figures is too great to explain away as a mere statistical problem.[17]

Although England seems to have been able to produce a good deal of the rope needed for its ships, much of the canvas used in the sails had to be imported. Some canvas was made at Bridport, but evidence for sailcloth manufacture elsewhere in England is thin. The Hanseatic ports, Brittany and south-western France were the main sources of canvas from the Middle Ages until well into the sixteenth century. In 1547 some Breton canvas-makers were brought over to England to teach the art of making their 'poldavis' canvas, and by 1558 at least two English canvas-makers were active in Suffolk. The areas around Wood-bridge and Ipswich later became famous for their canvas, but the overall impression is that the English canvas-making industry was virtually non-existent before the mid-sixteenth century. As might be expected in a wool-producing country such as medieval England, some use was made of a woollen cloth called 'bever' or 'belver' for making sails. It was used to make complete sails as late as 1371, but thereafter only occurs as a sail-patching material, last recorded in 1413–16.[18]

Even though England may not have been able to produce much sailcloth, English workers were well able to make the sails themselves. The sail of the small 24-oar barge built at Newcastle in 1304 seems largely to have been made by one man, assisted by another man in colouring the sail. Sailmaking teams, however, could be quite large, varying between eight and as many as twenty-four people. The sail-makers were often mariners, but women workers were also employed. When a sail was made for the 80-oar galley *Philippe*, building at King's Lynn in 1337, a site had to be hired for the work, and twenty-four women toiled for two weeks sewing the sail, paid at the rate of 2d each per day. For this work they were supplied with 'pack needles', a type of strong needle used for working with heavy fabrics such as sail- or sack-cloth. The women were supervised by a master mariner and the galley's 'constable' (second-in-command).[19]

A study of the costs of making eleven sails between 1295 and 1436 shows manufacturing costs averaging about 25 per cent of the total cost of the sail, with actual cost percentages ranging between about 5 and 50 per cent. There are indications that sail prices actually fell in the fifteenth century. For example, the single sail of the 100-oar balinger *Godegrace* cost £17 14s in 1401; the sails of the 60- and 80-oar barks *Sweepstake* and *Mary Fortune*, built in 1497, cost £14 19s and £10 12s respectively. The significant point here is that the *Godegrace* was a one-master; the other two vessels were three-masters with five sails apiece. Although the two barks had fewer oars than the earlier vessel, and were therefore probably smaller, they cannot have been very much smaller than the *Godegrace*. The fact that multi-masted ships were not necessarily more expensive to equip with sails than one-masters (in this case it was clearly possible for three-masters to have a cheaper sail-plan) means that cost was not a major barrier to rig development. A drop in the price of canvas in the course of the fifteenth century can be inferred from the fact that the canvas used to make the *Godegrace*'s sail in 1401 cost 24s per bolt, whereas that supplied to the royal ships in the 1490s cost between 10s and just over 13s per bolt.[20]

The basic structure of a traditional sail was very simple. It consisted of a series of canvas strips sewn together with vertical seams *c.* 1–1½ ins (25–38 mm) wide. Bolt-ropes were secured to the edges of the sail to stop the canvas fraying or parting, and to provide attachment-points for the sheets, tacks, bowlines and other elements of the running rigging. The sail was tied to the yard with lines called robands. The sail itself was a single unit until the first half of the fourteenth century, when seamen (probably in the Mediterranean) developed the 'bonnet'. This was a separate section of canvas that could be laced to the foot of the sail, or taken off, as required, giving mariners a rapid means to increase or decrease sail-area. The bonnet first appears in English sources about 1350, but developed rapidly; by the 1370s, some English ships had as many as three bonnets. The main part of the sail came to be called the 'course', from the Latin *corpus* ('body').[21]

It is possible that the development of the bonnet led to certain other methods of shortening sail going temporarily out of use. Reefs, small lines attached in rows to the forward side of the sail, have long been one method of shortening sail. The reefs in a lower row can be tied to those in an upper row (hence the 'reef knot'). They can be seen on some thirteenth-century illustrations of ships (see Figs 5.4 and 5.8), but the instances of equivalent terms for 'reefs' are insufficient to suggest that this method was common, particularly in the fourteenth century. Another method of shortening sail was to use brail-ropes (ropes attached to the sail and used to furl or unfurl it); 'brail' and its synonyms are likewise uncommon. Sandahl has suggested that the advent of the bonnet may have led to the abandonment of brails or reefs, although there are signs that by the early fifteenth century 'sail-shortening' ropes were coming back into general use.[22]

The written sources do not give a clear idea of the actual sizes of sails. There are many references to the amounts of canvas used in sails, usually in terms of 'ells' of cloth (in the fifteenth century an ell measured 'five quarters' of a yard, i.e. 45 ins (1.14 m)). Before about 1400 it was sometimes used, ambiguously, to mean a yard (0.9 m). The *Godegrace* sail of 1401 was made from 320 ells of Oléron canvas (from south-west France). Even if one assumes that each ell was a yard square, this would give a total area of 2880 sq. ft (266.3 sq. m) of canvas. This would have made a square of cloth measuring 53.66 ft (16.3 m) on a side, although this ignores canvas overlapped to make seams, and the likelihood that at least some of the canvas was used double in order to strengthen the sail, and that the sail was rectangular, not square. In one rare instance, however, it is possible to reconstruct a sail, made for the galley *Philippe* at King's Lynn in 1337. The building account describes the sail in some detail, stating that it consisted of the following: four cloths of bever cloth containing 640 ells (ie 26 cloths in width and 25 ells in length); 220 ells of bever to make *wynewes* (cloth strengthening-bands); and 60 ells of canvas for doubling the sail.

The 'length' figure of 25 ells gives us the depth of the sail. If the ell in this case equalled 3 ft, then the sail was 75 ft (22.9 m) deep. The twenty-six cloth strips (see Fig. 5.8) would have been joined by twenty-five seams: assuming each to be made using an overlap of 1 in., this would give a sewn width of 72 ft 7½ ins (22.1 m), and the sail would have been nearly square. Of course, if the 45-inch ell was being used, the sail would have been larger, some 91 ft 10 ins wide and 93 ft 9 ins deep (28.0 × 28.6 m). Debate over the evidence for this sail led to the statement that even the 75-foot sail was 'impossibly large', and the suggestion that a 2-foot ell was used. However, there is no evidence that a 2-foot ell was ever used in England, and while the sail based on the 45-inch ell would have needed a very large mast, the 75-foot sail seems more probable. After all, the barge *Marie* of 1307–08 is known to have had a 72-foot mast; the *Philippe* would only have needed a mast of about 90–100 ft. The 75-foot sail would have had an area of approximately 5448 sq. ft (506.1 sq. m). Five hundred *swyftes* (probably reefs) were supplied for the sail, and could have been attached in twenty-five rows of twenty-five each. These would have made the sail somewhat easier to handle, but with sails of this size one can see an incentive to split the sail into smaller, more manageable units (i.e. to develop detachable bonnets).[23]

There does not appear to have been any one standard proportional size for bonnets. The royal ship *Grand Marie* of the 1413–20 period had a replacement main sail course of 800 ells of canvas, and a new bonnet of 80 ells, suggesting that the bonnet equalled one-tenth of the area of the course. The contemporary balinger *George*, however, had three bonnets, of 60, 80 and 98 ells, showing little clear pattern of proportional sizes (unless there was a rule governing the reducing sizes of multiple bonnets). By the early fifteenth-century, most English royal ships had at least two bonnets for every sail, and vessels with three or four bonnets were not uncommon. Two of the 'great ships' (*Holigost* and *Trinity Royal*) had five bonnets each. Interestingly, of the eight large (400–600 ton) Genoese carracks captured by the English in 1416–17, six had two bonnets each, and two had only one bonnet per sail, indicating that Mediterranean methods of taking in sail may have been superior to those used by the English.[24]

The advent of the multi-masted ship may have made it possible for ships to use lighter sails. The tearing of a sail in a storm was a serious problem for a multi-masted ship, but for a one-master, it was the prelude to disaster. There was very good reason to make such a sail as strong as possible by adding reinforcements and thus weight. When

5.5 Schematic diagram of standing rigging.

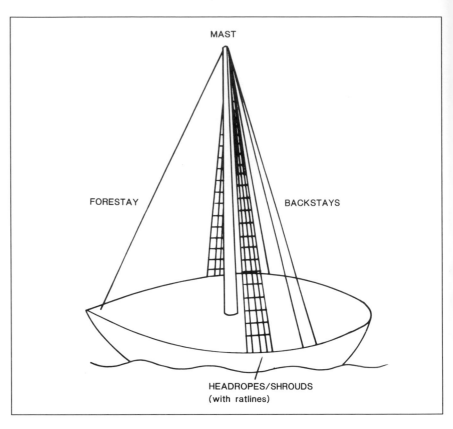

two- and three-masted ships were developed, the old one-masters were more than ready for replacement.

Masts, yards and sails needed standing and running rigging to support and work them, and the basic equipment was well established by the thirteenth century. Standing rigging commonly consisted of a forestay supporting the mast from the stem end, shrouds (called 'head-ropes' in Middle English) supporting the mast on either side, and backstays at the rear (see Fig. 5.5). The yard to which the sail was tied was raised and lowered by means of a rope-and-pulley system centred on one or more large pulleys at the mast-head, often supported by other ropes and pulleys. The sail itself was controlled by sets of ropes and pulleys that helped to raise or lower it, and to keep its side and bottom edge taut as sailing conditions required (see Figs 5.6 and 5.7). The standing rigging was not entirely static: it could be tightened or slackened off, using the wooden 'deadeyes' to which it was attached. The rigging controlling the yard and sail was fully movable, and for this reason is known as 'running rigging'.

Medieval sailors may well have had set formulae for working out the numbers of ropes that they used in the standing rigging of a ship, but no single, general formula can be discerned in the sources. On one-masted vessels, there was usually only one forestay, although a some double-

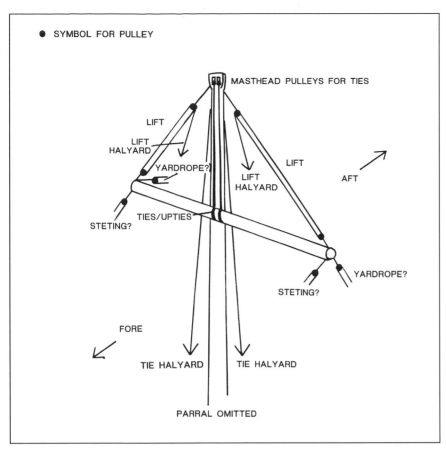

or triple-stays are known (see Table 8).

The use of multiple forestays declined in the fifteenth century, suggesting a growing confidence in improved technical capabilities. The single forestay must have been made stronger and more reliable.

The numbers of shrouds tended to increase with vessel (i.e. mast) size. From the seventeenth to nineteenth centuries, shrouds were put on to the mast-head in pairs and, as most medieval inventories refer to shrouds or headropes in 'couples', this was probably also the practice in the Middle Ages. Thirty-three examples of numbers of headropes set against ships' tonnage from the period 1400–97 give some indication of how the numbers of mainmast headropes increased with tonnage, but do not show any simple relationship between ship size and the number of headropes (see Table 9).

Backstays are most common in inventories of the first half of the fifteenth century, when they are often found to equal one-quarter or one-third of the numbers of headropes. They are less frequent in fourteenth-century inventories (listed in only twelve out of nineteen inventories of the period 1295–1378), and usually found in smaller numbers (in backstay : headrope ratios varying from 1:3 to 1:14). They

5.7 Schematic diagram of
basic square sail control gear.

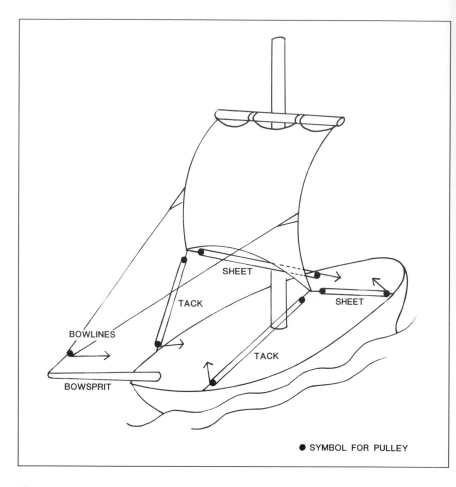

disappear entirely from the late fifteenth-century inventories, and were
probably subsumed under the heading of 'shrouds', or as Howard
suggested, they were supplanted by 'swifting tackles'.

'Swifting tackles' seem to have been a late fifteenth-century version
of gear earlier called 'polancres' or 'pollans' ropes. They are first encountered in English ship inventories of the 1370s, and were commonplace by the early fifteenth century: out of fifty-eight ships inventoried
in the period 1400 to 1436, thirty-six had polancres. Usually listed in
pairs, they were tackles used in association with the shrouds and
backstays, and had two or three pulleys each. Howard suggested that
they were used either because of weakness in the rope used for the
standing rigging, or 'to spread the pull of shrouds over a longer stretch
of topsides'. Either way, their purpose seems to have been to help
relieve the strain on the other parts of the standing rigging and on the
mast, rather like modern 'running backstays'. These are tackles to the
rear of the mast and are set up and made taut on one side of the ship
when the wind is blowing from that side (the tackle on the other side
being slackened). The later swifting tackles may have taken the place of

backstays, although they were used on some ships alongside Breton or Burton tackles (another late fifteenth-century innovation, presumably imported from Brittany) and the older polancres, suggesting that there were technical differences between these tackles.

The idea of using pulley-assisted tackles as part of the standing rigging may have originated in the Mediterranean, where pictures show that such tackles were common in the Middle Ages (see Fig. 9.7). It may be no coincidence that the earliest recorded ship in England to have them was the *Bayard*, a Genoese ship captured by the English in 1371. The Genoese carracks taken in 1416 and 1417 had them in much greater numbers than English ships, ranging from six to twelve pairs each as opposed to one or two pairs on the average English ship. By the late fifteenth century, English ships too were using the tackles in much greater numbers. The ability to vary the amount of support given to the mast or masts was clearly a technical advance, for it gave mariners a greater range of options as to how they sailed a ship, and contributed to both efficiency and safety. Like certain aspects of running rigging, the use of tackles on the standing rigging may have come from the Mediterranean.

English records seldom specify rope-length, but there is quite a lot of information regarding the weight of ropes, which can indicate whether ship riggers (almost always mariners) were using any form of planning or theory. Analysis of the accounts for gear supplied to twenty ships between 1337 and 1497 provides some interesting results. The total weights of the ropes used for the forestay, headropes or shrouds, backstays and 'upties' were examined. The upties, or ties, were ropes that went from the deck, up to and through the mast-head pulleys, and were tied to yards. They were the principal ropes used in raising or lowering the yard, and strictly speaking were part of the running rigging. In order to function, however, they had to be slightly longer than twice the height of the mast, and their weight helps to indicate the size of the mast. This analysis uses the total weight of the headropes as the base figure (this was the heaviest single element in the rigging), and in fourteen of the twenty cases, the headrope weight has to be estimated using the total number of headropes and the known weight of only one pair. The overall results, however, suggest that this approach works. For instance, a comparison of forestay, backstay and uptic weights with headrope weights for eighteen vessels over this period (excluding the *Philippe* and its barge) produced numerous weight ratios that can be expressed either as virtually whole numbers or as simple fractions (see Table 10).

In the case of the 80-oar galley *Philippe* and its 30-oar barge, both built at King's Lynn in 1337, the evidence of the use of proportions in the standing rigging is unequivocal (see Table 10). No forestay was listed for the 1337 barge, so its weight cannot be used as the index figure, but the relative weights of the galley and barge rigging were clearly not worked out according to the same system. For example, the headropes of the galley weighed six times the weight of its backstays; the head-ropes of the barge were eight times the weight of its backstays. In the case of the *Nicholas*, the headropes were about two-and-a-half times as heavy as the backstays. It is difficult to detect an overall scheme, but the evidence is that proportional rigging systems were in use. Surviving fifteenth-century shipbuilding treatises from Italy show that Mediter-ranean sailors used proportional methods to work out the amount of rigging required for a ship, and it seems that medieval English mariners also made use of basic arithmetical reasoning in rigging their ships.[25]

Much of the running rigging of a square-sailed medieval ship would be familiar to square-rig sailors of the twentieth century.[26] The northern European mariner of 1300 was able to raise or lower the yard of his ship by means of ties and lifts, and the yard could be braced (turned in the horizontal plane in different positions, according to wind direction and the point of sailing) with the help of yardropes and 'stetings', which were probably braces and 'preventer' (supplementary) braces. The bowline and the lof were available for securing the leading edge of the sail when the vessel was sailing to windward, and the lower corners (or clews) of the sail were held by ropes called sheets, which ran aft. Tacks, which ran forward from the clews, seem to have been used from Viking times, but they cannot be identified in English documentary sources before the mid-fourteenth century, when they appear under the name 'Loller' (superseded by 'tack' about 1400). The absence of tacks and some other items from the record before the fourteenth century does not mean that these items of gear were not in use; Middle English nomenclature can be obscure, and it is likely that most types of control-ropes used for yards and sails in the fourteenth and fifteenth centuries were similar to their counterparts of the sixteenth and seventeenth centuries.[27]

Just as the use of polancre ropes may have been imported from the Mediterranean, other items of rigging were possibly introduced from the south. These include the 'gire' or jeer, a rope-and-pulley system used to help raise or lower the yard. The main ropes normally used for this purpose were the ties, which went through the mast-head pulley to the centre-section of the yard, and the lifts, which ran through pulleys on either side of the mast out to each yard-arm. The gire or jeer was used mainly in the rigging of large ships, giving their crews much-needed extra purchase when raising or lowering the main yard. The earliest recorded ones were rigged in about 1415 or 1416 on two of Henry v's great ships, the *Trinity Royal* (540 tons) and the *Holigost* (760 tons). Gires were heavy pieces of tackle: the two or more in the *Trinity Royal* weighed 1236 lb (561.8 kg), almost as much as the ties. However, while the etymology of the word 'gire' indicates a southern origin, none of the great (400–600 ton) Genoese carracks captured by the English in 1416–17 had gires at the time of their capture, and only one of them was subsequently rigged with one. The extra tackles running to the main yard of the *Kraeck* may have been gires (see Fig. 4.5). The gire or jeer may thus have been a northern European invention, perhaps first developed in England.[28]

One clear example of technical transfer was related to lifting or lowering the yard. Two of Henry v's great ships, the *Holigost* and *Jesus*, were each equipped with an iron device called a 'flail' 'laid and fixed on the windlass ... to raise the sail more easily in the manner of a carrack'. The flail on the first vessel weighed 742 lb (337.3 kg), and that on the second 364 lb (165.5 kg). The flail and windlass in the *Jesus* were also furnished with iron *siropes* (meaning unknown) and wedges weighing 55 lb (25.0 kg). Both ships were equipped with flails in the period 1420–22, and that for the *Jesus* was bought from a Southampton black-smith, Robert Smyth, for 52s 4½d. The reference to 'the manner of a carrack' indicates that the device was copied from those used on Mediterranean carracks; the yards of the two great ships would have been easily as heavy as those of a carrack, and the flail was evidently designed to enable the crew to get more purchase on the yard.

Discovering what exactly the flail was, however, is less straight-forward. Medieval windlasses, like those of later times, were rotating horizontal drums with a rope attached to the centre section and holes for bars at each end. The windlass was turned by inserting bars in the holes in turn, removing the first set of bars as their holes turned underneath the windlass, and using the second set to provide continuing pressure, and to stop the windlass running back. Windlasses and capstans (vertical rotating drums) were used for a variety of tasks, including raising and lowering both the anchor and the yard. The Winchelsea seal of *c*. 1300 shows two of the crew working the windlass bars, engaged in raising the anchor (see Fig. 1.2). The flail has been associated with a 'whele' used 'for to wynde up the Mayne Sayle' of the great ship *Sovereign* in 1495: it may have been a large iron wheel attached to the windlass, and the 'siropes' and wedges were perhaps part of a braking device. Intriguing as the flail is, however, there is no evidence that it was used widely (none are listed, for example, in the inventories of the carracks captured in 1416–17).[29]

As well as needing to be raised and lowered, the yard had to be held against the mast. The earliest fittings for this purpose were simple rope loops or wooden yokes. The word 'rack' was used to describe this in Middle English by the end of the thirteenth century, although in the fifteenth century this term was superseded by the Latin word *apparatus* and its English equivalent, 'apparel' (hence 'parral'). Documents give no idea of the structure of parrals until the fifteenth century, by which time they were relatively complex. The Flemish engraving of the *Kraeck* (see Fig. 4.5) of *c*. 1470 shows a mainmast parral of highly developed form. It consists of five layers of trucks (wooden balls with holes in their centres, through which the parral-ropes pass) with vertical wooden ribs between the trucks to prevent them from jamming. The trucks acted rather like ball-bearings, allowing the yard to move smoothly up and down the mast. A set of spare parrals of this type was found in the wreck of the *Mary Rose*. The *Grace Dieu* of 1418 was supplied with twenty-nine ribs, indicating the great circumference of the ship's main-mast, and three 'sisters' (possibly a special type of rib or a double block used in rigging the truss). The truss was a rope used both to pull the yard back to the mast and to help lower it, and it would not have been difficult to combine this function with that of a parral. 'Truss-parrals' are first encountered in the fifteenth-century sources, perhaps initially as part of the lateen mizzen rigging, although by the 1490s it was a part of mainmast rigging. The overall impression is that the form and structure of the parral became a good deal more sophisticated in the fifteenth century.

The yard had to be controlled horizontally as well as vertically. In post-medieval ships, this job was done by braces, tackles attached to each end of the yard and led aft. However, the word 'brace' is not found before the mid-fifteenth century; before this date, two different types of gear apparently did the work of the brace: the 'stetings' and the 'yardropes'. One would assume, from their name, that the yardropes were the more important of these items, and it has been suggested that stetings were 'preventer' (i.e. supplementary) braces led forward. However, in four out of five examples between 1337 and 1420 in which we can compare the respective steting and yardrope weights on ves-sels, the stetings were significantly heavier. Comparing the weights of rigging elements supplied to a vessel with the weight of its uptie or tie is another way of calculating the relative importance of those elements. For fifteen ships between 1337 and 1420, the upties worked out as being, on average, about 2.6 times heavier than the stetings. In eleven vessels over the same period, the upties were on average 3.5 times heavier than the yardropes, indicating that stetings were generally heavier than yardropes, and that it was the stetings, not the yardropes, that were more important in bracing the yard.[30]

The basic ropes controlling the corners and edges of the sail were the sheets, which led aft, and the tacks and bowlines, which led forward (see Fig. 5.7). A study of ship accounts between 1460 and 1465 (thirteen examples) shows that sheets were generally heavier than tacks (on average, 2.6 times heavier). In nine cases over this period, however, it is possible to set the combined known weights of tacks and bowlines against the known weights of sheets. In four cases (a galley and three ships of up to 330 tons) the combined tack–bowline weights were roughly equal to those of the sheets; in the case of the 760-ton great ship

Holigost, the ratio was 1:1.33; but in four other cases (the 1000-ton *Jesus* of 1416 and three of the captured Genoese carracks) the tack–bowline weights were significantly greater than those of the sheets. Although these examples are too few to be conclusive, the results (apart from the *Holigost*) fall into two distinct groups: vessels of moderate size, in which the respective weights were almost equal, and very large ships, in which the tacks and bowlines were heavier than the sheets. The latter group may have represented an attempt to improve the ability of these cumbersome ships to sail windward, by using heavier and/or longer ropes for the tacks and bowlines which supported the weather edge of the sail from the forward part of the ship.[31]

From at least the mid-fourteenth century, there were ropes that seem to have been operated from deck level in order to furl sails, but in the absence of reef-points (see p. 98), such ropes would have been of limited use in shortening sail at sea. The reason for this is that the furled part of a sail needs to be tied up, and without reef-points this would have been very difficult. The various furling or brailing ropes were probably of more use in furling the sail completely in harbour, when it could be tied to the yard.[32]

The sailing ship may have been the most complex machine of the pre-industrial age (see e.g. Fig. 4.5), but it relied for its operation on one of the simplest of machines: the block or pulley. Inventories and accounts seldom list pulleys in large numbers: pulleys attached to ropes were probably normally counted as part of the rope. Most parts of the running rigging (and some other items of gear), however, would have been unworkable without pulleys, at least in all but the smallest ships. The building account for the 80-oar galley *Philippe* of 1337 lists the purchase of sixteen pulleys, with six of the most expensive (1s each) being used in raising the sail. The 80-oar barge *Paul* of London (built in 1373), had twenty pulleys, plus two 'winding-pulleys' (presumably used for the windlasses).[33]

In later centuries there were specialist blockmakers who constructed pulleys, but in the Middle Ages and the sixteenth century they were the work of wood-turners. Turners supplied royal ships with pulleys at both the beginning and end of the fifteenth century, and it is in the fifteenth century that more detail becomes available about different types of pulley and their construction. The wooden pulley shell contained a wooden or metal wheel, running on a small axle or pin. The axle was usually of wood, and there is one instance, from about 1415, of pins made of hard-wearing box-wood. Some larger ships used bronze pulley-wheels or sheaves; these seem to have been introduced in the early fifteenth century. Although bronze was heavier and more expensive than wood, it was much stronger and more durable, and represented a definite technical advance, at least for larger ships. The 1400-ton *Grace Dieu* of 1418 had fifty-seven such sheaves, made from copper, bell-brass and pan-brass, each weighing 41 lb (18.6 kg) on average. The 1514 inventory of the 600-ton *Mary Rose* listed some sixty-three brass sheaves in use in the ship, mostly in the rigging, along with three *spare shevers of Brasse grete & smalle*. They were undoubtedly itemised separately because of the high value of bronze or 'brass'. By the 1480s, bronze was being used to make the 'colkes' of pulleys, which were either the axles, or more likely small coaks (metal plates with circular holes) inserted into the pulley to give the axles more secure and durable footings.[34]

The recorded type-names of pulleys increase in the fifteenth century; before this time, the only adjectives used with the word 'pulley' tended to be simply 'great' or 'small'. In the early 1400s we begin to hear of 'truss-pulleys' (presumably used with the truss for the yard) and *hengepolives* ('hinged pulleys'). Sources later in the century refer to other types. For example, in 1485 the semi-derelict *Grace Dieu* (a vessel built in the late 1430s; see p. 13) had two pendants with double pulleys, a bowline pulley with two sheaves, five 'cheek' pulleys with brass sheaves, lift pulleys with two or four brass sheaves each, and a block with three sheaves, for the mizzen. The impression is that specialised pulleys were increasingly developed, probably to help cope with new rigging requirements created by the advent of the multi-masted ship. The earliest surviving set of rigging elements, those found in the wreck of the *Mary Rose* (1545), shows an interesting variety of single and double blocks. The double blocks included types with the sheaves set

5.8 One-masted ship on the town seal of Rye, Sussex, *c.* 1400. The reef-points are clearly visible on the sail, as are the seams joining the separate bolts of sailcloth together. The small 'flag' at the masthead is a fane or wind-vane, used to show wind-direction. Drawing after Ewe 1972.

side-by-side, those with sheaves set in series running in the same plane, and another group with the sheaves in series, but set at right-angles to each other. The shells of the blocks and the wooden pulley sheaves tended to be made from ash or elm, with wooden pins. Some of the larger bronze-sheaved pulleys had iron pins, a further technical advance.[35]

The fifteenth century seems to have seen an appreciable increase in the mechanical efficiency of running rigging, thanks to changes in the form and construction of pulleys. With the development of the multi-masted ship, rigging to some extent became more intricate, although a square sail and its yard operated in much the same way, whether used as mainsail, on a foremast or on a topmast. New ways had to be devised for operating, say, a top yard from deck level or from the top-castle, but otherwise no great technological leap was required in controlling the sail. Much the same was true of lateen topsails. The real technological leap lay in a new arrangement of masts, sails and yards (see Chapter 9).

Oars and oar-power

Northern European oar-powered vessels did not have anything like the technical complexity of the famous triremes of antiquity, nor, for the most part, were they as developed of those of the medieval Mediterranean. There is little doubt that they existed for two main purposes: war and piracy.

The ascendancy, fall and rise of the oared fighting ship in England is discussed in Chapter 8. This chapter is concerned with how English oared vessels actually worked. There is a good deal of documentary evidence, for most of the surviving building accounts relate to oared-vessel construction, and the picture that they give us does not suggest that there were any major changes in English rowing technology between the end of the thirteenth century (and probably much earlier) and the sixteenth century.

There were two basic ways in which an oar was pivoted on the side of a vessel. One way was to use thole-pins set in the gunwale of the craft, against which the oar moves, a system that will be familiar to anyone who has been in a modern rowing boat. This system was certainly used for large vessels in northern Europe in the early Middle Ages. However, there was always the possibility that a large oar might spring out of the thole-pins, even if it had been tied in place. By the ninth century, a different technique had been introduced, in which the oars were put through special oar-ports cut in the upper strake of the hull. This was both stronger and more secure. The oar-ports had to be large enough to take the oar handle (loom) and its blade. Some oar-ports had an extended cut to allow the blade of the oar to pass through, making it

mmck vatt hem mt eylant een frotne mmt vn goude
Als alle defe dmghe dus ghtolmtert en gh waen waen
volc vertoeth hem eje datt hn vvolnachtich was lovt
den den goden dat apollo ghtegsentert had dat sn
so zett beghtett hadden dat vat dat hn haer vonmolc
vaet en m vayse ende vieden hielt hier mede apollo
als haet vonmolc bleef vpt palays mt zethmuo en ze
thephmuo en mter ander dit hn m sn dienst onthielt
en van dien daghe voert de vonmolc apollo belradt
en regierde dat volc so visolo dat in den tut vn pn
ratie hn so bemmtvaro vn al sm ondersatt en vn sm
ghebutte dit an hem lande die vn hn ltems hadde

Thot de god mars den vonmolc apollo sende de
mamer hoe tguldn vlito ghtbvomr soude
vvesen of mors en anders met

possible to reduce the size of the port. This would have helped to seat the oar more securely, and to reduce the amount of water that might be shipped (see Figs 1.1, 5.9 and 5.10).[36]

So, by the thirteenth century, particular forms of rowing technology were well established in northern Europe. The port customs of London in the thirteenth century levied tolls on a variety of vessels, ranging from 2d for sailing ships to ½d for fishing boats. Two types of oared vessels were listed: ships being rowed or navigated *infra orlokes*, 'in oar-locks', at 1d; and ships navigated *cum thollis*, 'with tholes', at a halfpenny. The implication of the difference in tolls for the two types is that the vessels with oar-locks were larger. The latter were presumably ships with oar-ports in their sides (the tolls also distinguished between some fishing boats with tholes and oar-locks, at the same rates). Another interesting point is that these tolls indicate that the presence of oared merchant and fishing craft in the thirteenth-century port of London was a normal occurrence.[37]

Beyond some references to *galiote* ('galleymen') in thirteenth-century sources, there is little sign that medieval or sixteenth-century England had a specialised group of galley oarsmen such as existed in some of the Italian maritime republics. Italian and other European states used free

5.9 OPPOSITE Medieval north European images of oared craft are nowhere near as common as those of sailing ships. Although it lacks a mast and sail, this ten-oared vessel from a fifteenth-century Dutch manuscript has some of the attributes of a larger ship: an aftercastle and a bowsprit. The oar-ports are circular, set in the top strake, but for added strength the strake is topped by a gunwale.

5.10 A six-oared barge in a Flemish tapestry of the 1430s, the 'Otter and Swan Hunt' (one of the Devonshire Tapestries). In a small vessel such as this, each pair of rowers sits on the same bench or thwart. The oar-ports are rectangular.

men to crew their galleys in the Middle Ages; the 'galley slave' (a convict, captive or slave) did not appear in southern and western European galleys until the sixteenth century. From at least the late thirteenth century in England, galley crews were simply described as 'mariners', on the same pay-rates as the crews of sailing vessels, with no sign of a separate rowing specialisation.[38]

The rowing arrangements of medieval northern European ships have not attracted as much scholarly attention as those of the Greek trireme, but they were not as straightforward as one might think. The excavated remains of Viking ships show that those that operated under oars had a single bank of oars on each side, with the rowers either seated on benches set at right-angles to the keel, or standing up. This provides a simple model which was probably followed in some medieval and sixteenth-century English ships (see Fig. 5.10). The problem is that documentary sources show that in some ships the oars would have been set too close together in order for this model to work, while other vessels had oars of different lengths. The 1373 specifications for the barge *Paul* of London stated that the vessel was to have a keel length of 80 ft (24.4 m), a beam of 20 ft (6.1 m) and 80 oars. This would have given 40 oars on a side, with a spacing between each of little more than about 2 ft (0.61 m).

The same sort of two-foot spacing seems to have obtained with the Newcastle galley of 1295, and the 100-oar balinger *Godegrace* of 1401. The keel of the *Godegrace* was made up of three timbers, two measuring 40 ft (12.2 m), and is unlikely to have been much over 100 ft in length (30.5 m). On at least one occasion the balinger was rowed by 100 mariners, showing that none of the oars were 'spares'. A two-foot spacing between rowing positions would have been wholly inadequate if the rowers were seated on benches at right-angles to the keel, and even the most disciplined rowing team would have 'caught a crab' in such a situation. The best explanation for this apparent difficulty is that offered by R. C. Anderson (1976): that a system akin to Mediterranean *alla sensile* rowing was in use, with rowing benches set at an angle to the keel, and two rowers using oars of different lengths from the same bench. Certainly, this helps to explain why the Newcastle galley had oars of 16–17 ft (4.9–5.2 m) and 22–33 ft (6.7–7.0 m) in length, plus others of unknown length, and why in 1409 Henry IV's royal barge had twenty-six 'long' oars and twenty-two 'short' oars. Figure 5.11 is a schematic diagram showing the possible arrangement in the Newcastle galley. Assuming that the oar blades were intended to strike the water in the same line, despite their different lengths, there would have been about 6 ft between the rowers on the same bench, and 4 ft between the rowers on successive benches. There is no reason to believe that this system was borrowed from Mediterranean galleys. The Mediterranean galley trade to northern Europe only began in the last quarter of the

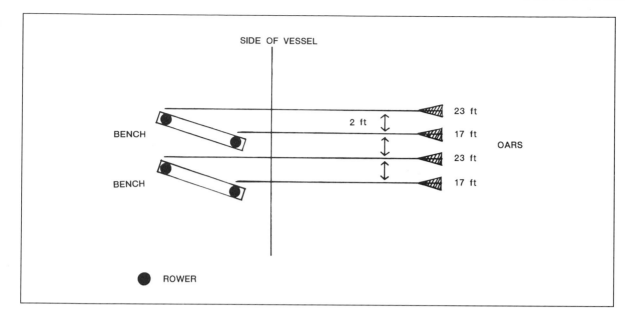

5.11 Possible rowing arrangement in English oared vessels with long and short oars.

thirteenth century and, given the long northern experience with oared craft, such a rowing method quite possibly developed independently.[39]

There is no evidence that the *al scaloccio* style of rowing was used in England before the sixteenth century. This technique, involving several men on a bench working the same large oar, did not develop even in the Mediterranean before the 1500s. The general evidence, however, is so slight that one cannot be dogmatic. The 120-ton royal balingers *Anne* and *George* were supplied (respectively) with sets of 68 and 71 oars of 24 ft (7.3 m) in length between 1416 and 1420, and the *George* is specifically described as having been made 'in the manner of a galley'. The fact that the oars on each vessel were of the same length suggests either that some special system was being used or that there was a relatively wide spacing between rowing benches; interestingly, the *George* is known to have put to sea on at least one occasion with a crew of 143 men, enough to allow two men per oar.[40]

It is, moreover, clear that oared vessels did not always make use of all of their oars. As mentioned above, in 1402, in the presence of the king, the *Godegrace* was rowed by a crew of 100 men; this may have been part of a special event on the Thames. All of the balinger's oars could be used, but in three subsequent voyages across the English Channel the *Godegrace*'s complement numbered no more than sixty. Other vessels were better-provided. On two occasions the contemporary 40-oar balinger *Anne* (a predecessor to that of 1416) had crews of thirty-seven to thirty-eight men: a 30-oar balinger of 1416 had a crew of thirty-four. Oared vessels were of course labour-intensive, but all could be moved under sail as well as by oars. Rare evidence of the size of a sailing crew of an oared craft is provided by the building account for a small 24-oar

(25 oars are actually listed) barge built at Newcastle in 1304. Constructed for Edward I, the barge was sailed north to join the king in Scotland, by a crew of ten, about 40 per cent of the number of men needed to row the vessel.[41]

Illustrations of oared craft are much less common in medieval art from northern Europe than from the Mediterranean. Apart from some special sources, such as the Bayeux Tapestry, it is difficult to illustrate such craft and their oars. Oars were made from long timber blanks called *orevenes* or *or-evens*. Some oars were supplied ready-made, while others were bought as blanks and fashioned into oars. The cost of manufacture was variable. In 1348, buying some timbers and making them into oars cost 9d per oar, of which only 1d represented the manufacturing cost (about 11 per cent). In the 1430s, a joiner was paid 5s for 'making' (possibly finishing) thirty-six great oars. The oars cost 3s each before they were worked on, and the joiner's wages amounted to about 4.5 per cent of the total.[42]

The overall cost of oars was also variable. The oars of the 1295 galleys were 11d–12d each. Price-levels remained fairly stable until the second half of the fourteenth century, when they seem to have started to rise (possibly as a consequence of the economic upheavals following the Black Death), reaching a figure of 2s to 3s in the early fifteenth century. Somewhat paradoxically, oars were certainly no more expensive, and in real terms probably cheaper, at the end of the century. Henry VII's oared fighting ships were equipped with oars costing from 1s to 2s: even some 24-foot oars were only priced at 1s each. Oars were made in England, but Henry VII was even known to buy some abroad, importing over two hundred from Normandy (the cost of transport of these items only added about 2d to the cost of each 1s oar). There is no easy technological or other explanation for the increasing relative cheapness of oars in the late fifteenth century.

Data on the lengths of oars is scarce. The 16–17 and 22–23 ft lengths of the oars of the Newcastle galley are some of the few known from the thirteenth century. Oars of 20–24 ft length were in use in both the early and late fifteenth century. As some of these were used on the greatest oared vessels of Henry V's fleet (the 120-ton *Anne* and *George*), the 24-foot oar probably represented the largest type used by the English at the end of the Middle Ages.[43]

The English did not adopt, so far as is known, the counterweighting of oars with lead weights. This was a Mediterranean practice, designed to improve handling. Henry IV's large (and probably unused) galley *Jesus Maria* had two hundred and forty leaded oars, along with twelve non-leaded ones, but no such oars are listed among the inventories and accounts of the other English royal ships between the late thirteenth century and the late fifteenth century. Such innovations may have crept into use during the reign of Henry VIII, given the king's interest in matters nautical. His 800-ton *Great Galley* of 1515 was described by Venetian diplomats as a 'galeass', a combination of broadside-firing sailing warship and oared craft that was well-known in the Mediterranean, but comparatively rare in north European waters. The *Great Galley* had seven guns per side, carried on a deck above the rowers. The galley is said to have had 120 oars, and is known to have been crewed by 160 Thames watermen in 1515, so it is possible that some of the oars were worked by two men. Henry also had a Mediterranean-style galley built in the 1540s, and it may have been that the ship built to take him and his queen to the Field of the Cloth of Gold in 1520 had at least one feature borrowed from southern European galleys. The building account for this ship, the *Katerine Pleasaunce*, includes the cost of two masts to make the *thowbem* and 57s 4d spent on the laying 'of the postywyches to Row' – evidently something to do with rowing. The word 'postywyches' may be an anglicisation of the Italian word *apostis*. Apostis were protruding rowing-frames that ran along the upper parts of both sides of a Mediterranean galley. They were mounted on transverse beams at either end of the hull, which may offer an explanation for the two masts used for the 'thowbeme(s)'. The apostis were designed to give the oarsmen greater leverage, and to enable the width of the hull to be reduced without reducing the space for rowers.[44]

CHAPTER 6

Life, work and equipment on board

COOKING AND EATING

If the crew were part of the 'machinery' that drove a ship, then food and drink were their fuel. The typical shipboard victuals of mariners in medieval and sixteenth-century northern Europe would have been depressingly familiar to their counterparts of the eighteenth century. The staple items were ship's biscuit (a mixture of flour and water slow-baked until it justified its alternative name of 'hardtack'), salted meat and fish, and beer. Basic rations may have been supplemented by fresh food: there is evidence that crews sometimes dined on fresh bread, eggs, cheese, meat and fish, vegetables, fruit and even spices. The royal ship *George* of the 1340s was supplied with 1800 hooks and fishing lines to enable the crew to supplement their diet with fresh fish, although not everyone was keen on this staple item. In 1466 Sir John Howard was prepared to buy white bread for those members of the crew of his new carvel *Edward* that did not eat fish (the fish in question being herring and salted fish of some kind). The bones of fresh pork and fish were found in the wreck of the *Mary Rose*, along with peas still in the pod, fruit-stones, venison and mutton bones, and even peppercorns. Some of these foodstuffs would have been the property of officers: the standard shipboard fare was monotonous, and perhaps not particularly nourishing.[1]

Ships of the Viking age were not equipped for cooking food, and it is evident that the cauldrons and hanging chains in some Viking ship burials were 'camping equipment', used for cooking ashore. There is no documentary reference to cooking facilities aboard an English ship until the 1330s, although it is likely that English ships had them before this date. The galleys of 1295 certainly carried items connected with cooking, eating and drinking. The Dunwich galley inventory included four cauldrons, four pots, ten tuns (water barrels?), twenty-four cups, a hundred plates and ten dishes, all for a crew of about a hundred men. The Ipswich and London galleys had similar equipment, with also a 'brass pot for ale' in the Ipswich vessel, and 'small tuns for keeping water' in the second London galley. The Newcastle galley had on board a 'mill' (*mola*) and six iron griddles. The mill would have been a hand-mill or quern for grinding corn or, more likely, oats, to make flour. This could then have been cooked on the griddles to make oatcakes. This may imply the existence of a cooking hearth in the galley, although the griddles could have been used for cooking ashore. The Newcastle galley also had three brass cauldrons and six brass pots of considerable size, weighing 157 lb (71.4 kg) in total, three other brass cauldrons, six great tuns, six cups, eighty dishes and forty saucers. Apparently the aim was to provide each galley crewman in 1295 with a plate or dish from which to eat.[2]

An adequate water supply was vital for any ship's crew, but particularly for a crew of oarsmen. In the naval wars of the medieval Mediterranean, ensuring sufficient water supplies for galley crews was a constant worry for admirals. It has been estimated that a Mediterranean galley rower would require a minimum of four pints (0.5 gallons; 1.82 litres) of water per day when at sea during the summer months, and there is evidence that southern galleys could carry between 800 and 1500 gallons (2909–5460 litres). Unfortunately, it is impossible to know if the 'tuns' carried by the 1295 galleys were equivalent in capacity to the wine tun of 252 gallons (917.3 litres). If they were, the ten tuns of the Dunwich galley and the twenty-two tuns of the Ipswich galley would have contained 2520 gallons and 5544 gallons respectively (9163.6 and 20,180.2 litres). At Mediterranean rates of consumption, the Dunwich vessel would have had enough water to stay at sea for about fifty days and the Ipswich craft for a hundred and ten days. This is highly theoretical however: Mediterranean galleys seem only to have been able to go for two to three weeks without replenishing their water barrels and, in northern Europe, coastal water supplies were nowhere near as scarce as they were in parts of the Mediterranean. An added consideration is the state of the contents of a water barrel after fifty days![3]

Working a vessel under sail or oars required a great deal of hard, tiring work, sometimes in highly unpleasant and dangerous conditions. The provision of hot food is very important for a ship's crew, for it is easy to lose body warmth, energy and morale in wet and cold conditions at sea. Shipboard cooking facilities were not just a way of making life more tolerable for the crew, they could actually help to improve the crew's ability to work the ship. The records indicate that the basic materials, and probably also the basic structures, of ovens in English ships did not change much between at least the 1340s and the first half of the sixteenth century. The royal ship *All Hallow's Cog* had an oven for baking bread in the 1330s, and in the following decade the king's ship *Cog Thomas* was fitted out with a hearth and one or more ovens made from Flemish tiles. The distinction between 'hearth' and 'oven' points to the existence of both open and enclosed cooking spaces, with the possibilities of boiling and frying food as well as roasting or baking it.

Ships' kitchens required tile, brick and stone in large quantities, in order safely to contain the heat generated by the cooking fire. This was true even in a comparatively small ship like Sir John Howard's carvel *Edward*, of 1466, which had an oven made of 800 bricks, 250 house tiles and 13 paving tiles. The 1000-ton royal ship *Sovereign* was provided in the 1490s with a new kitchen with two ovens and a new floor, the whole made from 6500 bricks and 600 paving stones. The bricks and stones were fixed together with lime cement, and a large quantity of salt was laid in the kitchen floor, perhaps as extra heat insulation. The construction work was carried out by a team of masons, a trade that one would not normally associate with work aboard ship, but fairly common in the building of ships' kitchens. Repairs to the kitchen of the *Jesus* in the early 1420s had involved 'cementers' (masons), plasterers and plumbers, the latter working with lead and solder, perhaps to fix cooking cauldrons in place.

The earliest English ship's kitchen to have been found is that of the *Mary Rose*. This contained the shattered remains of a huge firebox, made of thousands of bricks, which supported two large copper cooking cauldrons with wide leaded rims. The kitchen was built in the hold of the ship, which is where most earlier ships' kitchens are likely to have been constructed, because of their great weight. The *Mary Rose* kitchen was positioned roughly amidships, although in the wrecks of two later medieval cogs found in Danish waters, the cooking area seems to have been in the bows. The smoke from the fire had to be carried up to deck level by some form of chimney, although the only written reference to such a feature comes in the record of the purchase of clay daub to make a chimney for the kitchen in Henry IV's ship *Trinity* in the early 1400s. It is thought that smoke from the kitchen of the *Mary Rose* may have been carried up through the ship by means of a lead-lined timber hood.[4] (It should be pointed out that the word 'kitchen' is used here instead of the word 'galley' to avoid confusion, and because medieval and sixteenth-century sources in Latin, Norman-French and English use terms such as *coquina*, *cusyne* and *kychyn*.)

Just as the kitchens seem to have changed little between the fourteenth and sixteenth centuries, the general types of cooking and eating equipment do not appear to have altered much. One standard feature of fifteenth-century ships' kitchens was the 'kettle' (*cacabum*), usually made of brass. This seems to have been a large, portable cooking pot; those in the *Sovereign* in the 1490s were used 'to seth [boil] in ffleshe'.

They were made of brass, two with an iron band each, and two and four iron rings apiece, and one with a handle. There was a hook and iron chain to hang the kettles from, and a coal-rake, doubtless used for the hearth. Sir John Howard's ship the *George Howard* had three brass kettles in 1479, the largest of which could hold 20 gallons (72.7 litres), the second 10 gallons, and the third was a small one used for boiling pitch for ship repairs. Other kitchen equipment included an iron tripod, two gridirons, some pewter dishes and pots and an iron cover for the oven. Howard's other ship, the *Edward Howard* (the carvel built in 1466), was similarly equipped. Many of these items could be found in the inventories of English royal ships earlier in the century, along with pots, tankards, flesh-hooks, frying pans, and occasional refinements, like the mustard-quern and mortar in the *Christofre* of 1411, which may have been used for mixing herbs and spices. Late fifteenth-century royal ships, at least the larger ones, were not much different; items such as a brass water-cistern for a furnace and iron spits are listed, along with hand-baskets for carrying bread and 'maunds' (great baskets) used for meat. The contents of beer barrels were accessed by means of wooden taps and 'canelles' (channels, tubes); two dozen of each were bought for the *Sovereign* in 1496.[5]

The items bought for the crew's use in the late fifteenth and early sixteenth centuries were little different from those of two centuries before. In 1482 Sir John Howard purchased for his ship *Mary Howard* 52 tankards of various types, 126 drinking bowls, 120 plates, 120 saucers, 8 trays and 6 maunds. The *Mary Howard* was a big ship; in the following year she sailed in an expedition to Scotland with a crew of 400 men, who presumably required even more drinking bowls and plates. Plates, dishes, saucers, tankards and drinking bowls were the common table items of the Tudor mariner, even though most of them would never have sat at table while aboard ship: there are only occasional references to (trestle) tables in the fifteenth century. These seem to have been reserved for the use of the master or owner, or, on some occasions, for royal passengers. Trestle tables would have been very useful on board ship, for they could be taken apart and stowed away. The crew probably sat on deck to eat, while the master and captain sat in chairs. There is only one documented instance of a chair on board a ship before 1500, however, and that was a wainscot chair, apparently in the master's cabin of the *Regent*, with a trestle table.[6]

Almost nothing is known about the cooks. They are seldom noted separately in wages' lists, suggesting that they were paid at the same rate as ordinary mariners. It is worth remarking, however, on the 'kooke' of Sir John Howard's *Edward* in 1466 and 1467: Nicholas Blow-bolle is perhaps the earliest English sea-cook recorded by name.

Winding gear

Part of the hard shipboard work consisted of working the winding gear. This term covers the windlasses (horizontal winches) and capstans (vertical winches) needed to raise and lower the yard, to work the anchors and to lift heavy cargo or ordnance loads (see Fig. 6.1). The earliest ship's windlass known was found in the wreck of a small (11-metre) vessel of the thirteenth century excavated in Kalmar harbour in Sweden. Most of the 1295 galleys had no more than one windlass each, although the Newcastle galley possessed two: a rear windlass, and a forward one taken from a Dutch ship. Besides the highly specialised 'flail' and wheel (see p. 105), the only advance in turning the windlass seems to have been the introduction of iron winch-handles, which would have been set at either end of the windlass drum. The royal ship *Grace Dieu* of 1402 had two iron *wynches* on its windlass.[8]

The date of the introduction of the capstan is unknown, as is the origin of the word itself. It may have come from the Mediterranean, but is first known in English in a poem of *c.* 1325. This describes Noah's Ark as being '*with-outen . . . kable oþer* [or] *capstan to clyppe* [clasp] *to her ankrez* [anchors]'. The first non-literary reference to a capstan on board an English vessel comes in 1348, when a capstan costing 3s was installed in

6.1 Model of the Bremen cog of *c.* 1380, showing the capstan and the windlass in the aft part of the ship.

an oared fighting vessel. The Bremen cog, wrecked in about 1380, had a windlass and a six-bar capstan. The capstan was turned by men pushing on the bars; the central barrel of the capstan had a projection which went down through the deck, to which the cable or other rope was attached.[9]

Although capstans and windlasses were essential in the handling of large ships,[10] direct references to them are rare in fifteenth-century ship inventories, probably because they were counted as part of the fixtures and fittings. Most of the written references come from building or repair accounts, although their presence can be detected in the inventories in references to 'winding-ropes', 'winding-tackle' and 'winding-pulleys'. The winding-ropes could be quite heavy: for example, between 1416 and 1420, the royal ship *Marie Breton* was equipped with hawsers for the windlass weighing 1–2.5 cwt (50.9–127.3 kg). Some capstans were massive. A capstan for the 300-ton *Trinity* in 1400 took two carpenters eight days to construct and incorporated three iron bands, an iron ferrule and other ironwork weighing close on 1.33 cwt (148 kg). By the end of the fifteenth century, capstans had proliferated: the great ship *Sovereign* had three and the *Regent*, four. The windlasses on these ships may have been subsumed under the term 'wheel'.

ANCHORS

One of the things that would have been impossible without winding gear was the use of large anchors. Anchors are to be found in many medieval and sixteenth-century pictorial representations (see Figs. 6.2 and 6.3b), and there is no doubt that they followed what has become known as the 'Admiralty' pattern. This was an anchor consisting of an iron shank with two curved arms projecting from it at one end. Near the tip of each arm was a triangular plate called a fluke, made for digging into the sea-bed. At the other end of the anchor was a detachable wooden stock, set at right angles to the arms to ensure that they would be flipped into a vertical position on the sea-bed, allowing one fluke to dig in. At the stock end of the anchor there was an iron ring for the anchor cable, while the anchor buoy-rope was usually attached to the other end (the buoy, floating on the surface, marked the position of the anchor).[11]

Inventories show that all but the smallest ships had at least two anchors. Even so, there was no simple equation between vessel size and number of anchors. The Ipswich galley of 1295 (100 oars) had four anchors, its attendant barge (30 oars) had two; yet the 1295 Lyme galley, with a mere 54 oars, had the same number of anchors as the Ipswich galley, and the Dunwich galley (100 oars) had six anchors. Similarly, the 80-ton royal ship *Petite Marie* of the period 1413–20 had six anchors, as many as the contemporary *Cog John* (220 tons) and the carrack *George*

Coment Noee charge sa neef. e apres ses enfauns e sa femme en la neef. p une
cleele et de chesune chose: male e femmele. si com li angel deu li auoit comande p
le mounde sauuer. ~

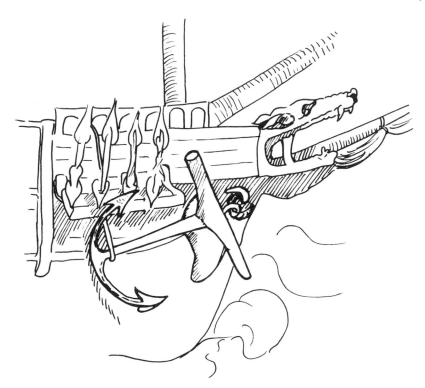

6.2 OPPOSITE Noah entering the Ark, early fourteenth century English manuscript (Queen Mary's Psalter). The Ark hull is that of a double-ended vessel with a stern rudder. The anchor on the right is what was later called an 'Admiralty pattern' type.

6.3 (a) an anchor in position at a ship's bow; (b) a ship's boat equipped with a pulley for warping a vessel out of harbour (after the Tunis Tapestry, sixteenth century).

(600 tons).[12] Illustrations often show an anchor carried on either side of the bow (see Fig. 9.5), where one would expect to find the main anchors, but exactly where any other anchors were stowed is debatable.

There is little data on the weights and dimensions of English anchors before the seventeenth century, but it is clear that English anchor-smithing had reached a high degree of sophistication as early as the first half of the fourteenth century. The usual raw material was imported Spanish iron, which was perhaps superior to the native product. In 1337 it was used to make four 14 ft-long anchors (4.27 m) for a royal galley at Winchelsea in Sussex. These cost 60s each, but, despite their great length, they must have been significantly lighter (and perhaps smaller) than three Spanish iron anchors made at King's Lynn in Norfolk in the same year for the royal ship *Grande Cogge*. These anchors cost between 228s and 260s, more than four times the cost of the Winchelsea anchors, and their weights ranged between 2324 lb and 2646 lb (1056–1203 kg). A fourth, smaller anchor weighed 938 lb, but even this equalled one-and-a-half times the Winchelsea price. The *Grande Cogge* was fitted out at King's Lynn at the same time that the 80-oar galley *Philippe* was being built there. Although the galley did not have individual anchors as heavy as those of the cog, its two largest anchors weighed around half a ton apiece, and its whole set of six anchors weighed just over 2 tons. The *Grande Cogge* anchors were as heavy as any anchors known to have been made in the fifteenth century. The largest single anchor in the 1000-ton great ship *Jesus* of 1416 weighed 2511 lb (1141.4 kg), slightly less than the heaviest *Grande Cogge* anchor, although the total weight of the five great anchors of the *Jesus* amounted to 9543 lb, just over 4.25 tons (4338 kg).[13]

Rare detailed measurements survive for two English anchors of the fifteenth century: these were taken in 1450, when they were granted for use in a ship (later in royal ownership) called the *Grace Dieu*, sailing in an expedition to Bordeaux. The anchors were from two of Henry v's old great ships (ironically, one had belonged to the *Grace Dieu* of 1418, destroyed by fire in 1439). The other anchor actually had a name, *Marie Tynktawe* (meaning unknown), and was recorded as far back as 1411. It had been used in both the *Trinity Royale* (540 tons) and the *Holigost* (760 tons). The reason for naming this anchor was probably to give a 'personality' or even a religious dedication to this grand piece of ironwork, much in the way that some of the great iron cannon of the Middle Ages acquired names, such as 'Mons Meg'. The measurements are not always easy to interpret, but they give overall lengths and widths for the two anchors. The document refers to the width of the *virga* ('yard') of each anchor, which in this context must mean the two arms, and not the anchor stocks (the measurements seem to have been intended to ensure that the anchors were identifiable, for a safe return: the iron arms were a fixed feature, but wooden stocks were not). The

Grace Dieu anchor was 17 ft 2 ins (5.23 m) long and 11 ft 5 ins (3.48 m) across the arms; the equivalent measurements for the anchor *Marie Tynktawe* were 15 ft 9 ins (4.80 m) long and 11 ft (3.35 m) across.

The width of the arms of the *Grace Dieu* anchor was almost exactly two-thirds (0.67) of the length of its shank, and the other anchor was close (0.70) to this figure, suggesting that the anchor-smiths were working to some system of proportions. Further evidence of the massiveness of these items is provided by the width of the flukes of the *Grace Dieu* anchor, each of which measured 25 ins (0.635 m) across. This anchor would have been one of those made for the great ship between 1416 and 1420, constructed on a special 'iron apparatus for hanging anchors during the time of their making'.[14]

Anchors for large ships were expensive. Average costs for the anchors of the 1295 galleys ranged between 18s and £2. The two largest anchors for the *Philippe* of 1337 cost over £11 in total, and the four great anchors made for the *Grande Cogge* at the same time came to nearly £42, enough to build a boat of reasonable size. The costs of the 'great ship' anchors of the early fifteenth century are not known, although they are liable to have been considerable. Three anchors bought for the 1000-ton *Regent* in the 1490s were around £12 each. The only anchor parts mentioned with any frequency are anchor stocks, but these references show little apart from the facts that the stocks were made of timber and relatively cheap. Two anchor stocks for Edward II's ship *Swallow* in about 1312 cost 1s apiece, while those supplied for the *Trinity* and the barge *Holigost* almost a century later cost between 2s and 3s 4d. An anchor stock for the contemporary balinger *Godegrace* was 1s 8d, one-eighteenth of the value of one of the vessel's anchors. In 1497, an 8d anchor stock for the bark *Mary Fortune* was thirty-three times cheaper than the least expensive of the bark's anchors. Anchors in general may have been costly, but the stocks were cheap and easily replaced. This was an advantage, for they were susceptible to rot and damage. The 300-ton ship *Trinity* needed seven replacement anchor stocks between 1399 and 1402.[15]

Names for different types of anchors are seldom recorded before the late fifteenth century, beyond the simple distinction between 'great' and 'small' anchors (this does not, of course, mean that different type-names or types did not exist). The royal ships of the 1490s had a variety of anchors, including starboard and port (*lathebourde*; 'larboard') anchors, bowers, 'destrells', sheet anchors and *caggyng* (kedge) anchors. The meaning of 'destrells' is not clear, although they seem to have been reasonably large anchors, for the buoy-ropes of the destrells of the *Sovereign* measured 6 ins in circumference, as opposed to 13 ins for the largest cables in the ship. The bowers were the anchors carried attached to cables on either side of the bow, and the sheet anchor was kept in reserve, should the bowers fail. The kedge was a light anchor used to 'warp' a ship out of harbour. This process involved the anchor being taken forwards in a boat, attached to the warp-rope, and then dropped and allowed to dig into the sea-bed. The capstan was then used to haul the ship forward on the warp-rope; the anchor was raised, and the process was repeated. In the 1490s the great boat of the *Sovereign* had two chains in the bow 'for armyng the Ankers', together with a sheaved davit, items that might well have been used for warping the ship. A similar sort of arrangement may be seen in a boat in the sixteenth-century 'Tunis Tapestry' (see Fig. 6.3b).[16]

The earliest details of anchor-handling equipment, other than windlasses and capstans, date from the early fifteenth century. The *Trinity Royal* of 1415 had two iron chains with hooks 'for painting the anchors', also with two brass sheaves for the purpose. The contemporary *Holigost* had two iron hooks on two ropes in the forecastle, used for 'hauling' the anchors. 'Paint' in a nautical context means 'to make fast', and iron *peyntynghokes pro ancor'* are to be found in a number of ship inventories of the early fifteenth century, including one weighing 36 lb (16.4 kg) in the 290-ton *Holigost Spain*, another of Henry v's vessels. The other examples of painting-hooks seem to have been confined to three of the king's large Genoese carracks, suggesting that specialised anchor-handling gear of this type was only needed on large vessels with heavy anchors.[17]

Large ships of the late fifteenth century had even more sophisticated anchor-handling equipment, including hooks 'to fish the Ankre with', cat-hooks, bow-hooks, shank-hooks, bow-seizings, bow-painters and shank-painters. Some of these terms may have been synonymous, but on the basis of later evidence a cat-hook was secured to the anchor-ring, and used to raise it from the water to a horizontal position close to a projecting timber called a cat-head. Fish-hooks were used to pull the flukes of the anchor to the side of the ship, and shank-painters, from their name, were used to lash the anchor-shank to the ship. Bow-seizings and -painters were presumably used to secure the end of the anchor closest to the bow. The picture is one of greater complexity than that of the early fifteenth century. The multiple hooks and lashings would not only have made the work easier, but they would undoubtedly have brought an element of redundancy into the system (as happened with 'preventer' ropes in rigging), which meant that the failure of just one rope was not the prelude to disaster.[18]

Little is known about anchor-buoys. References to buoy-ropes are more plentiful than references to the buoys themselves. Buoys were certainly in use by the late thirteenth century, for the Lyme and Newcastle galleys had two each, the two *signis* (buoys) for the Lyme galley costing a mere 7d in total. Buoys had to be light, and some are known to have been made of cork. The barge *Paul* of London had two *boyes de corkill'* in the 1370s, and fifty years later the great ship *Grace Dieu* had two cork buoys and five double wooden buoys. Two buoys used in the *Holigost* at the same period were made from a hundred pieces of cork. The *Mary of the Tower* some sixty years later had a mixture of cork and double wooden buoys, similar to those in the old *Grace Dieu*.[19]

The other major item of ground-tackle was the mooring-rope. It is not often specifically named, but any spare cable or hawser would have served the purpose. Sometimes cut-up pieces of old cable or rope called 'junks' were set aside for mooring use (they were also used to make fenders for the side of the ship), but there was also a specialised type of mooring-rope called a 'baste'. Bastes were made from the inner bark of the lime tree, cut into strips and spun into ropes. They seem to have been imported from the Baltic, and were sometimes described as 'Prussian ropes'.[20]

The main elements of ground-tackle, with the probable exception of sheaved anchor-handling equipment, were in existence by the thirteenth century. The main change that seems to have taken place, from the first half of the fourteenth century, was the development of the ability to make massive anchors for large ships, which in turn led to a requirement for sheaved anchor-handling equipment. English anchors of 1500 were not much different in shape from those of 1300, but the changes in the intervening years meant that the seaman of the early sixteenth century was able to 'cat' and 'fish' his anchors in ways that were to become standard for the next three centuries or more.

PUMPING GEAR

All vessels take in water to some degree, and getting rid of this water before it rises too high has been a problem for sailors since prehistory. The simplest type of bailer used in the Middle Ages was a hand-held water scoop, variously called a *baile*, *spucher*, *spogeor* or *scope* ('scoop'). In 1337, purchases for the *All Hallow's Cog* included 2d spent on 'a wooden instrument called a *spuchour* for pouring out and expelling water from the ship'. The bailers were normally made just of wood, although some iron-bound examples were recorded.[21]

The first point at which water gathers in the hull is of course at the bottom, or the bilge. In wooden ships this meant that the ballast tended to be permanently wet, and could clog any mechanical pumping apparatus that might be used (see below). To prevent this, 'limber holes' were usually cut into the floor timbers, allowing water to pass through. To keep the holes clear of ballast, a 'keel-rope' was used, which ran the length of the ship and could be pulled through the limber holes to remove any detritus. Only one documentary reference to a keel-rope is known, in the ship *All Hallow's Cog* of 1337, described as a 'keel-rope placed in the bottom of the ship for making a good flow of water'. Despite this unique appearance in the records, a keel-rope is something that few medieval or sixteenth-century ships could have afforded to be without. Blocked limber holes would have led to water pooling in the lower parts of the hull, causing timbers to rot, and endangering the ship itself.[22]

Medieval pumping apparatus could be quite complicated. Chain-pumps were used in ships in the Roman and early medieval Mediterranean, and remains of rope-and-timber chain-pumps have been recovered from wrecks of this period. The chain-pump was a device consisting (in post-medieval times) of a continuous piece of chain, attached to a rotating wheel at deck level, passing down through a tube to the bilge of the ship. The chain had valves or water-scoops set on it at intervals so that as it passed through the bilge-water, water was scooped up and carried to deck level in another tube, where it was discharged into the scuppers and so over the side. Chain-pumps were noted as being more efficient than suction-pumps in removing water, and men could work for longer at the chain-pump than they could at the suction-pump. Chain-pumps, however, were labour-intensive over long periods, prone to breakdowns, and required much maintenance.[23]

Chain-pumps were certainly used in at least some English ships of the fourteenth century, although in these cases the 'chain' was actually made of rope. The 1337 galley *Philippe* had two 'wyndigbalies' with 'two windlasses for putting water out of the ship', costing a mere 3s 4d, accompanied by a 28 lb (12.7 kg) winding-rope for the windlasses, costing 2s, and two bailers (*spoiours*) worth 4d each. The bailers were used for putting water into the winding-bailers. The system was completed by twelve gutters, made from four stones of lead, one of a number of references to the use of lead guttering in the pumping systems of medieval ships. The Dunwich galley of 1295 may have had such a device, for its inventory included 'thirty scoops for the windlass', along with twenty-four other scoops. The scoops may have been valves for a chain-pump system. Two winding-bailers formed part of the equipment of the barge *Paul* of 1373, and another English royal ship of the 1370s, the *Dieulagard*, had a *waterwyndas* (water-windlass). Such items were not confined to English ships, for the *Bayard*, a Genoese ship briefly in English hands in 1371, also had a 'waterwyndas'.[24]

The use of water-windlasses seems to have died out in England – and indeed, Europe as a whole – after the fourteenth century. They disappeared from memory to such an extent that their reintroduction in the sixteenth century was thought by contemporaries to be an innovation.[25]

The water-windlass or chain-pump was supplanted by the suction-pump, a machine of a type most familiar as the village water-pump. The suction-pump consists of a tube with a handle at the top; the handle works a piston, and either suction or pressure is used to raise water from the bottom of the tube to the spout at the top. In ships, the top of the pump was situated at weather-deck level, by the scuppers, and the bottom of the pump tube reached down into the bilge. One would think that such a pump is of great antiquity, but the English word 'pump' is not recorded before the fifteenth century, and was perhaps a specifically nautical term in middle English, possibly of Dutch/Low German origin.

The earliest-recorded instance of 'pump' in English, given by the *Oxford English Dictionary*, comes in a word-list of *c.* 1440, which defines it as a 'Pumpe of a schyp, or other lyke, *hauritorium*'. An earlier written reference, pre-dating the *OED* by over thirty years, does indeed come from a nautical context. In 1408–9, six pieces of fir timber were used to make *cuiusdam Pompe*, 'a certain pump' for Henry IV's household barge. The timber cost only 2s, so the pump must have been of fairly light construction, but the idea rapidly caught on. Between 1413 and 1422, seventeen English royal vessels (two of the great ships, one carrack, seven ships and seven balingers or barges) are known to have been fitted with pumps. In each case this took place either during construction or after the vessel in question had been acquired by the Crown. There is no evidence that any of the Genoese, Breton, Spanish or other foreign vessels taken by the English during this period had pumps. This, together with its etymology, suggests that the pump may have been an English invention, developed for use on board ship in the first decade of the fifteenth century.[26] Whether or not the 1408–9 reference marks the first use of the pump, is impossible to say: keeping the royal feet dry may not have been sufficient motive to develop a new piece of technology.

There are no clear references to the old water-windlass system after the 1370s, and there can be little doubt that the suction-pump was an improvement. A pumping system relying on ropes and windlasses is liable to have been bulky and prone to breakdown or rot. The suction-pump was much more compact. Larger ships, such as the *Grace Dieu* of 1418 and the *Regent* of 1495 had two pumps, although most smaller vessels needed only one. Pump positions are generally uncertain, although the *Regent* had one pump by its mainmast and the other by the mizzenmast, and the *Mary Rose* of 1545 may have had a pump near the mainmast.[27]

The precise constructional details of pumps are unclear. Wooden pump-boxes seem to have worn out fairly quickly, for twenty had to be bought between 1422 and 1427 in an effort to keep six royal ships afloat at their moorings on the River Hamble. Some leather was used in scuppers and pumps, to provide hoses and perhaps even flexible valves or seals, and some fifteenth-century pumps may have had iron valves. The pump-handles themselves were probably mostly wooden, although a weighty 59 lb (26.8 kg) 'pump-yard' bought for Henry V's *Holigost* gives some indication of the arduous nature of 'pumping ship'.

The pump-barrels in the larger ships had to be long, for they had to reach from deck level to the bottom of the hull. When the royal ship *Mary and John* was repaired after a fire in 1512, two new pumps were bought. The *Mary and John* was not a large ship (between 180 and 260 tons) but the pumps, with their boxes, measured 23 ft and 24 ft in length (7.0–7.3 m). The pumps were also supplied with timber for pump-staves, and two hoses.[28]

Whatever the effectiveness of pumps, they could not prevent the damp, enclosed bilges of medieval and sixteenth-century ships from acquiring a very foul smell, caused by stagnant water and human and food waste. The anonymous author of *The Pilgrim's Sea Voyage* (c. 1450) gave a heartfelt description of the unfortunate pilgrim compelled to bed down in the hold of an English ship:

> For when that we shall go to bedde
> The pumpe was nygh our bedde hede
> A man were as good to be dede
> As smell therof the stynk.[29]

CHAPTER 7

Ships for trade

England's trading network between the thirteenth and sixteenth centuries was very wide, given that the country was nowhere near as populous and wealthy as some of its European neighbours. Goods reached England from as far north as Scandinavia and the Baltic (and, from the fifteenth century, from Iceland) and from as far south as the Mediterranean. In the words of the historian J. L. Bolton, 'England was ... one of the nodal points of European trade' (see Fig. 7.1). But to what extent was English overseas trade served by English shipping? In the fifteenth century much of England's foreign trade was carried in foreign ships, particularly those from Flanders and Holland, and it has been doubted whether the English shipbuilding industry was able to expand enough to supply more ships when, in the later Middle Ages, English merchants began to take over a larger share of English trade.[1]

The general outlines of English sea trade in the Middle Ages and sixteenth century are clear. The enrolled customs accounts have enabled historians to chart the fortunes of the country's two main exports, wool and cloth, from the late thirteenth century to the sixteenth century. The enrolled, or summary, accounts were compiled from the detailed 'particular' accounts prepared in each port area. Only a minority of these have survived, and they have certain drawbacks. The port areas were very large (that for Chichester in Sussex, for example, stretched from Chichester to Folkestone in Kent), often making it impossible to know exactly which port was being entered. No national customs were charged on coastal shipping, leaving out a major element in the total sea traffic. Surviving accounts, however, document the movements of many thousands of ships over more than two centuries, and, despite their faults, they are a source of great importance for economic and maritime history. Local customs tolls, affecting coastal shipping and fishing vessels, were charged in some ports, and some of

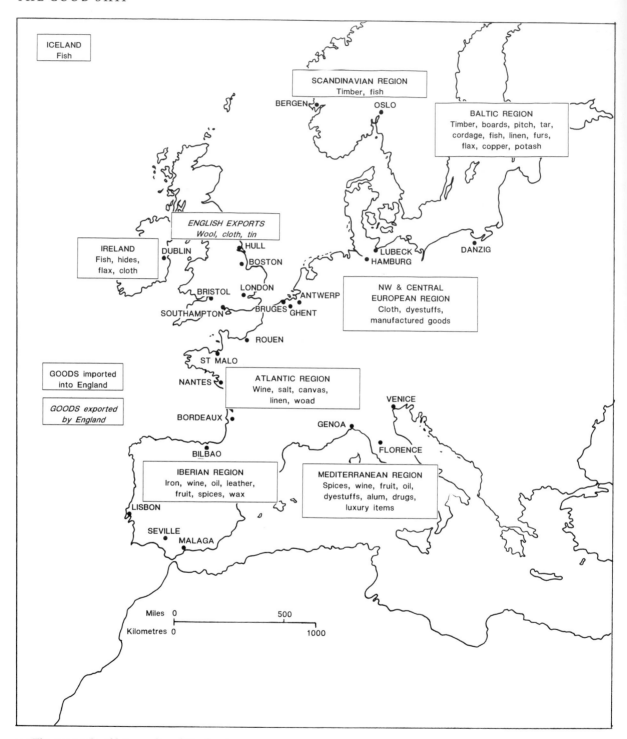

ICELAND
Fish

SCANDINAVIAN REGION
Timber, fish

BERGEN

OSLO

BALTIC REGION
Timber, boards, pitch, tar,
cordage, fish, linen, furs,
flax, copper, potash

ENGLISH EXPORTS
Wool, cloth, tin

HULL

IRELAND
Fish, hides,
flax, cloth

DUBLIN

BOSTON

LUBECK
HAMBURG

DANZIG

BRISTOL

LONDON

ANTWERP

**NW & CENTRAL
EUROPEAN REGION**
Cloth, dyestuffs,
manufactured goods

SOUTHAMPTON

BRUGES
GHENT

ROUEN

ST MALO

GOODS imported
into England

NANTES

ATLANTIC REGION
Wine, salt, canvas,
linen, woad

VENICE

GOODS exported
by England

BORDEAUX

GENOA

FLORENCE

BILBAO

IBERIAN REGION
Iron, wine, oil, leather,
fruit, spices, wax

MEDITERRANEAN REGION
Spices, wine, fruit, oil,
dyestuffs, alum, drugs,
luxury items

LISBON

SEVILLE

MALAGA

Miles 0   500
Kilometres 0   1000

7.1 The sea trade of late medieval England.

these survive in part for places such as Exeter, Southampton and Newcastle.[2]

References to English ships on trading voyages before the late thirteenth century tend to be confined to isolated episodes, such as wrecks, piratical attacks and the granting of safe-conducts. For example, in 1267 Brother Geoffrey of the Abbey of St Benet of Hulme, in Norfolk, was given a royal grant of safe-conduct for the Abbey's ship, men and goods, which were in his keeping (it is unclear if he was the master or a sort of supercargo). In the following year the ship *La Stelle* ('Star') of Beaulieu Abbey in Hampshire received two grants of protection. Such grants, to both religious and secular shipowners, are fairly common in English records and point to a high degree of insecurity, both at sea and in port. In 1243 a certain John Bonet was granted protection for his ship the *Sauvette* to trade along the whole English coast, without molestation, between the beginning of March and the end of September. Thirteenth-century conditions were far from any idea of 'free trade'.[3]

If it is the volume, not the value, of trade that affects the usage of shipping, there was more employment for English shipping in the early fourteenth century than in the fifteenth. Cloth exports did not require a great volume of shipping, and the key bulk English trade was the transport of wine from Gascony. In the early 1300s, England took each year about one-fifth of the 90–100,000 tuns of wine exported annually from Bordeaux and the other Gascon ports, and it is no accident that in England and many other countries the wine tun of 252 gallons became the theoretical measure of a ship's capacity (see pp. 32–3).

The Bordeaux customs records, which noted the name, home port, amount of cargo and other details of each ship lading wine, give a good idea of the scale of the trade in the early fourteenth century. Between June 1303 and June 1304 there were over 900 shipping movements in the wine trade at Bordeaux. Each 'movement' represented a vessel being loaded with wine for export. Although this figure included a substantial number of ships making two voyages in the year, it still indicates the impressive scale of the trade. A few years later, between September 1310 and early July 1311, there were just over 500 shipping movements in the port – a smaller figure, but still considerable, compared to the situation after the outbreak of war between England and France in 1337, which began the long series of conflicts known as the Hundred Years War. In the mid-1350s, annual numbers of shipping movements at Bordeaux varied between 154 and 245, and those for the later fourteenth century and the first half of the fifteenth were no better, with 193 movements in 1385–6 and 218 in 1416–17. Once it had dropped to its new, lower level, the trade did not suffer any further significant decline until the mid-fifteenth century, and indeed it underwent something of a revival in terms of the total tonnage of wine moved in the late fourteenth century. English imports in the fifteenth century averaged 9,000–10,000 tuns per year, about half that of the early four-teenth-century figure, but that trade was being carried on in ships of greater size, leading to no increase in the numbers of vessels required on the Bordeaux route.[4]

The coal trade from the north-east of England was another major employer of shipping, although again it is debatable how much of this was English-owned. Much of the coal trade was carried along the coast, with London as its main destination, but as no national customs dues were charged on coastal traffic, it is impossible to ascertain the owner-ship or nationality of the vessels used. There was an active export trade in coals from Newcastle upon Tyne by the 1290s, and probably much earlier, with a great deal of demand from Holland, Zealand and Flan-ders. In 1377–78 there were 158 sailings from Newcastle, carrying 7320 chaldrons (c. 6000 tons) of coal, a level of shipping movements close to those experienced at Bordeaux. Ships from the Low Countries, however, far outnumbered those from Newcastle, with only five New-castle ships involved out of the total of 113 sailings in 1390–91. The coal itself was measured in terms of chalders or chaldrons (from 'cauldron') and it was normally transported down the Tyne, or from the quay to ships anchored in the river, by boats called 'keels', which in 1421 were said to contain about 20 chalders. It is not certain how the coal was loaded into the ships, but it would have been much easier to handle if it had been packed in containers.[5]

Another trade in which English ships were employed, albeit un-certainly, was the Bourgneuf Bay salt trade. English ships had been loading salt in 'The Bay', on the west coast of France, since at least the early thirteenth century, but the dislocations of salt supply and other areas of trade in the second half of the fourteenth century, caused by plague and war, benefited the Bourgneuf trade and enabled it to grow. Before this date, England seems to have been an important supplier of salt, but it was eclipsed by the Bay, and changed from being a net exporter to a net importer. The salt was mainly used for preserving fish, and European salt production and the sailing of salt fleets had to be geared to meet the demands of the main fishing seasons and markets. After the mid-1300s, two-thirds to three-quarters of English salt imports came from the Bay.

The numbers of English ships employed in the trade is not known; they sometimes travelled in convoy, as did the Bordeaux wine fleets, but none of the English convoys matched the size of the Hanse salt fleets, which could exceed 100 vessels. The value of the cargo itself was low in relation to its bulk, making it an ideal cargo in terms of the employment of shipping. Most shippers of salt appear to have hired cargo space, rather than owning their own vessels, often splitting their salt between different ships to reduce risk. A great deal of the salt was exported in sacks, although some was certainly carried loose. The

And in this schippe ageine alle schoures
Ther were castels and eke toures

7.2 A one-masted ship with a lading port in the port side, from an English manuscript *c.* 1426. The ship has some of the form of a carrack (see also Fig. 4.5).

loading and unloading of a ship was generally carried out by special porters, working from the quays, although there were cases in London in the fifteenth century when salt ships were found to be too large to tie up at the wharves and had to anchor in the river where they could be unloaded by lighters.[6]

How were ships physically adapted for trade? Most vessels with decks were probably loaded through deck-hatches, although some evidently had a lading-port in the side (see Figs. 7.2 and 4.5). The ways in which cargo was stowed are very poorly documented. One rare exception is an account for work carried out at Harwich in Edward II's ship *Nicholas of Westminster* in 1312–13. This ship was fitted out to carry a total of sixty-three containers of wine: thirty tuns and thirty-three pipes (half-tuns).

One might imagine that the barrels would have been most easily stowed merely by laying them in tiers, relying on the sides of the ship and the weight of each tier to hold them steady, but the process was clearly much more involved than this. The lowest barrels were bedded down on top of 'dunnage', a soft material, possibly straw, used to cushion them against damage from the ballast. Wooden *garners* ('gran-aries') were made for bedding (*por coucher*) the tuns and pipes. The granaries were made of 66 stanchions, 400 laths and over 300 timber *cortins* ('curtains' or 'partitions'; eight were also used for dunnage), along with other timber, 200 spike-nails for fastening the stanchions, 900 lath-nails for fixing the laths to the granaries, 400 *romnayl por coucher les toneaux*, and other nails. The fact that the number of stanchions is only three more than the number of barrels suggests that there was one granary to each barrel. They may have been 'barrel-cradles' of some type, possibly made before the barrels were stowed, as carpenters were paid 12d for making the granaries and 6s for bedding the tuns. The barrels were evidently brought aboard using a windlass, for payment was made *en wyndag' de xxx toneaux de vin & xxxiii pipes*, at about 1.5d each. The windlass was probably a quayside crane, for there would have been no charge for the use of the ship's windlass.[7]

The use of the term 'granary' to mean an item used for stowing cargo is not listed in any of the standard dictionaries and is seldom found in documentary sources. Granaries were, however, used to stow wheat in English ships as early as the 1170s, and when three west-country ships were fitted out in the mid-1320s to carry tuns packed with flour, they were also supplied with timber and nails to make granaries (in this instance, the dunnage was composed of hay hurdles). The small number of references to shipboard granaries reflects the dearth of early records about ship stowage; such information as survives points to medieval cargo stowage being considerably more complex than might have been thought.[8]

Although horses were sometimes carried as cargo or as the property of important passengers, they were often transported by sea for military reasons. Fourteen Dorset ships were used to transport horses in the same Gascony expedition of the mid-1320s as the three ships carrying flour, mentioned above. Each ship was issued with materials to provide secure stabling for the horses. The amounts varied from ship to ship, but every vessel received boards, nails, hurdles (of wood), *rackes* (two per ship, perhaps feeding racks), 14–16 yards (12.8–14.6 m) of canvas, 16–20 (29.3–36.6 m) fathoms of rope, a dozen iron rings and staples, and a number of tuns of fresh water (*aqua dulce*). The boards may have been used to help strengthen the ships, as one account of the 1340s states, and the canvas will have been made into slings (*mangeria equorum*) to go around the horses' bellies, to support them and stop them from moving. English materials and practices seem to have been similar to those used in the Mediterranean in the thirteenth century, although whether one region influenced the other is difficult to say. The hurdles were sometimes used to separate one horse from another, fourteenth-century hurdles measuring as much as 7 × 9 ft (2.1 × 2.7 m). The gang-

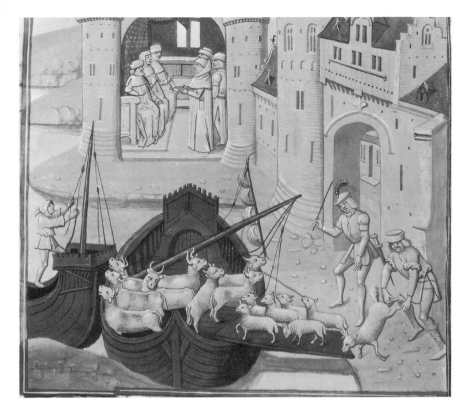

7.3 Loading cattle and sheep on to a vessel. Flemish manuscript, late fifteenth century. The animals are being driven up a gangway: similar gangways would have been used for horses.

ways used for embarking animals were larger, up to 5 × 30 ft (1.5 × 9.1 m) (see Fig. 7.3). Horses and other animals were probably brought aboard in this way, although a few pictures show animals being hoisted aboard using tackle attached to a yard-arm.[9]

Apart from the movement of people to and fro across the English Channel from designated 'passage' ports such as Dover, the only major passenger-carrying trade in which English ships participated (under licence) was the transport of pilgrims to the northern Spanish port of Corunna, *en route* for the shrine of Santiago de Compostella. Pilgrims had been going from England to the shrine since the twelfth century, but the pilgrim trade reached its peak in the fifteenth century, with Devon ships playing an especially important role. Recent research has shown that between 1390 and 1485, Devon ships made one-third of all licensed crossings to Spain. This was the case in the peak year for the trade, 1434, when the passage of 3120 pilgrims was licensed. Most pilgrim ships carried between 40 and 60 passengers on average, although some could take up to 200 people. The conditions experienced by the passengers were cramped and unpleasant, aptly summed up in *The Pilgrims' Sea-voyage* (see p. 130). Even the movement of 980 pilgrims from Plymouth in 1434, however, only involved the use of fifteen Devon ships, making a total of twenty-two voyages over a short sea route (a 3- to 5-day journey in good conditions). In 1435–6, thirty-three

7.4 Merchants awaiting the arrival of ships – evidently with some anxiety – in an English manuscript of the fourteenth century.

Devon ships were involved in the Bordeaux wine trade. The pilgrim trade cannot have been a major employer of shipping.[10]

The names, types and sizes of thousands of medieval and sixteenth-century merchantmen are recorded, and trade was the engine that drove most sea traffic (Fig. 7.4). The technological aspects of medieval ships engaged in 'honourable trade', however, are nowhere near as well documented as those of another kind of vessel, the warship.

CHAPTER 8

Ships for war

Few English naval battles of the Middle Ages are well known, even to people interested in naval history. One dictionary of 'the principal sea battles of history' lists a mere six, from William Longspee's victory over the French at Damme in 1213 to the Duke of Bedford's defeat of the French at Harfleur in 1416. Five of these battles were English victories: Damme, Dover 1217, Sluys 1340, Winchelsea 1350 and Harfleur. The sixth, at La Rochelle in 1372, was a resounding defeat for the English (see Fig. 8.5). The same book lists three battles for the reign of Henry VIII, the two combats off Brest in 1512 and 1513, and the encounter between the English and French fleets off Portsmouth in 1545. Each of these three battles was characterised by spectacular individual disasters: the loss of the *Regent* and *La Cordelière* in 1512; the death of the English Lord High Admiral in 1513; and the capsizing of the *Mary Rose* in 1545. Most, apart from La Rochelle (and this may be significant), were fought in a small sea area close to the English coast between Flanders, the coast of Kent, Sussex and Hampshire, and the mouth of the Seine. All were conducted against the French or their allies.[1]

It is difficult to call many medieval sea battles 'decisive', for it was land campaigns that finally determined the outcomes of wars. Some sea battles, however, did have important results. The battles of Damme, Dover and Sluys severely dented French seapower, and forestalled invasions of England. The battle of Harfleur in 1416 lifted the French siege of the English forces trapped in the town, and led to the capture of some Genoese carracks; but it has to be seen in the context of the Earl of Huntingdon's victory off the Chef de Caux in the following year, in which the remaining carracks were taken and the way was cleared for Henry v's invasion army to sail. It has been argued that even the humiliating defeat inflicted by Castilian galleys at La Rochelle in 1372 only spurred the English on to make greater efforts at sea.[2]

8.1 English manuscript of 1271 showing two ships in combat, with troops stationed in the castles. The basic tactics, and some of the weapons, are little different from those to be found in the Warwick Roll illustration of over two centuries later (Fig. 8.2).

Battles naturally attracted particular attention from chroniclers, but they were just one part of conflict at sea in the Middle Ages and the sixteenth century: the spectrum of violence ranged from full-blown battles between state navies to skirmishes between small groups of ships on official sea patrols, individual efforts by privateers, and outright piracy. Piracy was sometimes impossible to distinguish from wartime privateering (and the distinction would have been academic to the victims); but it had its own spectrum of activities, ranging from spectacular acts such as the capture by English pirates of a 110-strong fleet of German, Dutch and Flemish salt-ships in 1449 to opportunist boardings by passing ships (nautical 'muggings') and the outright pilfering of cargoes in harbour. One of the ugliest manifestations of seaborne warfare was the raiding of coastal towns and other settlements. Attacks of this sort were perpetrated by both sides during the Hundred Years War, and they also took place during Henry VIII's wars with the French. Such was the fear of seaborne attack that in 1381, during the Peasants' Revolt, the Kentish rebels marching on London ordered all those living within twelve leagues of the sea to stay at home, in order to be ready to defend the coast against the French. The basic tactic used by the English, French and others was to land a force on the coast, then pillage and destroy every settlement within reach, retreating before any effective defence could be organised.[3]

Medieval illustrations of sea battles tend to show either stylised combats between single ships, or pitched battles with masses of ships laid side-by-side (see Figs 8.1, 8.2, 8.3 and 8.4). In general terms, these images were probably quite accurate. Boarding was the main sea-fighting technique in northern European naval warfare, and the manoeuvrings of ships were generally directed towards either boarding or avoiding being boarded. The only effective long-range weapons were the longbow, and to a lesser extent, the crossbow, with guns coming a very poor third, at least before the late fifteenth century (see pp. 150–6).

As in later naval combats, it was usually best to be to windward of an opponent, to 'have the weather gage', for this meant that an attacking ship could choose the positioning, mode and timing of an attack. Being able to turn so that the wind was behind you, or on the beam, meant that a vessel could acquire considerable momentum, making ramming feasible. In 1440 an English ship, the *George* of Wells (120 tons), was deliberately rammed by the 320-ton *Christopher* of Dartmouth, just off Start Point in Devon. Complaints made in the Court of Chancery by three of the merchants who were on board the *George* make it fairly clear that the intentions of the *Christopher*'s crew were hostile. It was said that the master of the *Christopher*, seeing the *George* following three miles behind, turned his ship around and bore down on the smaller vessel, with three 'well harnessed' (i.e. wearing helmets and armour) men in the topcastle, and forty other armed men about the ship. The *Christopher*

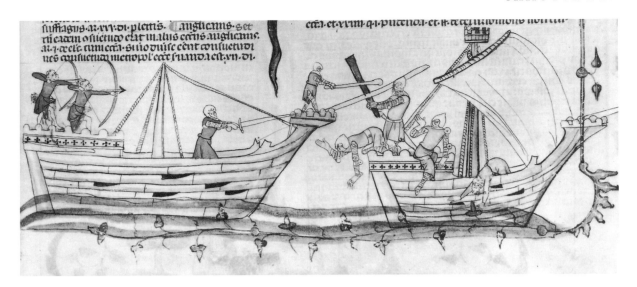

suffragus.ar.xxv.or.plenis. Canglicanus.set
rti eam ofueaudo erat in albis certis anglicanis.
ar.q.ecle eminerā.s.no ouise cent consuetuoi
nes consuetuam meuopl'ece suano a est.vn.or.

cca.et.rxvm.q.putecoi.et.ff.ete aluomos nou eu

came down with full sail and *a large wynde* behind it, and hit the *George*
so hard that the latter's 'foreship' (probably forecastle) broke off and
fell into the sea. Ramming could be a shock tactic of considerable
effectiveness, knocking an opponent's crew off their feet and damaging
their ship.

How the forty-four people in the *George* survived the attack is not
made clear. One or more of the merchants called out to the *Christopher*
that they were English, and that they stood to leeward, with the
mainsail set low ('lay upon the lee wyth ther corse low set', i.e. not
ready to fight or flee). Their survival is attributed to the grace of God,
without further explanation, although the ship and an alleged £600
worth of goods may well have been taken. The *Christopher* belonged to
Thomas Gyll, a prominent Dartmouth citizen and shipowner, who
despite being a powerful man in his own district, eventually found
himself having to pay back something to his victims.[4]

The earliest-known set of official 'fighting instructions' in English
dates from *c.* 1530, in a brief memorandum set down by a lawyer. As the
historian Julian Corbett pointed out, the tactics described are essentially medieval. The admiral of a fleet was urged to try 'to get the wind
[i.e. get to windward] of the enemy by all means he can, for that is the
advantage'. Ships were to seek out opponents of roughly equal size to
their own vessel, and to leave the boarding of the enemy flagship to
their own admiral's ship. Some pinnaces (small oared craft) were to be
left uncommitted to help out those ships that were in danger of being
overwhelmed, with a small vessel detailed to support the admiral's
flagship (perhaps also one of the duties of the balingers that acted as
'followers' to some of the English great ships in the early fifteenth
century; see Fig. 8.5). Cannon, small-arms and 'crossbow shot' (and
also, presumably, longbow shot) was to be used to clear an enemy's

8.3 Two cogs in combat, from
an English manuscript, early
fourteenth century. This
small-scale, rather one-sided
battle bears more
resemblance to piracy than to
warfare.

8.2 OPPOSITE This scene from
the Warwick Roll of *c.* 1485
ostensibly shows an English
ship in battle with two enemy
carracks in the time of Henry
v, although the vessels
themselves (apparently
clinker-built) belong to the
late fifteenth century.
However, the weapons used,
including cannon, bows,
crossbows, a spear, topcastle
gads, and even a rock, would
not have been out of place in
the early fifteenth century, or
even (apart from the cannon)
in the thirteenth. It was not
uncommon to find heraldic
devices on the sails of large
ships.

8.4 Late fifteenth-century Flemish manuscript of Froissart's *Chronicles*, depicting the battle of La Rochelle, 1372. This is not a literal rendering of the battle: the English were defeated by Castilian galleys, none of which are shown here, and the ships are stylised versions of carracks. The same manuscript's representation of the 1340 battle of Sluys looks very similar! (see Fowler 1980, p. 32). However, the picture probably does give a good impression of what a medieval sea-battle was like: a deadly melée of hand-to-hand fighting with ships laid against each other.

O m voert te weten dan waer om dat dese
vier steeplime dus poedern en vñ dart
m was de hystorie seyt dat haer minnghe was
des griekien sip te achter volghe En mt een wat
de rominde octes mt vier hondert manen mt hē
wyter stat die hm alle hatselic hadde doen wapenē
om diestbel dat hm vischert was dat sm dorhter
medea mt rason werh was En sal v segghē hoe
hut quam te weten dese rominde octhes die drowmch
was als gheseyt is was sec vol gheperm dat hm

8.5 Large English sailing warships of the fifteenth century often had 'followers', large, oared boats which acted as auxiliary vessels to the warship, but could also operate independently. This fifteenth-century Dutch manuscript shows a sailing ship with a retinue of oared vessels.

decks before boarding. It was also said that an attempt should be made to capture the topcastles of the other vessel before boarding, although how this was to be done was left unclear. If a captured ship looked like being rescued, the memorandum's bleak advice was to first take off the enemy captain 'with certain of the best with him' (i.e. the richer and more ransomable officers) and then scuttle the ship with its crew, to prevent them turning on their captors.

Gunfire was to be avoided when chasing another ship, for it slowed your vessel down, but it was advocated as a means of escape when being chased, using the smoke from cannon to cover an attempt to get to windward of the pursuers. There was no notion of using guns at a distance to batter an enemy ship to pieces or to sink it. These tactics would not have been out of place two hundred years before. The instruction to attack a ship of similar size was common sense: the defending ship would not have a height advantage which could have allowed it to make the attacker's decks untenable, and in ships of similar size the crews would probably be of similar numbers.[5]

FIGHTING SHIPS: OAR AND SAIL

One of the earliest-known 'facts' about the history of the English navy is the famous order in 897 by King Alfred of Wessex for the construction of a group of large oared warships, of 60 oars and more. These were to be used to help repel Danish seaborne attacks. At least some of these vessels were built, and scholarly attention has tended to focus on what the craft may have been like. Of much greater importance, however, is the evidence that ninth-century Wessex had sufficient shipwrights, shipbuilding resources and expertise to enable it to build large oared fighting ships at fairly short notice. Anglo-Saxon naval arrangements did not long survive the Norman Conquest, and it was not until the early thirteenth century that England began to require a large royal fleet again.

King John's loss of Normandy in 1204 turned the English Channel coast from a transit-point for people crossing from one part of a cross-Channel kingdom to the other, into a threatened frontier. John rapidly created a royal fleet: in 1204 he had forty-five galleys based at different ports in England and a further five in Ireland. His reign was one of the great periods of naval expansion in English medieval history, driven by pressing military needs. Between 1209 and 1212, twenty new galleys were built for the Crown along with thirty-four other vessels. As Professor Warren observes: 'The galleys (*galeae*) were the principal warships, equipped with sail but fitted also with oars for speed and independence of the wind'. Sailing ships were built for the king, but galleys were the main fighting vessels, and were to remain so throughout the thirteenth century. When Edward I sent out orders to various ports to build warships, in 1276 and 1294, the aim was to construct galleys and their attendant oared barges. The 1294 order was for twenty galleys of 120 oars each, with barges, and the burden of the work was to be borne by twenty-six towns. Only eight of the galleys are known to have been built, but their construction accounts are among the most important medieval English shipbuilding records (see Chapter 3). Constructed between 1294 and 1296 (but conventionally known as the 'galleys of 1295'), few of them seem to have lived up to the 120-oar specification, but most were substantial vessels.[6]

As a way of describing large, native-built fighting craft, the term 'galley' started to fall out of favour in England in the fourteenth century. The 80-oar galley *Philippe*, constructed at King's Lynn in 1337, seems to have been similar to the 1295 galleys, but by the later fourteenth century the main English oared warships were being called 'barges' and 'balingers'. In the fifteenth century, the English generally used 'galley' to denote foreign oared vessels (particularly the Italian trading galleys). Henry IV's large *Jesus Maria*, described as 'newly made' in 1411, was called a galley, but the galley's inventory includes certain features that suggest it may have been of Mediterranean design, if not construction (see pp. 172–3).

What exactly balingers or barges were is not easy to determine. They were usually oared fighting craft, and barges may have tended to be larger than balingers, but few sources suggest much difference between them and galleys, and there are no identifiable pictures of either type. The word 'balinger' derived from an Old French word for a whaling boat, but why it came to be used in English as a name for a warship is unclear. Balingers ranged in size from the smallest, such as the *Paul* of 1413, with about 20 oars, to the 100-oar, 100-ton *Godegrace* of 1401. Balingers enjoyed a certain popularity with pirates, suggesting that they were speedy and manoeuvrable. The 56-ton balinger *Craccher* ('Spitter'), given to Henry V in 1416, may well have been an ex-pirate ship, for she was given to the king by John Hawley of Dartmouth, a notorious pirate. Whatever the exact nature of the balinger, it seems to have eclipsed the galley, in name at least. In 1377 and 1401, the Crown once again sent 'round-robin' orders to large numbers of ports for the construction of warships, but on these occasions the vessels specified were balingers and barges, not galleys. Merchant balingers did exist, although it is not known if they were oared, but by the early sixteenth century 'balinger' no longer meant an oared warship. The term 'galley' came back into fashion during the reign of Henry VIII, following a brief period in the fifteenth century when some oared fighting craft were called 'barks'.[7]

The changes affecting English oared warships were not merely semantic. The fourteenth century saw the rise of the sailing ship in naval warfare, although oared vessels remained important. The information on English royal oared ships between 1295 and 1422 for which the numbers of oars are known shows that warships of more than 100 oars were very rare. The two biggest owned by the English Crown in the fourteenth century were the *St Edward* (132 oars) and the *St George* (152 oars), constructed at Bayonne in southern Gascony in the mid-1320s. The *Jesus Maria* of 1411 had over 240 oars, but is not known to have been used. It is plain, however, that oared vessels of between 50 and 100 oars were an important feature of English royal fleets between the reigns of Edward I and Edward III. Henry IV's fleet (1399–1413) saw very little action, but contained a fairly large proportion of sizeable oared ships. Henry V's fleet (1413–22) saw a great deal of war use, and the absence in it of the larger balingers and barges is highly significant. Oared warships were still numerous, but the main fleet units of Henry V's navy were sailing ships. Henry VIII's fleet of a century later (1509–47) contained a high proportion of oared ships – galleys, galleasses, rowbarges and others – and extensive use was made of them, but there can be little doubt that the most important vessels in the royal navy were the king's great broadside-firing carracks (see pp. 153–6). The day of the oared fighting vessel was by no means over in England by the early fifteenth century, but it had ceased to be the main fighting unit. The oared warship dominated northern European sea warfare from at least the eighth century to the fourteenth, and its decline marks the beginning of the end of a major seafaring tradition. Why did it happen?

One highly likely explanation is given by Ole Crumlin Pedersen who points out the fact that such ships as the cog were higher than the oared longships that developed out of the Scandinavian and other northern European shipbuilding traditions. In combat the cog had an automatic height advantage – one of the crucial factors in medieval sea warfare. Crumlin Pedersen suggests that the development of castles represented an attempt by the builders of longships to nullify the height advantage of cogs and other high-sided ships; but this was an 'arms race' that low-built vessels could not win, for shipwrights began putting castles on cogs.

To illustrate the magnitude of the change, Crumlin Pedersen quotes the example of the Danish naval defence system, the *leding*, which in the thirteenth century maintained some 1100 longships. In 1304 the *leding* was converted to using the cog, and the Danish island of Zealand changed from maintaining 120 longships to 5–10 cogs.[8] As we have seen, the earliest datable images of ships with castles, from *c.* 1200, show them on both longships and cog-types, suggesting that castles had actually developed in the twelfth century (see Chapter 4). If so, the ascendancy of the high-sided sailing ship evidently took at least a century to establish in Denmark and perhaps 150 years or more in England. Large oared ships were expensive to build and to man, and cash-strapped medieval monarchies would not have kept building them merely out of sentiment or blind adherence to tradition. Crumlin Pedersen's explanation of the rise of the sail-powered warship brings out an important factor in the decline of the longship, but it may not represent the whole explanation.

The fleet that the French fielded at Sluys in 1340 included 198 vessels, of which only 28 were oared craft. The 170 sailing ships in the force, gathered from the coasts of France, were large by contemporary standards – 149 of them exceeded 100 tons burden, and the largest was a ship of 240 tons. The oared galleys and barges represented the bulk of the king's fleet, moved from its base at Rouen, the Clos des Galées. Despite their relatively small numbers, these ships were very large, fourteen having crews of 100 men or more, and eight with crews exceeding 200. They were larger than any oared vessels possessed by the English. The fleet's destruction did not lead the French to abandon galleys: the Clos des Galées remained in use as a galley and barge dockyard until it was burnt to the ground by Henry V's troops.

When the French hired foreign vessels to fight Henry V at sea, the Genoese mercenary force included not only eight great carracks, but also twelve galleys. The limitations of oared ships in combat, however, is well illustrated in the attempt by English balingers to capture a carrack. At about 1 pm on Thursday 24 August 1416, a large carrack was sighted between Calais and Dover, sailing up-Channel. The Earl of Warwick, captain of the English garrison in Calais, and several leading knights, armed six balingers and 'passagers' (small vessels used to transport passengers between Dover and Calais) and prepared to attack. The carrack was out of sight before the English vessels were ready, but they still set off, under sail (the English are said to have departed almost without any victuals: the crews were exhausted by the time they eventually reached harbour). One of the balingers became separated from the rest during the night, but the remaining five carried on and caught up with the carrack at dawn on the Friday. The deck of the carrack was more than 'a spear's length higher' than the highest deck of the balingers (perhaps about 10 ft or 3 m), but the English ships still attacked, taking turns to grapple with the side of the carrack. The attack went on for a long time, until the English had to break off for lack of missiles and boarding ladders. The English account reports a great number killed on the carrack, some English fatalities, and many seriously wounded on both sides. Another source says that when the carrack finally reached Sluys, only four of the sixty-two soldiers on board were uninjured. The English force was separated by a storm on the following night, but despite some danger, all eventually returned safely to harbour in England or Calais, the last on 28 September. English relief at the return of the vessels was tempered by the bad news of the failure, and by the death of a young knight, who was donning his armour at the foot of the mast of Warwick's vessel when a stone being hoisted to the topcastle fell out of its sling and dealt him a fatal blow on his unhelmeted head. The bravery of the English crews was considerable, but this story further reveals that it was quite possible for a large sailing ship such as a carrack to be under continuous attack from five low-built oared vessels in a long, running fight, to suffer heavy casualties, and still reach a safe harbour.[9]

There was no one, simple path in the decline of the oared fighting ship in northern Europe. Such vessels were never totally abandoned, at least before the mid-sixteenth century, but, despite their 'revival' in the reign of Henry VIII, they were gradually downgraded in terms of size and importance. It was the fourteenth century that saw the rise of the sailing warship in England.

WEAPONS

Hand-held weapons remained an important factor in sea warfare until at least the nineteenth century and, as any devotee of C.S. Forester or Patrick O'Brian will know, they were still significant in the age of Nelson. The hand-weapons used at sea were little different from those used on land. The early fourteenth-century image of two cogs in a fight (see Fig. 8.3) shows a sword, bows and arrows, and even clubs in use. Swords are seldom found in ships' inventories and the lists of hand-portable shipboard armaments found in the medieval sources probably do not give a complete picture of the weapons actually carried on war voyages. Soldiers probably carried most of their weapons with them, on and off the ship, so that they did not become a part of the inventory.

A list of some weapons and armour present in the 760-ton *Holigost* in the spring of 1416 gives an idea of the range of such items carried by a medieval warship. The weapons included seven breach-loading cannon, with twelve chambers, fourteen bows and ninety-one sheaves of arrows, six crossbows, three pole-axes, twenty-seven bascinets (helmets) and some other pieces of armour. The equipment of the topcastle included 102 iron 'gads' (long spears thrown down on to the deck of enemy ships); these can often be seen protruding from topcastles in medieval illustrations (see Figs 4.5, 8.2, 9.3), and two crane-lines, used to winch ammunition up from the deck (see Fig. 4.5). There were also five dozen darts, which may have been thrown from the topcastle. The ship also possessed two iron grapnels, each with iron chains 12 fathoms (22.0 m) long, which would have been used for grappling the *Holigost* to another ship during a boarding action.

A century or so later, in 1514, the weapons inventory of the *Mary Rose* included many hand-weapons as well as cannon. There were 74 'wyldfyre' (incendiary) arrows and balls, 143 bows, over 504 sheaves of arrows (probably more than 12,000 individual arrows), 238 bills (pole-arms with blades on the end), 91 'hacbusshes' (a type of musket), 900 lead pellets for the hacbushes (and the means to cast more), 180 helmets, nearly 150 complete sets of leg- and body-armour (and many more breast- and backplates) and 159 'morris pikes'. The items found in the wreck of the *Mary Rose* show that, apart from the greater use of firearms and incendiary weapons, the basic fighting equipment of the sea soldier did not alter much between the time of Henry v and that of Henry viii.[10]

What were the effects of warfare on medieval and early Tudor ships? The only way that one can get any idea of how much gear a ship used up in a given period is to examine the lists of gear disposed of as 'broken', 'worn' and (a favourite term of medieval administrators) 'feeble'. Unfortunately these accounts usually cover periods of several years, making it difficult to link damaged or lost gear with specific events. Two rare exceptions occur in the enrolled accounts of the king's ships for the period 1416–20. These specify gear lost by the *Trinity Royal* (540 tons) in the Battle of Harfleur in 1416, and equipment lost by the *Holigost* in both the Battle of Harfleur and the Earl of Huntingdon's battle off the Chef de Caux in the following year.

At Harfleur, each ship lost a seizing grapnel and chain, together with a good deal of ground tackle: four cables, six hawsers and two buoys from the *Trinity Royal*; and five cables, two buoy-ropes and an anchor from the other great ship. The loss of the grapnels and the ground tackle suggest that both ships were anchored, and grappled with other ships in a boarding action. The *Trinity Royal* lost its sailyard, but the *Holigost* suffered greater rigging damage, with roughly half the standing rigging and twenty-five running rigging ropes going by the board. The losses to the ship in 1417 were much lighter, mostly restricted to a few tools and ropes, although one of the ship's cannon is listed as one of the items 'captured and taken away by the enemies of the lord king'.

The stilted officialese of the account says nothing about damage to the ships' hulls or about casualties among their crews. The contemporary Latin panegyric, *Gesta Henrici Quinti* ('The Deeds of Henry v') puts the French dead at the battle of Harfleur at 1500, with nearly 100 dead on the English side. Details of the action are few: the wind favoured both sides, and they had been drawn together at the mouth of the Seine by the time the battle started in the early dawn. The ships grappled, and many died 'under the heavy rain of missiles', iron gads, stones and other projectiles. The 'long drawn-out and most bitter' fight lasted five or six hours before the French surrendered. Three carracks were taken, probably with other ships, although much of the French fleet is said to have escaped among the sandbanks of the Seine. The account is fairly typical of medieval descriptions of sea battles: little detail and much blood. As a counterpoint to some of the attractive depictions of sea battles in medieval art, it is worth recalling that even the author of an 'heroic' chronicle such as the *Gesta* could not bring himself to gloat over the battle, just though he believed the English victory to be. The most compelling image in his account of the battle is that of the bodies of the dead, left floating for days afterwards in the Seine, carried backwards and forwards by the tide, 'as if seeking other burial than that the fishes would provide'.

Although some of the ships present at the Battle of Harfleur had cannon, they do not feature in the *Gesta*'s account, perhaps a sign of their relative unimportance compared with that of more traditional weapons. Gunpowder was known in Europe by the 1260s, but the earliest certain reference to a cannon in Europe is in an illustration to a treatise of *c.* 1326 written by the Englishman Walter de Milemete. This shows a cannon shaped like a large pot or vase, lying on its side on a wooden trestle, with a large arrow emerging from its mouth (see Fig. 8.6). Cannon are mentioned in Italian documents of the 1320s and early 1330s, which may have been the point at which they were first introduced into Europe. The first instance of a cannon on board ship comes in an account for work on an English royal ship, the *All Hallow's Cog*, between March 1337 and the end of September 1338. The *All Hallow's Cog* was a big ship, with a maximum war crew of ninety-five men, and included in the account is a section dealing with 'equipment and diverse necessaries purchased on different occasions' (largely without more specific purchase dates). This section features a sum of 3s spent on 'a certain iron instrument for firing quarrels [crossbow-bolts] and lead pellets, with powder, for the defence of the ship'. Three shillings was not a great price for a piece of ship's equipment, even by fourteenth-century standards; a great iron-bound tankard for the ship cost 23d, almost two-thirds as much, so the cannon cannot have been of

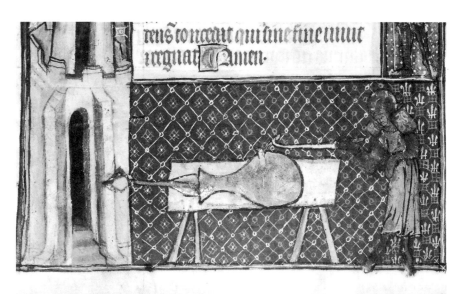

8.6 The earliest-known representation of a gun. From an English manuscript *c.* 1326. The gun resembles a metal vase, and is set on a wooden trestle. It is firing a large arrow, as the cannon in the *All Hallows Cog* of 1337–8 was able to do.

any great size. As the Milemete treatise and other sources show, it was not at all uncommon for early guns to fire arrows as well as lead, iron and stone balls.[11]

Until well into the fifteenth century (and perhaps later), guns remained of limited importance in sea warfare. Henry v's fleet, the most powerful royal naval force of fifteenth-century England, had only fifteen gun-armed ships out of an effective total of about thirty, with no more than forty-two guns between them. Apart from the balinger *Roose*, which had two guns in 1420, all Henry's armed vessels were sailing ships, but none of them had guns in sufficient numbers to make much difference in a naval combat. The most heavily armed was the 760-ton great ship *Holigost*, with its seven cannon. The *Trinity Royale* (540 tons) had five cannon, and most of the others only two or three. Almost all the guns seem to have been breech-loaders, weapons with their powder charges contained in separate, removable breech-chambers. Most guns had at least two breech-chambers, to allow a spare to be kept fully-loaded at all times. The words 'cannon' or 'gun' were used fairly indiscriminately, with no suggestion of technical differences.

Where a material is referred to, the cannon and guns seem to have been made of iron (wrought iron, at this date). Ammunition and powder are rarely mentioned, and the sources give no 'standard' figures for amounts of either. Between 1413 and 1416, for example, the 180-ton *Thomas* had four guns, with a total of twelve chambers, and thirty gunstones (probably cannonballs made of stone). In 1420 the 600-ton carrack *George* had three cannon, six chambers and seventy-two gunstones. Neither figure reveals much about the way guns were used.[12]

By the later fifteenth century guns were becoming much more numerous. In 1479, two ships belonging to Sir John Howard, the *George Howard* and the *Edward Howard* (the 'carvel' that he had built in the 1460s), were captured by foreign vessels, and Sir John's complaint to the Crown included brief inventories of each vessel. The first ship seems to have been a four-master, while the second was a three-master. The *George* had 16 'bombards' with 72 chambers, and the *Edward* had 15, with 64 chambers, along with 24 bows each, 100 sheaves of arrows apiece, with spears, armour and some other weapons. In 1485 the derelict old *Grace Dieu* (the ship built in the late 1430s) had 21 'gonnes feble' along with 89 chambers, and a formidable armament of 140 bows, 810 sheaves of arrows, 140 bills, and even a few axes and crossbows. The contemporary *Mary of the Tower* had 48 guns, with 110 chambers and 12 'hakebusses'. The inventories of large royal ships of the 1480s, 1490s and 1510s make it clear quite how much the provision of cannon had increased since Henry v's time (see Table 11).[13]

Even by 1485, a single royal ship could carry more guns, of various types, than Henry v's entire navy. Identifying some of the gun-types by

8.7 A large, gun-armed four-master of *c.* 1485, in the Warwick Roll. The three cannon in the waist of the ship are pointing over the gunwale (literally, the wale over which the guns fired): this word was first used in connection with Sir John Howard's carvel *Edward* of 1465–6.

the names current in the late fifteenth and early sixteenth centuries is a specialised task. 'Stone-guns', of which the *Sovereign* had twenty in its waist in 1497 (the 'waist' was the open weather-deck area between the fore- and aftercastles; see Fig. 8.7), may have been wheeled pieces like the medium-sized iron breach-loaders found in the wreck of the *Mary Rose*. 'Serpentines', which formed the majority of the ship's guns, were mounted in the castles, and were probably light swivel guns, mounted on metal swivels pegged into the side of the ship ('miches' were listed for each gun; the word originally meant a 'forked stick', like a mike or 'mekhoke', hence a forked gun-swivel).

Gun-type etymology, however, is as confusing as that of ship-types, and it is not proposed to pursue it here; the main point is that by the 1480s, at the latest, the fire-power of large English ships had increased ten- or twenty-fold from what it had been in 1420. This was probably a Europe-wide phenomenon, although information is lacking as to how many smaller ships were armed with guns, and how many they carried.

The appearance of shipboard guns in the 1330s was perhaps the first phase of the revolution in naval ordnance brought about by gun-powder, although its immediate effects were negligible. The second phase, occurring some time between 1420 and 1480, saw a massive increase in the numbers of guns on board the largest ships.

The third phase was the invention of the gunport and the gundeck. Cutting rows of lidded gunports in the sides of a ship, below the open weather-deck, meant that it became possible to carry more heavy cannon; being closer to the waterline, they were less likely to make a ship unstable. The weight penalty of heavy guns had made it difficult for ships to carry many of them on the weather deck, still less in the castles. The invention of the gunport has been attributed to a French shipwright named Descharges, in 1501. It is difficult to trace this claim further back than the nineteenth century, although it is not impossible that it is true; as the historian L. G. Carr Laughton pointed out, the cutting of single lading ports in ships was not uncommon, long before gunports were used (see Figs 4.5 and 7.3).

It was only possible to cut gunports in any numbers in a skeleton-built hull, for to introduce more than one or two significant breaches into the hull of a clinker-built ship would have weakened it seriously. The 'invention' of the gunport and the gundeck was not just a matter of cutting holes in the side of a ship. Just as important was the realisation that rows of ports could be made on both sides with hinged lids that could be sealed tight when not in use. This led eventually to the creation of batteries of heavy guns on both sides of the ship, able to fire broad-sides of the type that conditioned sea warfare from the late sixteenth century to the middle of the nineteenth. It also seems to have led to the transformation of the ship's stern from the old rounded stern to the flat, transom stern, which was both better adapted to take cannon and (as R.

C. Smith has pointed out) improved the run of the stern through the water without requiring its breadth to be reduced.

Ultimately, however, the chronology of the development of gunports may be impossible to unravel. The documentary sources provide little information. Archaeological evidence, in the form of the *Mary Rose* (see Fig. 1.8), shows that they were a major feature of this ship, which sank in 1545 (a fatal feature, in fact: water flooded in through the open gunports). As the vessel's last major overhaul had taken place in the 1530s, gunports must have been developed by that date. The great illustrated list of Henry VIII's navy produced by Antony Antony in 1546 shows that, by then, gunports were nearly ubiquitous, even on quite small craft. Similar evidence from the period 1500–45 proves elusive. The ship *Mary Gonson* had ports specified as part of its structure, but the construction specifications for this vessel cannot be precisely dated: they may date from 1514, but could be one or two decades later. At present, it seems plausible to suggest that the gunport and gundeck were inventions of the early sixteenth century.[14]

Guns must have made sea battles much more terrifying and deadly for those taking part, but they seem to have had little effect on the basic nature of sea battles. Spanish fighting instructions of about 1530, and English fleet orders of 1545, introduced a much clear tactical organisation into the management of fleets, but the main aim of most ships in a force remained the capture or destruction of their opponents by means of the traditional boarding action, with ships grappled side-to-side. Even the 'state-of-the-art' Spanish tactics saw heavy guns as a means of 'softening up' an enemy before grappling, perhaps causing them to surrender or run. They did not regard cannon as a means of battering a ship or sinking it; this was not to come until much later.[15]

Another eventual consequence of the development of the gunport and gundeck was that it made the warship a much more specialised instrument, making it far less easy to use impressed merchantmen in the role. Even in the 1540s, however, this development was a long way off: the inventories of fourteen German, English, Spanish and Venetian ships, of between 120 and 500 tons, arrested for royal service on the Thames in July 1545, show that guns were common on merchantmen and still made them an asset in naval expeditions. One of the group, a 200-ton English merchantman called the *George Bonaventure*, carried as many as seventeen breech-loading guns.

Despite the gun, the medieval northern European system of sea fighting was to endure for decades more. Well into the sixteenth century, English seamen, like most of their foreign contemporaries, remained wedded to the notion that a successful boarding action was the ultimate aim of a ship in battle. By the time of the Spanish Armada in 1588, however, the English forces fought their battles with heavy gunfire, trying to disable and even sink their opponents.[16]

CHAPTER 9

Inventions or Accidents?

Despite the fact that the developments in medieval European ship-building that culminated in the ocean-going vessels of the six-teenth century arguably had a far-reaching influence on the course of world history, the exact nature of these technological achievements remains poorly represented in general historical studies. For example, the great French historian Fernand Braudel seems to have believed that northern European clinker construction was adopted by Mediter-ranean shipwrights, and that the Portuguese caravel of about 1430 was square-rigged and clinker-built.[1] In reality, it was Mediterranean skele-ton construction that was adopted in the north; the caravel of 1430 was skeleton-built and almost certainly lateen-rigged rather than square-rigged (see below, pp. 175–7). The blame for confusions of this kind lies, in part, with maritime historians and archaeologists, who have tended to see their field as a separate discipline from the normal run of human history, ironically reflecting the historical division between seamen and landsmen. Nevertheless, as the historian Carlo Cipolla acknowledged in the title of his book, it was *Guns and Sails* that enabled Europeans to have such an impact on the wider world in the fifteenth and sixteenth centuries, and later.[2]

THE INVENTION OF THE MULTI-MASTED SHIP

The easiest changes to identify in the pictorial evidence are changes in rig. Whatever may have been the time lag between a new mast or sail being introduced and its appearance in art, a clear technological pro-gression can be identified in European representations of ships be-tween the fourteenth and sixteenth centuries. Until the fourteenth century the rigging traditions of northern Europe and the Mediter-ranean seem to have been entirely separate. Square-rigged northern ships may have ventured into the Mediterranean on crusades or even for trade and, from the late fourteenth century, lateen-rigged southern galleys started sailing to northern Europe, but there is little sign of any real technical transfer before about 1300.

Around the turn of the fourteenth century, Mediterranean shipbuilders and seamen began to make use of the cog type, which had been brought into that sea by Basques from northern Spain. The typical large southern merchantman of the thirteenth century was a two- or even three-masted lateen-rigged ship steered by side rudders. In the early fourteenth century, this was gradually abandoned in favour of a large skeleton-built version of the northern cog, with a single square sail and a stern rudder. Known in the Mediterranean as a *cocha* (and later, in northern Europe, as the 'carrack'), the new type was developed for reasons that were probably both technical and economic. The lateen sail was much better adapted for sailing into the wind than the square sail, but it was also more difficult to handle, especially when sailing with the wind from behind, and it was considerably more labour-intensive than the square sail. From this point of view the cog was much cheaper to crew. The beamy, flat-floored hull-shape of the cog made it ideal as a bulk carrier, perhaps a better hull-form for the purpose than the old lateen-rigger, and the stern rudder was less susceptible to collision or battle damage.[3]

It is the sharp prow and the square sail of the *cocha* that begins to predominate in the iconography of Mediterranean shipping in the fourteenth century, but it is from a documentary source that we have the earliest evidence of the appearance of a lateen-rigged mizzenmast on the *cocha*. This is in a Catalan contract of 1353 for a *cocha* or *nau* that was about to sail from Barcelona to Alexandria. The vessel had a bowsprit, mainmast, yard and sail (a square sail, with bonnets), and an *arbre de mis* or mizzenmast, with its yard and sail. Such ships appeared in pictorial form within a short time; an illustration on a portolan chart of 1367 shows a square-rigged *cocha* with a lateen sail set behind the mainmast. Although the lateen mizzen could probably have been rigged to provide extra driving power when the wind was blowing from the stern or the side, there is little doubt that its primary purpose was to improve the *cocha*'s manoeuvrability, making use of the lateen's better windward sailing capabilities to help turn the ship. Improved handling qualities made the *cocha* more efficient as a sailing ship, and thus as a cargo-carrier. The large *cocha* was also easy to defend (see p. 149) and could carry large amounts of cargo and supplies, making it ideal for long-distance trade where the risk of piratical attack was high, but where the economic returns were also considerable. From the 1340s, the Genoese abandoned the use of galleys in their northern trade to England and Flanders, and went over to the *cocha*.

Exactly why northerners started calling these vessels 'carracks' is uncertain, for the word was seldom used in the contemporary Mediterranean, though it was in general use in England and other northern countries from about the mid-fourteenth century. Many of the carracks voyaging north from at least the 1360s were probably two-masters, with the square mainsail and the lateen mizzen, but there is no sign that they began to have any impact on the rig of northern ships for some fifty years.[4]

By the first half of the fourteenth century, the square sails of larger craft were clearly becoming over-large, unwieldy and expensive (see pp. 98–9). The development of bonnets at this period helped to make the square sail more manageable, but could do little to reduce its cost. As has been shown (see p. 97), it was not automatically the case that two- or three-masted rigs were more expensive than single-masted rigs that relied on one large sail; and having more than one sail not only made a vessel more manoeuvrable, it also meant that the mariner was not dependent on just one piece of canvas.

The evidence for the introduction of the two-masted rig into England occurs mainly in written records. None of the surviving ship inventories and accounts for ships in England before about 1410 indicate that English ships were anything other than single-masted and square-rigged. This is backed up by English and northern European iconographic evidence. Matters began to change in 1409. In that year, a Genoese carrack called *Sancta Maria & Sancta Brigida* was captured in Milford Haven by pirates, and in 1410 it was seized by the Crown. Known simply as *Le Carake* in English service, the ship's inventory showed it to have 'one great mast' and 'one small mast', as well as 'one sailyard of two pieces' (a feature both of some Mediterranean square sail yards and of lateen yards). Unfortunately, little is known of the carrack's upkeep while it was in English hands. In September 1411 it was sent on a voyage to Bordeaux with other royal vessels, to lade wine, but the carrack was not listed among the royal ships when Henry V came to the throne in 1413.[5]

Six of the eight Genoese carracks taken by the English in 1416 and 1417 were two-masters, as was the 30-ton balinger *Roose*, forfeited to the English Crown at Bayonne in 1419. The first two-master known to have been built in England was the 120-ton balinger *Anne*, constructed at Southampton between June and October 1416. On 21 September 1416 a Southampton man named Robert Flores was paid 10s for a small mast for use as a 'mesan mast' for the balinger, and 2s 4d for a small sailyard for the 'mesan'. This was just over a month after the capture of the first group of carracks at Harfleur. The mizzenmast and yard cannot have been large, relative to the mainmast and spar: the cost of the mizzenmast (the same as that of the bowsprit) was one-twentieth that of the balinger's mainmast and the mizzen yard was a little over one-tenth of the value of the main yard. The only other multi-masted ship built by the English Crown before the 1430s was the 1400-ton great ship *Grace*

Dieu, which was also constructed at Southampton, between 1416 and about 1418 (for rigging development, see Figs 9.1 and 9.2).[6]

The accounts for the king's ships in the period 1416–22 reveal that only five of the royal ships – three carracks, the balinger *Roose* and the great ship *Grace Dieu* – had complete sets of mizzenmast, yard and sail during this period. In five other cases (two ships, a carrack, a balinger and the 1000-ton great ship *Jesus*) elements of mizzen rigging – mainly masts and sails – were supplied, but seemingly these vessels never had enough ancillary gear to allow them to be used. Even the *Anne* never seems to have been supplied with a mizzen sail. The impression is that the English were making efforts to use the newly introduced rigging technology, but doing so only in a faltering fashion.

The fact that these attempts post-date the capture of the carracks in 1416 strongly suggests that the two-masted rig was copied from them. Carracks, great ships and balingers comprise all but two of the vessels linked to these 'experiments'. All three types would have had their sailing performance adversely affected by their size and/or length, and the mizzen sail would have been an invaluable adjunct to their steering.[7]

The word 'mizzen' or 'mesan' was used at first to denote the mizzen

9.1 Schematic diagram to illustrate European rig development from two to four masts, with dates from which different masts or other features are known to have been in use. In the sixteenth century, items 1–4 and 6 were the most common elements in a ship's rig: the other masts tended to be used only on the very largest ships.

1: MIZZENMAST
    by *c.* 1350,
        Mediterranean
    by *c.* 1416, N. Europe
2: FOREMAST
    by *c.* 1435 N. Europe
    by 1453 Mediterranean
3: MAIN TOPMAST
    by 1465
4: SPRIT YARD
    by 1465
5: BONAVENTURE MAST AND
    OUTLIGGER
    by late 1470s
6: FORE TOPMAST
    by 1495
7: MAIN TOPGALLANT
    by 1495
8: MIZZEN TOPMAST
    by 1514
9: FORE TOPGALLANT
    by 1514
10: MIZZEN TOPGALLANT
    by 1514
11: BONAVENTURE TOPMAST
    by 1514

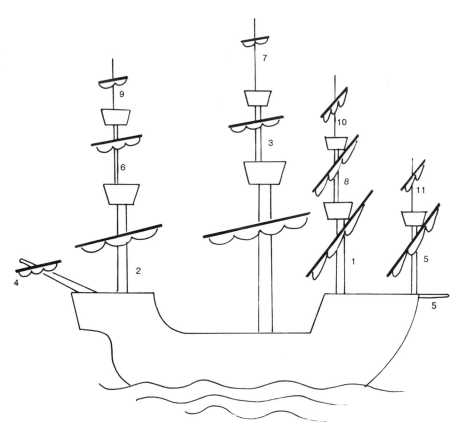

9.2 A two-masted vessel, carved on a bench-end of *c.* 1415, formerly in the Chapel of St. Nicholas, King's Lynn, Norfolk (dated by the style of the woodwork). The vessel has the hull-form of a carrack, a square mainsail and a lateen mizzen. It is arrayed for war, with gads in the topcastle, a two-stage forecastle and what seems to be a three-stage aftercastle. The carving appears to be so close in date to the capture of Genoese carracks by Henry v's forces, that it is possible that there was some connection. At the very least, it dates from the time of the introduction of the lateen mizzen into England.

sail. Its first recorded occurrence in English was in 1416; in 1411 there had been no word to denote the second mast of *Le Carake* beyond calling it a 'small mast'. 'Mesan maste' was in use by 1420, and although it was briefly rivalled by the term *countremaste pro le mesan*, it became the accepted description for the mast sited aft of the mainmast. The word *mesan* came from either Spanish or, more probably, Italian. It is difficult to say whether or not England was the first country in northern Europe to adopt the two-masted rig, which it did between 1416 and 1420;[8] the seizure of the two-master *Roose* in south-west France in 1419 may indicate that it was not. The French Crown had had two-masted galleys based at Rouen since the thirteenth century, but these were built and maintained by Mediterranean craftsmen, and there is no evidence that they had any influence on local Norman craft. A Danish prior's seal of about 1425 shows a two-masted vessel, seemingly with a square-rigged foremast and mainmast, but it is impossible to find contemporary pictorial parallels for this and it may even have been an adaptation of an image of a Mediterranean lateen-rigger of the thirteenth century.

The mainmast and mizzenmast were two of the three parts of what was to become the 'classic' three-masted rig; the third was a square-rigged foremast, stepped in the bow of the ship. The earliest evidence of such a foremast comes from England. Three-masted lateen-riggers had been known in the Mediterranean as early as the thirteenth century, with the largest sail rigged on the foremast. The square foresail was a rather different proposition. In its earliest form, it was undoubtedly a manoeuvring sail, serving to help bring the ship's head round. The 1420 inventory of the *Grace Dieu* shows that the ship had a great mast, two other masts, two sails, a 'mesan' sail and two sailyards: in other words, three masts, three sails, but only two sailyards. It is not known if the third mast was ever used, but it is possible that it carried a square foresail. Clearer evidence of a foresail occurs in the accounts for re-building the 36-oar royal balinger *Petit Jesus* in 1435–36. The rig of this vessel comprised one mainmast, yard and sail, one 'mesan' mast and sail, and one 'ffokesail'. This was probably a square foresail of the kind well known later in the fifteenth century. The absence of a reference to a 'ffoke-mast' or yard has led to suggestions that this 'ffokesail' might have been either a triangular jib or a spritsail, but the jib was not known until long after the fifteenth century, and the etymological evidence does not indicate that the *ffokesail* had anything to do with the spritsail.

The rig of the *Petit Jesus* was certainly incomplete (besides the missing foremast and yard, there was no 'mesan' yard) but the document does suggest that the fundamentals of the three-masted rig were known in England by the mid-1430s. The clinker-built *Petit Jesus*, and perhaps also the *Grace Dieu*, provide the earliest-known references to the three-masted square rig in Europe. What is also interesting is that the word 'ffokesail' is of Middle English or northern derivation and not,

9.3 Carving of a three-masted ship, in the Hotel Jacques, Bourges, built between 1442 and 1451. This is probably the earliest closely-dated image of a three-masted, square-rigged ship (although the mizzen sail in this case may also be square!).

9.5 OPPOSITE Three-masted carracks, and Mediterranean galleys, in a manuscript of 1464 (decretal of Pope Pius II raising a Crusade against the Turks).

like 'mesan', from a Romance language. This points to the foresail having been an English, or at least northern European, invention.[9]

The earliest-dated image of a three-masted, square-rigged ship is a carving from the Hôtel Jacques Coeur at Bourges in France (see Fig. 9.3). The Hôtel was built between 1442 and 1453 for the great French merchant Jacques Coeur, a man with trading and shipping interests in the Mediterranean, Atlantic and North Sea. The carving depicts an oared, clinker-built vessel with square main and foresails and a mizzen sail that may have been lateen or square (the carving is unclear at this point). As with many ship illustrations until well into the second half of the fifteenth century, the foresail is much smaller than the mizzen sail. If the mizzen sail on the Hôtel Jacques Coeur carving was square, it was a rarity. The vast majority of mizzen sails represented in European art in the second half of the fifteenth century were lateen sails (see Figs 9.2, 9.4, 9.5, 9.6 and 9.7).[10]

There is a lack of written information about the construction and rig of English ships between the 1430s and the 1460s, partly because the royal fleet was allowed to run down until it was no more than a collection of rotting hulls and rusted gear. This is unfortunate, for this was clearly the period in which the multi-masted rig was spread around Europe, and in which skeleton construction began to be adopted in northern Europe. A Spanish caravel, inventoried at Barcelona in 1453, was a three-masted square-rigger, perhaps the earliest-known ship to combine the three-masted rig with a skeleton-built hull. It also shows that the 'new' rig was known in the Mediterranean by at least the early 1450s.

The first *carvel* (skeleton-built ship: see pp. 175–80) known to have been built in England was also a three-master. This was a vessel built for the East Anglian landowner Sir John Howard in the port of Dun-

9.4 An early three-masted ship carved on a Norwegian merchant's calendar-stick of 1457 (after Liebgott 1973).

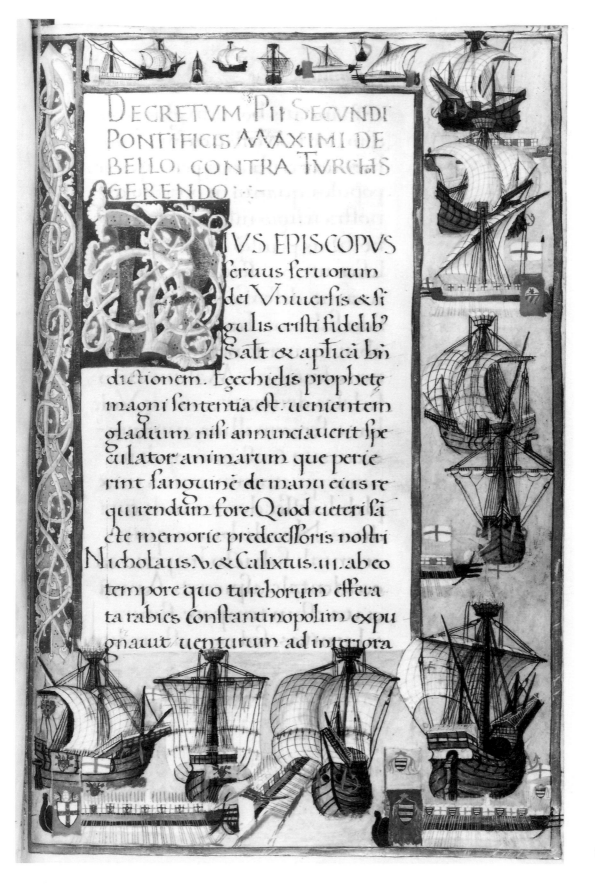

DECRETVM PII SECVNDI
PONTIFICIS MAXIMI DE
BELLO CONTRA TVRCHIS
GERENDO

IVS EPISCOPVS
feruus feruorum
dei Vniuerfis & fi
gulis crifti fidelib'
Salt & aplicã bñ
dictionem. Egechielis prophete
magni fententia eft. uenientem
gladium nifi annunciauerit fpe
culator animarum que perie
rint fanguine de manu eius re
quirendum fore. Quod ueteri fã
cte memorie predecefloris noftri
Nicholaus. v. & Calixtus. iii. ab eo
tempore quo turchorum effera
ta rabies Conftantinopolim expu
gnauit uenturum ad interiora

9.6 OPPOSITE Three-masted ships anchored off Antwerp, from a panoramic map of the river Scheldt, 1468. A large treadmill-powered harbour crane can be seen on the quay.

9.7 Three-masted carrack in an Italian engraving, *c.* 1470–80. The standing rigging of the three masts consists of pulley arrangements, in the Mediterranean manner, rather than deadeyes and shrouds, as was the case in northern Europe. The triangular topsail was another Mediterranean feature, found in some other sources (even as a triangular mainsail, rigged on a horizontal yard), but very little is known about how it was used.

wich in Suffolk between 1463 and 1466. Later known as the *Edward*, this vessel had fore-, main- and mizzenmasts, but also carried a spritsail and a topmast. The spritsail was slung on a yard underneath the bowsprit, and was used both to drive the ship and, like the foresail, to help bring its head around. However, the spritsail had an unfortunate tendency to bury a ship's head in the waves, a tendency counteracted by a square topsail, rigged on a topmast set at the head of the mainmast. As the *Edward* had a topmast, it was presumably able to rig such a sail.

The topsail helped to lift the ship's bows and could also be used to take advantage of the more constant breezes at mast-head height.

Whether the topsail or the spritsail came first is impossible to say. What is more important is the evidence that the basic three-masted rig was already being embellished by the 1460s. This form of rig evidently proved highly serviceable: one of the few facts known about Columbus' *Santa Maria* of 1492 is that it had a sail-plan similar that of the *Edward*. Three-masters are a regular feature of European ship iconography of the 1460s, 1470s and later, suggesting that the three-master was common enough by then to constitute the typical image of a ship. For example, the title page of a papal decree of Pius II in 1464, calling for a crusade against the Turks, has three-masted carracks crowded in its illuminated border; a chapel built at Tiverton in Devon by a wool merchant named John Greenway in 1517 is festooned with images of three-masted ships (see Fig. 1.3). Just as the two-masted lateener had been the standard artistic ship motif in the thirteenth-century Mediter-

9.8 A four-master of *c.* 1500. Detail of *The Legend of the Hermit Antony,* by the Master of the Heilige Sippe.

ranean, or the one-masted square-rigger had been its equivalent in medieval northern European art, so the three-masted ship rapidly became the usual image of the ship in the second half of the fifteenth century. The difference was that the three-master could stand for an English, French, Italian, Dutch, Spanish or other type of ship. Combining elements of the rig of both northern and southern Europe, it was perhaps the first truly European vessel, ending a major division in the Continent's maritime technology that had persisted since the early Middle Ages.

Four-masted ships, with a second lateen-rigged mizzenmast, were in existence by the late 1470s (see Figs 9.1, 9.8 and 8.7). The fourth mast, sometimes known as the 'bonaventure' mast, can be seen in many late fifteenth- and early sixteenth-century illustrations, perched precariously atop the stern, as if it really would have required 'good luck' (*bona ventura*) to enable it to stay in place. A wooden spar called an 'outligger' was usually attached to the stern, protruding outwards, to provide a fixing for the pulley controlling the sheet of the bonaventure sail. The *George Howard* of 1479 had five masts, and it is possible that one of these was a bonaventure mizzen, or 'after-mizzen' as the English called it. The old ship *Grace Dieu* in 1485 had a second mizzen sail, with a sail-plan that worked out as follows:

		Topsail		
Foresail	Mainsail	Main mizzen sail	After mizzen sail	
	3 bonnets			
Spritsail				

Two of the other royal ships of 1485, The *Mary of the Tower* and the *Governor*, had the same type of four-masted rig, but within two years there had been further developments. In 1495 the sail plan of the 600-ton *Sovereign* was as follows:

	Fore topsail	Main topsail		
	Foresail	Mainsail	Mizzen sail	Bonaventure sail
	2 bonnets	3 bonnets		
Spritsail				Outligger

The rig of the 1000-ton *Regent* in 1495 was even more elaborate:

		'Topgallant' sail		
	Fore topsail	Main topsail		
	Foresail	Mainsail	Main mizzen	Bonaventure sail
	1 bonnet	3 bonnets	sail	
Spritsail				Outligger

Both of these ships had been built in the late 1480 and, as many of the sails listed in 1495 were described as 'feeble' or 'rotten', it is likely that these sail-plans represented the original rig of each vessel. It is apparent from these inventories and from contemporary illustrations that the foremast and its topmast were beginning to outstrip the mizzenmast in size and importance, as the foresail became a major driving sail rather than just a manoeuvring sail. By the 1510s, the 'mast upon the topmast', as found on the *Regent*, was being called the 'topgallant'. In 1514 the 600-ton *Mary Rose* (built 1510) had a rig similar to that of the *Regent* in 1495, with a main topgallant sail, but also had a main mizzen topsail. The 1000-ton *Henri Grâce à Dieu* in the same year had the additional refinements of a fore topgallant, a main mizzen topgallant and a bona-venture topmast (see Fig. 9.1).[11]

The extra masts and sails were used to help cope with the problems of moving and manoeuvring large, unwieldy vessels. The four-masted rig was generally confined to large ships, and one early seventeenth-century writer summarised the reason for having two mizzenmasts: 'when a ship will not keepe the wind ... sometymes we geve a ship 2 Missons to keepe her head to the winde'. In other words, the two mizzens were used to help prevent a ship which was sailing to windward from falling away from the wind.[12]

Rig was the single most 'plastic' feature of a sailing ship; it could be changed with relative ease. Sailors were used to having to trim sails with speed and, while adding or taking away masts was more complicated, it could be done fairly quickly, giving room for experiment that was simply not available in the cases of hull design or structure. The piecemeal addition of top and topgallant masts between the 1460s and 1510s may well have resulted from such a process of experimentation, a way of finding out if a ship could sail and turn better with extra sails. These additions could scarcely be termed 'inventions'; the true inventions were the original mizzenmast and foremast. It is unlikely however that they were mere 'accidents', and as has been shown (see p. 107) the more obvious masting and sail-plan developments took place against a background of improvements in the mechanical efficiency of running rigging. These helped the new ship to be a more effective machine.

The revolution in rig occurred during the period that Mediterranean skeleton-building techniques began to be adopted in northern Europe, but there is no evidence that the one depended on the other.

From clinker to carvel

It is clear that clinker construction (see Chapter 3) was the predominant shipbuilding technique in northern Europe from at least the early Middle Ages until the fifteenth century. In clinker construction the shell of overlapping planks provides the main strength of the structure, with the frames taking a subsidiary role.[13] By contrast, from at least the early eleventh century, and probably much earlier, Mediterranean ship-builders relied on the skeleton construction technique, in which the shape and strength of the hull is provided by a skeleton of frames. Unlike clinker-built vessels, the plank edges in skeleton construction are butted against each other, giving the hull a smooth appearance (see Fig. 4.2).

Ancient Greek and Roman hulls had been assembled by means of a complicated form of shell construction that involved joining the planks edge-to-edge with mortise-and-tenon joints (these joints consisted of small wooden pegs that fitted into holes in adjacent plank edges, and were usually then held in place using trenails). As the planks were butted against each other, the hull surface was smooth, but like clinker construction, it was the shell of planking, not the framing, that was the main load-bearing element. This technique demanded a great deal of both skill and time, and thus expense. Wreck evidence has shown that by the seventh century, Mediterranean shipbuilders were gradually moving over to a method that made less use of mortise-and-tenon joints, and more use of the framing. The change was certainly complete by the early eleventh century, for a wreck of Byzantine or Arab origin excavated off the Turkish coast at Serçe Limani was found to be skeleton-built, with no sign of mortise-and-tenon joints.[14]

The 'fine piece of furniture that was the Roman ship' was the product of a well-developed economy able to provide the skills, slaves, money, materials and time required to build it. The disruption of the Mediter-ranean economy after the collapse of the Western Roman Empire in the fifth century meant that most of these things were in short supply. A current view is that skeleton construction developed because there was a lack of skilled shipwrights. Shaping and positioning the frames for a hull was a skilled task, but one that could be carried out by a relatively small number of specialist craftsmen. Fastening the planking on to the hull required more men but did not require a team of skilled shipwrights.

Technological change was thus the child of necessity – in this case, poverty. By the thirteenth century, however, the maritime resources of some Mediterranean states were anything but poor. Contracts for transports ordered from Genoa and Venice by Louis ix in the thirteenth century point to the existence of ships with capacities as great as 600 tons, far larger than anything afloat in northern Europe at the time. There is little doubt that such ships were skeleton-built, and that the technique was the predominant ship construction method in the Mediterranean. What is of especial interest from the point of view of technological history is just how, and why, skeleton construction was adopted in northern Europe in the fifteenth century.[15]

Northern European craftsmen appear not to have constructed skeleton-built ships before the fifteenth century. The technical transfers resulting from sea traffic between northern and southern Europe seem mostly to have gone from north to south, rather than the other way. The French royal dockyard at Rouen, the Clos des Galées, established in the late thirteenth century, was the only place in northern Europe at which skeleton-built craft were based; and these were Mediterranean galleys, built and maintained by Mediterranean craftsmen who were not, it would seem, permanent residents of Rouen. Between 1294 and 1416 there were at least thirteen occasions on which southern shipwrights were brought north to Rouen, at great expense, to build or repair galleys. These men came from such places as Genoa, or from Marseilles, Aigues Mortes or Narbonne in southern France. The local Norman craftsmen were charged with building and maintaining the clinker-built barges that accompanied the galleys, but it does not seem that they ever learned the secret of skeleton construction.[16] The situation could be compared to that of a Third World country in the 1960s, maintaining an air force of modern jets but relying on the West or the Soviet Union to provide maintenance crews.

The English Crown sometimes acquired southern-built ships, but only in a haphazard fashion. For example, a subject's act of piracy made Edward III (briefly) the owner of a Genoese one-master in 1371: Henry IV bought a Portuguese ship, the *Katerine*, in 1402, and owned it for about five years, but it not known if this was a clinker-built or skeleton-built vessel (it was in bad condition when given away): *Le Carake* (see p. 159) of 1410 was another southern acquisition. Perhaps the most unusual of Henry IV's ships was a large galley, with over 240 oars, known as the *Jesus Maria*. This craft was probably bigger than any other galley that had ever been used in England; it is first encountered in the accounts of the clerk of the king's ships for 1409 to 1411, where it is described as 'newly built'. Whether the vessel had actually been built in England, or acquired from elsewhere, is unknown. Certain features of the vessel's inventory, however, suggest a Mediterranean origin: for example, the large number of oars; the fact that most of the oars had lead counterweights (see p. 114); shrouds set up on pulleys rather than deadeyes; a single main yard made of two pieces (like a lateen yard); and a set of four sails (lateen-riggers had sets of sails of different sizes). An officer in charge of the galley was described as a *comiter*, a southern European term. The *Jesus Maria* is a puzzle, but whatever its origins the galley saw little use, and by 1415 was a waterlogged hulk lying in a dock at Ratcliffe on the Thames. One suspects that its structure and design (and perhaps also its rowing system) were too alien for the English to make proper use of it.[17]

The details of a pile of junk in the storehouse of the king's ships in 1413 suggest that Henry IV may have been trying to have other Mediterranean-style galleys built. The junk included '10,902 nails called *Galey-naill* of diverse sorts ... [and] ... 100 *courves* (or *cowrbe*) coming from three newly-begun galleys [and] 108 pieces of small timber for making the same galleys'. Orders had been issued in 1412 to the clerk of the king's ships to take 800 oaks from the king's park at Eltham to make three galleys, but they never seem to have been completed. The references to the nails and other bits and pieces in 1413 are the last that is heard of them. The fact that the nails were called 'galley nails' rather than anything else (and the English had a rich terminology for nails) suggests that they were either of novel design, or were used for a purpose that was new to the English, namely building a special kind of galley. The puzzling *courves* or *cowrbe* could have been taken from the medieval French word *courbe* or the Italian *curva*, meaning a ship's knee (an angled bracket used to join two pieces of timber), but again the English had a perfectly serviceable word for such a feature. There is, however, another medieval Italian word, spelt variously as *corbe* or *chorba*, meaning 'frame', which is found in Italian galley-building treatises of the fifteenth and sixteenth centuries. Again the English had words for 'frame', but these were applied to the frames of clinker-built vessels. If the three vessels were to be skeleton-built, one can understand why special terms – not found in any other medieval or sixteenth-century source – would have been coined to describe their nails or frames. The fate of the three galleys does not support the notion that the *Jesus Maria* was English-built.[18]

The capture of the eight Genoese carracks in 1416 and 1417 put the English Crown in possession of some of the largest skeleton-built ships in Europe. The problem for the English was that they did not know how to maintain their hulls, as is revealed by a petition to the Crown, discovered some years ago by Dr Susan Rose, which came from someone charged with the upkeep of the carracks. These were mostly based at or near Southampton, and the petitioner may have been William Soper, a Southampton citizen and shipowner who from 1420 was keeper of the king's ships. Internal evidence dates the document to the period between 24 August 1417 and 13 October 1418. The former date was the day on which the last carracks were taken, the latter the day on which a damaged royal ship, the *Thomas*, was docked for repairs; the document lists the *Thomas* as one of four other royal ships badly in need of repair (two of these were actually sold in November 1418).

The petition states that the carracks are made 'in such manner' (*en tielle gyse*) that they need repair every three years. These vessels, having been in the water for four and five years (note that the groups were captured in two different years) need repairing before they can put to sea again. Large quantities of pitch, oakum timber, board and other materials would need to be purchased, but in a telling phrase the petitioner goes on to ask permission to hire 'carpenters and caulkers of foreign country[s] ... for in this country we shall find few people who know how to renew and amend the same carracks'. Statements, even negative ones, about the capabilities of English shipwrights in the Middle Ages are so rare that this document assumes considerable importance. What actually happened to the carracks suggests that the petitioner was telling the truth.[19]

Between 1416 and 1422, more than £2714 was spent on the upkeep of the seven carracks (the eighth had soon been lost, smashed against the walls of Southampton in a storm). Despite this, by 1422 only two, the *George* and the *Christofre*, were seaworthy, doubtless because about 60 per cent of the money was devoted to them. In about 1420, a decision seems to have been made to give the lion's share of the maintenance resources to these two, the Crown cutting its losses as regards the other five. These vessels may have been too badly decayed by that date to be worth saving. Two sank at anchor in the port of Hamble during storms in 1420, and two others had to be beached in 1421 to prevent them from going the same way.[20]

Specialist and foreign craftsmen were employed to work on the carracks. In 1417 a man named William Savage, 'carrek carpenter' (and perhaps a foreigner with an Anglicised name) was used in work on the great ships, carracks and balingers because of his 'special skill'. Other 'carrack-carpenters', 'carrack-shipwrights' and 'carrack-caulkers' worked on the carracks between 1417 and 1420. In the summer of 1419, fourteen Venetian and Catalan mariners spent a total of twenty-seven days removing rudders and masts from some of the carracks so that they could be repaired. They were employed 'on account of their ability and skill', a phrase (perhaps echoing the petition) justifying the use of foreigners.

A Portuguese and a number of Venetian caulkers who worked on the *George* and the *Christofre* in the early 1420s used a standard Mediterranean technique, 'careening', in order to carry out the work. Careening involved hauling a ship over to one side on the shore so that the bottom can be cleaned and caulked, with a raft used by the caulkers to get access to the seaward side. A raft ('raffe') bound with rope was made for work on the *Christofre*, and another one was made from fifty barrels for 'carranynge' the *George*. This is the earliest known usage of the word in English, and perhaps an isolated one for the period, as English practice for cleaning hulls usually seems to have involved docking (see pp. 52–4). The evidence all appears to show that in the 1420s, English shipwrights did not know how to repair (or build) skeleton-built hulls. If the Crown, with its powers of search and coercion, could not find English craftsmen to carry out the work, then it is probably true to say that careening was a technique largely unknown in England at that date.[21]

The 600-ton Tudor warship *Mary Rose* was built at Portsmouth in

1510, and perhaps rebuilt on the Thames in the 1530s. The recovered hull-remains of the ship show that a century or so later than Henry v's carracks, English shipwrights were able to construct large skeleton-built vessels. Not only this: clinker construction, the technique used in the *Grace Dieu* of 1418, was obsolescent in England, at least as regards the production of great state warships. The wreck found at Woolwich in 1912 was of a ship that had originally been clinker-built (Fig. 5.2); the distinctive 'steps' cut in the framing for clinker planking had been dubbed smooth, and the hull had been rebuilt skeleton fashion. If this wreck really was the 600-ton *Sovereign* (originally constructed *c.* 1487–8 and rebuilt in 1510) the conversion of the frames would tie in with a contemporary statement regarding the preservation of the ship's hull form. This in turn would suggest that 'big ship' clinker construction was still in use in England in the late 1480s, but was dying out by about 1510–20. The 800-ton *Great Galley*, launched at Greenwich in 1515, was probably the last large clinker-built warship to be constructed in England, but the vessel had to be rebuilt carvel- or skeleton-fashion in 1523, because of its dangerous condition (Sir William Fitzwilliam, the Lord High Admiral at the time, described the *Great Galley* as 'the dangeroust ship under water that ever man sailed in'). The archaeological evidence supports the documentary and pictorial sources: England, and much of northern Europe, had adopted skeleton construction by the early sixteenth century.[22]

The full details of how this Mediterranean method came north will never be known. However the technique was transmitted, it was passed from one largely illiterate group of craftsmen to another similar group, and, even if the precise building-places of skeleton-built wreck finds could be established, this would still not tell us exactly how the shipwrights in those places learned how to build ships in that manner. The written sources give some clues, however, and discussion of this historical process tends to centre round the study of one word: 'carvel' (see Fig. 9.9 for a possible image of a 'carvel'). Since the end of the Middle Ages, the words 'carvel' or 'carvel-built' have been more or less synonymous with skeleton construction. 'Carvel' in English, and its near equivalents in other northern languages such as Dutch, German and Swedish, derive from the Portuguese word *caravela*, or 'caravel'. This in turn seems to have come from an early medieval Mediterranean ship-type, although it is first recorded in Portuguese as the name of a kind of thirteenth-century fishing boat. By the mid-fifteenth century, 'caravel' denoted a small, skeleton-built vessel, usually with two lateen-rigged masts. Caravels had speed and manoeuvrability, qualities that made them ideal for the Portuguese voyages of exploration, which were beginning to reach further and further south along the coast of Africa. By the 1430s and 1440s, caravels were also starting to appear in northern Europe.[23]

A caravel is said to have been built at Sluys in Flanders in 1438–40, and in 1439 Philip the Good, Duke of Burgundy, paid some Portuguese shipwrights for building him *une caravelle* in the vicinity of Brussels. There is a reference in a Chancery document to a 'carvel' of Fowey in Cornwall, but this can only be dated to 1443–50, and one cannot be sure if this was the first reference to a carvel in England. The earliest securely dated English reference to the type is contained in a royal grant of protection given on 3 May 1448 to 'a certain ship or barge called *le Carvell* of Oporto in Portugal', This was a vessel of 80 tons burden or less, given leave for one year to trade to England. The precise value of such a 'protection' was demonstrated a couple of months later when English pirates seized two or possibly three Portuguese 'carvels' off the Isle of Wight. A document of 1450 names a notorious south coast pirate, Clais Stephen (a man of Dutch or Flemish origin, by his name), as the master of *le Carvell* of Portsmouth. This may have been one of the Portuguese ships taken in 1448; Stephen was allegedly using it to pursue his chief occupation. Confusingly, Stephen is also named as the master of the *Carvel* of Calais, a 60-ton vessel that formed part of a royal fleet gathered at Portsmouth in 1449. This was probably the same vessel as the *Carvel* of Portsmouth. Whatever the precise chronology or identifications, it is clear that at least two carvels were in English hands by 1450, at Fowey and Portsmouth.[24]

Other 'acquisitions' took place at about the same time. In 1449, a 55-ton carvel from *Vermewe* (Bermeo?) in Spain was captured off the Irish coast and taken in to Kinsale. At least four more carvels are known to have been seized by English pirates in the first half of the 1450s (three from Portugal and one from Spain). Charting this part of the story from piratical seizures is a little like trying to work out volumes of car production from statistics for car theft, but it does at least show one way in which the type was transferred into English hands, albeit with 'menaces'. Some other carvels may have been bought: William, Lord Saye, for example, claimed to have purchased his carvel at Sandwich in 1453. Between 1453 and 1466, there are references to over twenty English-owned carvels. Some of these may be instances of the same vessel recorded twice or more, but the sudden upsurge in references from the late 1440s is significant.[25]

Carvels and carvel construction were spreading to other parts of northern Europe at about this time. The king of Scotland owned a vessel called a *Kervel*, which he had under repair in 1449–50. This carvel was called both a 'ship' and a 'little ship' (*navicula*). A carvel was built in the Norman port of Dieppe in 1451, for a Breton owner. Also, in the 1450s there is a reference to a ship being built *a carvelle* (carvel-fashion) in France, the phrase probably denoting the skeleton-building technique rather than the ship-type. Local records for Dieppe list the construction or repair of nineteen carvels between 1451 and 1484. It was a French

9.9 A small two-masted ship engraved in the style of the Master W by Isaac van Meeckeren, *c.* 1470–80. The combination of square-rigged mainmast and foremast was not unknown in the sixteenth century (see Chapter 10). The bowsprit is set to one side of a huge, scimitar-like stempost, making the bowsprit look like an afterthought. The smooth planking and the heavy wales suggest that the hull is skeleton-built. Dr Pieter van der Merwe suggested some years ago that this vessel might represent a carvel, a north European version of the Portuguese caravel.

'carvel', the *Peter* of La Rochelle, that is said to have led to the ship-wrights of the Baltic port of Danzig (now Gdansk, Poland) learning the technique of skeleton construction. At 600 tons burden, the *Peter* was probably a skeleton-built carrack-type rather than a version of a caravel. The ship was abandoned at Danzig in 1462, and local shipwrights are said to have learned the new construction technique by studying the *Peter*'s hull. Elsewhere, skeleton construction may have been learned from individuals, such as the peripatetic Breton shipwright named Julian, who was said to have taught it to the craftsmen of Zealand in the Netherlands, in about 1459. There are signs that the Bretons had an important role in spreading the technique around northern Europe. Certainly, the Bordeaux customs accounts for the late fifteenth century show that the Bretons owned many carvels.[26]

The first carvel known to have been built in England was Sir John Howard's *Edward*, constructed at Dunwich in Suffolk. The first note of the carvel comes in an entry of 10 July 1463, but the bulk of the building work was carried out between 1465 and 1466. Over £140 was spent on constructing the *Edward*, and while it is known that the carvel was a three-master (see pp. 167–8), information regarding the hull is sketchy. Apart from general purchases of timber and boards, few hull components are named. The exceptions include thirty-four 'great knees' (for seventeen beams), 'collars' for the mast (mast-partners), gunwales and some other items. Nail-types named include spikings, hatch (deck) nails, door nails, great spikes and bolts. There is little overt evidence that this carvel was skeleton-built, apart from the absence of any references to the use of clench-nails and roves. These are mentioned in every previous English ship construction account as far back as the 1290s and in most medieval ship repair accounts as well. Their non-appearance in the *Edward* account was probably because they were not used: in a skeleton-built hull, they were not needed.[27]

'Carvel nails' do not appear in English sources before the late fifteenth century, and it is difficult to know if the term referred to a specific form of nail, or if it was an existing type of nail renamed because of the use to which it was put. The iron spikes and bolts and wooden trenails used since the thirteenth century and earlier would have been entirely adequate for fastening a skeleton-built hull. 'Carvel boards' appear as a distinct item in the late fifteenth and early sixteenth centuries: again, this may have been a renaming of an existing item, but when a Dartmouth merchant ship, the *Marie Bricxam* (Brixham), was repaired at Bordeaux in 1502, the work required the use of ninety-six *taules de carvelle* ('carvel boards'). Each board was twenty Bordeaux feet long and one foot wide; over 1900 ft of planking was replaced (approximate length and width of each board 23.0 × 1.1 ft (7 × 0.35 m) with total plank runs of 2184 ft (666 m)). The reference here is clearly to a form of board used specifically with skeleton construction. Two other English merchant ships repaired at Bordeaux in 1502 and 1504, one from King's Lynn in Norfolk and the other probably from Weymouth in Dorset, were also carvel-built.[28]

The 'rise' of the carvel coincided with a Europe-wide phenomenon that saw a decline in the numbers of large ships. Various explanations have been put forward to explain this change: small vessels were better suited to medieval harbours; their construction required less capital; carrying smaller cargoes, they were less of a risk for merchants; they were cheaper to crew and to operate. One other possibility, however, is that the ascendancy of the small ship, at least in northern Europe, was due to the adoption of skeleton construction. The carvels that the northerners copied were small vessels, and with a new technique there was a natural tendency to start small. The (relatively rare) great skeleton-built ships mostly came later, in the early sixteenth century.[29]

The English evidence offers an opportunity to test out the theory that skeleton construction offered economic as well as technological advantages over shell construction. The technological benefits were relatively straightforward; the heavier framing of a skeleton-built hull made it stronger and more durable than one built clinker-fashion. Flush-laid carvel planking was probably also much easier to repair than the overlapping strakes of a clinker hull and the former tended to use more in the way of trenails, which were much cheaper than iron clench-nails, and slower to degrade. The economic evidence is less clear-cut. Clinker construction did require a high proportion of skilled workmen (see pp. 42–6) and the late medieval period was one in which general wage-levels were rising. As we have seen, the construction and repair accounts for Henry VIII's ships do not suggest that the proportion of skilled workmen declined sharply, and the perceived economic benefits of skeleton construction may have related more to cheaper materials. Carvel hulls did not use as many iron fasteners as traditional northern methods, and those that they did use were simpler and cheaper than clench-nails and roves. Also, skeleton-built hulls did not 'waste' planking by having to overlap the planks, as in clinker construction.

The economic conditions favourable to a change from clinker to carvel construction may have existed as early as the second half of the fourteenth century. The reason why it did not happen then was probably due to the types of Mediterranean ship that northerners usually encountered. Until the 1440s, these were mostly great carracks and galleys. These ships might be copied in shape, but, as the story of Henry V's carracks showed, they were too large and complex for northern shipwrights to be able to make much sense of how they were built. Caravels, or carvels, were much smaller and a great deal more accessible as primary 'educational tools' for northern European shipwrights.

The 'carvel revolution' may have been largely complete in England by about 1500 to 1510, with clinker-building in sharp decline as a means of constructing major sea-going vessels, but in some other parts of Europe 'big ship' clinker construction may have lingered into the mid-sixteenth century. Some German ships arrested on the Thames for royal service in late July 1545 included a number of ships in the 400- to 500-ton range that were described unequivocally as 'Clenchers'. In the same month, some foreign clinker-built vessels (probably the same ones) were taken to Portsmouth with a view to using them in the royal fleet; the Lord High Admiral dismissed them with some contempt as 'clenchers, both feeble, olde, and out of fashion'.[30]

CHAPTER 10

At the edge of the ocean

A t least part of the reason why European colonies in the New World prospered as they did lies in the fact that, by the end of the medieval period, the Europeans had ships with durable hulls and manoeuvrable rigs.[1] England, however, played very little effective part in oceanic trade and colonisation until the seventeenth century. Even in 1600, the country was not a front-rank power as regards the size of its merchant marine, although between 1585 and 1603 it managed to hold its own in a sea war with Spain that ranged as far as the Americas. Spain was the greatest sea-power in Europe, able to call on the shipping resources of Habsburg subjects in the Iberian Peninsula, the Mediterranean and elsewhere. The failure of the famous invasion Armada of 1588 was in part due to bad weather and bad luck, but had the English not been able to muster a strong royal and merchant fleet to pursue and harry the Armada, a landing could have been effected. The subsequent Armadas were dispersed by bad weather and English counter-raids were ineffective, but the mere fact that the English could sustain such a long-running sea conflict says much for the basic strength of their shipbuilding and shipping industries.[2]

The growing dominance of the Antwerp cloth trade in the second half of the fifteenth century, and more particularly in the first half of the sixteenth century, meant that a good deal of England's shipping resources was tied up in the short-range trade between England and the Low Countries and this was not a trade that required large ships. The loss of Gascony to the French in 1453 virtually killed off England's Bordeaux wine trade for decades, and when English ships began to reappear in the Bordeaux customs records of the late fifteenth century, they were usually small vessels, most of not much more than 100 tons. Large ships continued in use in the English voyages to Iceland well into the second half of the fifteenth century, but they began to disappear even from this long-distance route by the 1490s. The decline in the

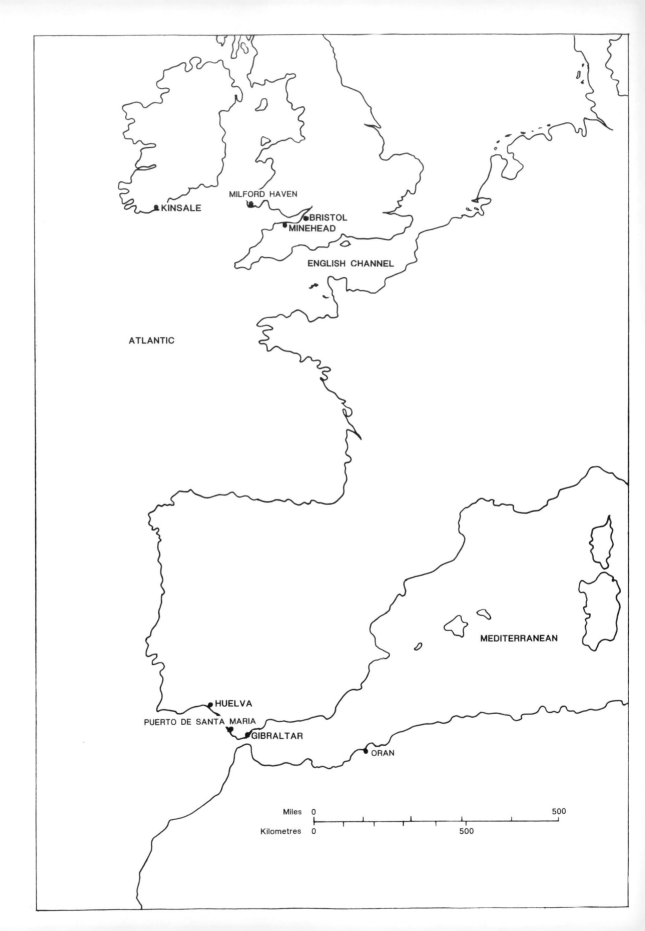

KINSALE

MILFORD HAVEN

BRISTOL

MINEHEAD

ENGLISH CHANNEL

ATLANTIC

MEDITERRANEAN

HUELVA

PUERTO DE SANTA MARIA

GIBRALTAR

ORAN

Miles 0   500

Kilometres 0   500

numbers of large ships was a major historical change. Even as late as 1582, ships of 100 tons or more were vastly outnumbered by the smaller ones. The great Elizabethan shipping survey of that year listed 1453 craft of between 20 and 100 tons and only 177 (10.9 per cent of the total) of more than 100 tons, with a mere three of 300 tons or more.[3]

A good example of an early English long-distance voyage is to be found in the rare surviving accounts of a ship's purser, John Balsall. Balsall was purser of a Bristol ship, the *Trinity*, a vessel of perhaps some 300 to 360 tons. The *Trinity* had been engaged in trade to Gascony, and latterly Lisbon, since the mid-1460s but in 1480–81 it made a voyage into the Mediterranean. This is the one recorded in Balsall's account (Fig. 10.1). The ship had a crew of sixteen mariners, eight soldiers, two gunners and three boys, plus the purser and four men of indeterminate duties (thirty-four in all). The ship left Bristol in October 1480 and, sailing via Minehead in Somerset, Milford Haven in Wales and Kinsale in Ireland, made for Huelva in southern Spain. The details of the *Trinity*'s main cargo are not known, although some cloth was carried, but the ship was at Huelva for some four or five weeks before making for Puerto Santa Maria and Gibraltar, where a pilot was taken aboard. The ship then sailed for Oran in North Africa (now in Algeria but then part of the Moorish kingdom of Tlemcen). The *Trinity* had taken on extra armament at Huelva for the journey to this 'lucrative but dangerous' port, and may even have formed part of a Spanish naval expedition. Whatever the reason for the voyage, the *Trinity* returned safely to Spain, was beached for repairs, and then made for home, making one only stop to revictual.

The account tells us little about the rig or construction of the *Trinity*, but it gives a good idea of the routine expenses on a voyage. At Minehead, a stone of tallow was bought, and in Huelva a pot for rosining the ship. In Spain, the overlop (deck) was caulked, using oakum and pitch, by two caulkers who spent four days at the work. When the ship was grounded, two skins were bought for mops (probably for tallowing), along with material to be burned to soften the pitch and burn off marine growths, so that the hull would be clean for re-caulking. 'Twists' and hasps were bought for doors in the ship, and the mention of the overlops (plural) may mean that the ship had more than one deck. The *Trinity* was a multi-masted vessel and probably at least a three-master; the mizzenmast was replaced in Spain, for 218 Spanish *maravedis*, and two small masts (almost certainly topmasts) were also bought at a cost of 310 *maravedis*. While the ship was beached, the mainmast was struck (i.e. brought down), and two new mast-partners were inserted and fixed in place with iron nails and bolts. It is not known how many guns the ship had, but some of them may have been swivel guns, for purchases included *myches* (probably swivel mounts, see p. 154), forelocks and bands for the guns, as well as gun-

10.1 Map showing the ports visited by the *Trinity* of Bristol, 1480–1.

powder. The *Trinity* also possessed crossbows, but the most unusual items in its armoury seem to have been supplied in Spain. These were pots for 'wyld ffyer', incendiary hand grenades designed for throwing on to the deck of an enemy ship. Some brimstone was bought, along with oakum, pitch and vinegar 'for the gunners'. As the entry for the purchases of the last three items is followed by the payment to the gunners for making the wildfire, they may have been the main ingredients of the mixture (similar *alcancias*, or ceramic fire grenades, were found in the wreck of the 1588 Armada ship *Trinidad Valencera*). The ship's return cargo, which included barrels of wine and fruit, seems to have been brought out to the *Trinity* in the ship's boat, and it was bedded down with the aid of ten bundles of cork and 'rommage' nails.

Full details of the victuals loaded at the outset of the voyage are not known but, once in Spain, purchases included sardines, biscuit, flour for making biscuit, and various other types of seafood including congers and dogfish. The crew were bought a pig for their Christmas dinner, and it seems that the ship's company also had a special celebration on New Year's Day at Puerto de Santa Maria. The *Trinity* returned to Bristol about the middle of 1481.[4]

One of the three owners of the *Trinity* was a man named John Jay, a Bristol merchant who in 1480 (with a partner) sent an 80-ton ship out into the Atlantic on a fruitless search for the mythical 'Isle of Brasil', said to lie to the west. While the *Trinity* was at Huelva, the Franciscan friars of Santa Maria de la Rabida were paid by John Balsall to offer up prayers for the ship. A few years later the convent was to supply Columbus with important backing in his search for royal sponsorship for his voyage westwards. The editors of Balsall's account established an ingenious and thought-provoking connection between the *Trinity*, the exploration schemes of its part-owner John Jay, and the convent's later known support for Columbus' proposed enterprise.

Whether or not 'the ffyres at our lady of Rebedewe' actually heard of Jay's voyage is impossible to say, but what is certain is that when the *Trinity* returned to Bristol it was rapidly fitted out by Jay and others for another Atlantic voyage. In July 1481 the *Trinity*, in company with the *George* of Bristol, sailed out on another expedition to the island of Brasil. What became of them is not known, although it has been suggested that the large amount of salt that they carried (specifically described as being for the sustenance of the ships, and not for trade) may have been for salting catches of fish. It is possible that Bristol ships reached the rich fishing grounds of the Grand Banks off Newfoundland at some time in the 1480s, and may even have made landfall before John Cabot's celebrated voyage to Newfoundland in 1497. Cabot's *Matthew* was a tiny ship, a vessel of only 50 tons (according to one source) with a crew of eighteen to twenty men. The ship returned safely, and in triumph; but Cabot's subsequent voyage, in 1498, was a disaster in which he and most of his fleet of five ships seem to have vanished. In terms of its size, the *Matthew* was typical of the majority of English ships that were to be used in Atlantic voyages for the next century or so. English participation in the Newfoundland fishery was fairly limited in the early sixteenth century, but by the 1580s and 1590s, when the scale of English involvement was greater, most of the ships used were of 60 tons or less. As in many other spheres of English maritime activity, ships of less than 100 tons predominated.[5]

Discussion of what sixteenth-century English ships were like has often centred around the construction and equipment of the well-documented royal warships: apart from copious historical sources, there are many good paintings and engravings, and in the *Mary Rose* there is an archaeological find of enormous significance. Beyond such books as Dorothy Burwash's *English Merchant Shipping 1460–1540* and a few other works, however, little has been written about what the privately-owned vessels were like (see Figs 10.2 and 10.3). Important sources for this subject exist in the copious archives of the High Court of Admiralty, and information from the 1580s helps to put the developments of the period up to 1520 into some sort of context. The High Court of Admiralty (HCA) was charged with the regulation of legal matters relating to the sea. This included the official appraisal of vessels that had come into the Court's hands, whether as a result of a legal action, seizure, capture or for some other reason. The study of 115 appraisals dating from the period 1579 to 1590 throws new light on the ordinary English and foreign shipping that floated alongside the better-known 'galleons' of the Elizabethan navy.[6]

The origins of one hundred and nine of the vessels are known. Sixty-eight were English, with a further nineteen from Holland, eight from France, six from Spain, and the remaining eight were from Germany, Flanders and Denmark. One might expect that the HCA would deal with many cases concerning foreign ships, but even so, the fact that forty-one (nearly 38 per cent) of these vessels were from abroad gives an idea of just how much foreign-built shipping was to be found in English waters and, often, in English ownership. The tonnages of forty-nine of the vessels are recorded, and suggest that most were very small; only four were of 80 tons or more. The types named included ships, barks, pinnaces, 'fly-boats' and others, and were clearly the sort of vessels that artists sketched in to fill in the backgrounds of sea paintings or engravings, the unregarded little craft that were the mainstay of much sixteenth-century sea trade (see Fig. 10.3).

The appraisals give details of the rig of seventy-seven of these ships: forty-one were three-masters, twenty-five two-masters, and eleven vessels had one mast only. The two-masters tended to have main- and foremasts (see Fig. 9.9) rather than the medieval main-and-mizzen combination. The three-masted rig was the commonest type (as con-

10.2 An English three-master, redrawn from a rutter (set of sailing directions) of the late fifteenth century. The crew is using a sounding-lead to find out the depth of water under the keel. The sounding lead, compass and hourglass ('sandglass') were the basic navigational instruments of English ships from the mid-fourteenth century, if not earlier.

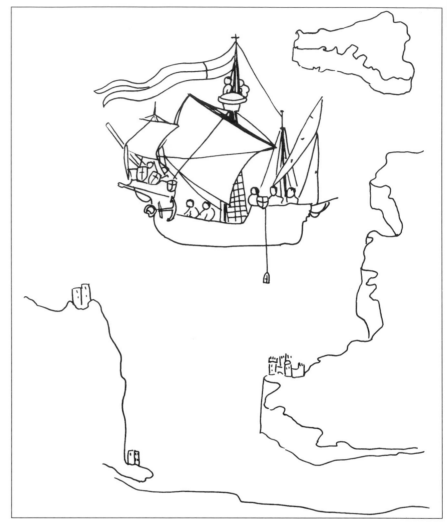

temporary illustrations suggest) in about 53 per cent of the cases, and there is nothing to suggest that any one nation had a monopoly of the type. The three-masted 'revolution' had had a great effect, but even 150 years or more after its introduction, it had not entirely supplanted other types, nor would it ever do so.

The appraisals offer few clues regarding the hull structures of the vessels, but it may be significant that only one of them was described as a 'clencher' (clinker-built) and this was a derelict, 'all rente in peeces and nothinge worthe', appraised in 1582. Armament was more common in those ships appraised after the outbreak of war between England and Spain in 1585 (only eighteen of the fifty-eight ships appraised between 1579 and 1585 had weapons) but one of these was a bark of a mere 16 tons which possessed a single breach-loader, three calivers, five old 'rustye rapyers' and seven pikes. Other private vessels were warships in all but name. The 120-ton *Galleon Fenner*, a Sussex ship

arrested in 1585 on suspicion of having been used 'pirateously', had fifteen cannon and thirteen smaller guns. This shows just how far the gunnery 'revolution' of the fifteenth century had affected shipping (incidentally, the *Galleon Fenner* carried a set of ten French flags, at a time when England and France were at peace, making it almost certainly a pirate ship). Guns were costly (in decayed ships they might be the most valuable items aboard) but they were also quite common.[7]

Pre-sixteenth-century English records give little information about how long ships lasted. Genoese carracks (see p. 173) seemed to be able to go no more than about five years before they needed major repairs or rebuilding. Indeed, it is often difficult to differentiate between a major repair and a rebuilding. For example, between July 1413 and 1422 over £530 was spent on the upkeep of the *Grand Marie*, a royal ship of about 140 tons. The vessel was finally beached at Itchen near Southampton in October 1422, because of its poor condition, so that it could be 'newly built and constructed'. The subsequent account describes the work as

10.3 Drawing of a small, three-masted ship of *c.* 1530 by the German artist Hans Holbein. Probably intended to convey the idea of a 'Ship of Fools', this Renaissance sketch has the human figures in about the right scale for the ship. Although many rigging elements have been omitted (see Howard 1987, p. 62), some other details, such as the standing rigging, anchor and topcastles, are very credible. Little ships of this type represented the 'normal' type of English and European merchantman for much of the sixteenth century.

the 'complete repair' of the ship. This cost £182, and required more than 140 loads of timber, so it must have been a major operation, closer to a 'rebuild' than a repair. The *Grand Marie* was in active use until at least the summer of 1420 but, in the absence of particular accounts for the royal ships between 1413 and 1420, it is impossible to determine the scale of repair work undertaken. Some ships are known to have stayed afloat for long periods (the great ship *Grace Dieu* of 1418 was afloat for some fifteen years before it finally had to be docked), but merely 'staying afloat' is not at all the same as a ship being used actively at sea.

The medieval data for the ages of ships, even for royal ships, are too thin and problematical to allow generalisations. By contrast, the HCA documents give fairly precise age estimates for thirty-seven of the ninety-seven vessels which received full appraisals. Most of the appraisers were shipwrights, mariners or master mariners, chosen for their specialist knowledge, though how exactly they arrived at these age estimates is impossible to say. In some cases, they may have known when a particular ship was built, although many of the judgments may have been 'by eye'. Of the thirty-seven precisely dated, only twelve were judged to be ten years old or less: twenty-two (59 per cent) were thought to be between eleven and twenty years old; and three were said to be even older, one vessel being said to be fifty years old! Given that a further twenty-eight vessels were described as 'old' or 'very old', it seems that a significant amount of the shipping stock, at least in the 1580s, was of some age. Conversely, the appraisals indicate that it was not at all uncommon for ships to last fifteen years or more. For a vessel active in trade, this would have meant that the original investment in building the ship would have been repaid many times over.[8] A ship's potential to bring wealth and prosperity, however, was only one part of the picture; for those non-European peoples who were contacted in the fifteenth and sixteenth centuries by the ocean-spanning three-masters, the 'good ship' was to bring anything but good.

Notes and references

ABBREVIATIONS

BL	British Library, London, Additional MSS
C1	Early Chancery Proceedings (PRO)
C54	Chancery, Close Rolls
C76	Chancery, Treaty Rolls (PRO)
CCR	*Calendar of Close Rolls* (PRO)
CIM	*Calendar of Inquisitions, Miscellaneous* (PRO)
CPR	*Calendar of Patent Rolls* (PRO)
E28	Exchequer, Treaty of Receipt, Council of Privy Seal (PRO)
E36	Exchequer Book (PRO)
E101	Exchequer, King's Remembrancer, Accounts Various (PRO)
E364	Exchequer, Lord Treasurer's Remembrancer, Foreign Accounts (PRO)
E372	Exchequer, Pipe Rolls (PRO)
E404	Exchequer, Warrants for Issue
EcHR	*Economic History Review*
EHR	*English Historical Review*
HCA	High Court of the Admiralty (PRO)
HCA24	High Court of the Admiralty, Libels and Answers (PRO)
IJNA	*International Journal of Nautical Archaeology*
MM	*Mariner's Mirror*
NMM	National Maritime Museum, Greenwich, MS PLA/18
PRO	Public Record Office, London
RBT	Rochester Bridge Trust Records
Rot. Norm.	*Rotuli Normanniae* (PRO)
SP1	State Papers, Henry VIII (PRO)
TRHS	*Transactions of the Royal Historical Society*

Most other publications referred to in the following notes are cited by author/editor and date only; full publication details are supplied in the bibliography.

1 EVIDENCE

1. *Calendar of State Papers, Milan, I, 1385–1618*, p. 184, C. Ross, *Edward IV*, London 1974, pp. 218–19; Anderson 1919.
2. Kemp 1979, p. 424.
3. For scholarly naval histories of the medieval period, see Clowes 1897 and de la Roncière, Vols I and II, Paris 1899 and 1914. Oppenheim published his *History of the Administration of the Royal Navy 1509–1660* in 1896.
4. Howard 1987, pp. 51–3.
5. See Chapter 4.
6. Chazelas 1977.
7. PRO E101/42/39, m. 12; E101/43/6, m. 10; and E101/43/7, m. 6; Reeves 1983, pp. 1–5; E364/54 D. m. 2.
8. Davies 1965; Loades 1992, pp. 74–102.
9. PRO E101/5/7, *passim*.
10. PRO E36/11, ff. 18v–19.
11. Friel 1983.
12. Friel 1994.
13. Ewe 1972.
14. Ewe 1972, pp. 173–6.
15. Unpublished study by the author in the collection of the National Maritime Museum; cf. Greenhill 1976, pp. 283–5.
16. Spencer 1980, p. 20.
17. McGrail 1974; L'Hour and Veyrat 1989; Rose 1982, p. 249.

2 SHIPS AND SHIPMEN

1. Greenhill 1976, pp. 129–54.
2. Bailey 1992, pp. 3, 15–18, 43, 59, 120 and 141.
3. Kowaleski 1992, pp. 69–70; Platt 1973, pp. 235, 256.
4. *Fifth Report of the Royal Commission on Historical Manuscripts*, London 1876, pp. 536–7; Finn 1911, pp. 27, 29–32; Margam: CCR 1231–1234, p. 360; Neath: CPR 1232–1247, p. 108. Ellen Lambard: CPR 1247–1258, p. 72; Scammell 1962, pp. 105–22; Crawford 1992, p. xxii.
5. Sweetman 1875, nos. 686 and 816.
6. PRO E364/43, *passim*.
7. PRO E364/54 D, m. 2r – F, m. 2v, *passim*, and E364/59, m. 2r.
8. Childs 1992, p. 85; E364/92, A, m. 1v – B, m. 1r.
9. Childs 1992, loc. cit.; Dunning and Tremlett 1971, pp. 49–50.

10. Dietz 1991.

11. Kowaleski 1992.

12. Taylor and Roskell 1975, pp. 20–21; Allmand 1992, p. 78 and n. 48.

13. 1327: group of ships, about to sail to Gascony for wine, arrested in English and Welsh ports but with most detail for ports north of the Thames and in Kent: *Calendar of Memoranda Rolls 1326–1327*, pp. 128–33). Notes of estimated losses of wine custom caused by the arrest suggest that another 6400–6500 tons of shipping, perhaps another 65 vessels, was not listed. We do not know the origins of most of the ships listed, although as they were arrested in English and Welsh ports, it is reasonable to assume that the majority of them were English or Welsh. In the mid-1320s, therefore, there may have been some 250 English ships engaged in carrying wine from Bordeaux. 1346: Edward III's major expedition to France for the siege of Calais and the Crecy campaign; the list of ships only survives in late and imperfect sixteenth- and seventeenth-century copies; Oppenheim 1968, p. 14. 1417: *Rot. Norm.* – mostly small ships, by no means the whole fleet – origins and the 99 foreign ships suggest bottom of seapower barrel was being scraped; other dates: see note 19.

14. Oppenheim 1896a, pp. 174–6.

15. National Maritime Museum 1988, pp. 152–3.

16. *OED*, s.v. Tun; Friel 1983, pp. 54–6; Platt 1973, p. 71; Oppenheim 1896b, pp. 124 and 132–3.

17. Burwash 1969, pp. 89–90.

18. Salisbury 1964; Burwash 1969, pp. 88–9.

19. 1327: *Calendar of Memoranda Rolls, 1326–1327*, pp. 128–33; April 1356 to March 1355: PRO E101/173/4; 1359 list payments of ships arrested for royal service in ports from Kings Lynn in Norfolk to Maldon in Essex: PRO E101/27/25 Total tonnage 5498: total crew = 1529 masters and mariners, and 143 pages = 1672. 107 of the vessels were in the 10–30 ton range; October 1372 to April 1373: PRO E101/179/10; October 1385 to June 1386: PRO E101/183/11; 1400–1412: references to ships and their tonnages, culled from *Calendar of Close Rolls* between 1400 and 1412; November 1409 to March 1410: PRO E101/19; October 1412 to February 1413: PRO E101/185/7; November 1435 to February 1436: PRO E101/192/1; September 1444 to January 1445: British Library Add. MS. 15524; 1450 expedition to Normandy and 1451 expedition to Gascony: PRO E364/92 A, M and N; 1512–14: English ships hired by the Crown as victuallers (supply-ships), Burwash 1969, p. 183.

20. Tinniswood 1949, p. 276; PRO E101/11/28, m. 2; Riley 1868, pp. 368 and 374.

21. PRO C54/217, m. 14v; CCR 1377–1381, pp. 32–3 and 43; Sandahl 1951, pp. 102–4 and n. 3.

22. Laughton 1923; Anderson 1934.

23. Anderson 1960; Mary Rose Trust 1986, pp. 14 and 18–19.

24. Burwash 1969, pp. 101–44; Crumlin Pedersen 1965 and 1979.

25. Beresford 1988, p. 496; Crumlin Pedersen 1972, pp. 187–8; Unger 1980, pp. 168–71.

26. Runyan 1974, p. 324.

3 BUILDING A SHIP

1. Lancashire 1984, nos 1194 (2) and 1560 (8).

2. McGrath 1985, pp. 3–6.

3. Ridge 1939, pp. i—iii, v, and Sharpe 1911, pp. 78, 143, 144; Farmer 1979, pp. 225, 357–8.

4. Warren 1966, p. 139; Ratcliffe: PRO E101/29/14 (1 m.) and Runyan 1974; Southampton and the River Hamble: PRO E364/61 G, m. 2v and E364/69 S, m. 2; Clos des Galées: Chazelas 1977; Venetian Arsenal: Lane 1934; Portsmouth dockyard; Oppenheim 1896a, pp. xxxiv–xxxix; Dietz 1991.

5. Sources for Fig. 3.2: Whitwell and Johnson 1926, pp. 162–83; Anderson 1928, pp. 222–3, 228; PRO E101/571/3; E101/5/21; Friel 1986; E36/5, ff. 179–88.

6. Taylor 1974, p. 397; for population data, see n. 62.

7. E36/5, ff. 179–88.

8. McDonnell 1978, pp. 99–100.

9. Carpenter-Turner 1954, p. 58.

10. Rose 1982, p. 237.

11. PRO E101/5/8, m. 1; Brown 1894, pp. 119–20; E101/7/25 (1 m.); E101/9/27; Rees Davies 1942, p. 24.

12. PRO E101/571/3, mm. 5–6.

13. PRO E101/53/5, ff. 10v–12v.

14. Whitwell and Johnson 1926, pp. 162–3; PRO E364/54 D, m. 2; *OED*, s.v. Berder.

15. Anderson 1928; PRO E101/5/21; E101/42/39; E101/43/6.

16. PRO E364/57 I, m. 2; *CCR 1399–1402*, p. 78.

17. Greenhill 1976; McGrail 1981.

18. Albion 1926.

19. Rackham 1976, pp. 99–100.

20. Rackham 1982, p. 213.

21. PRO E364/54 G, m. 2v.

22. Rose 1982, pp. 72–7.

23. PRO E101/571/3; E101/5/8; Whitwell and Johnson 1926; E101/11/28; E101/19/31; E36/11.

24. PRO E101/42/39, E101/43/6, E101/43/7, E101/44/9, E101/44/11, E101/44/12, E101/44/17, *passim*.

25. PRO E101/19/31, m. 2; E101/42/39, E101/43/6 and E101/43/7.

26. Cleere and Crossley 1985, pp. 88–90, 103–4; Childs 1981, pp. 25–47.

27. PRO E101/42/39, E101/43/6, E101/43/7 and E101/44/9, *passim*; Thrupp 1977, pp. 363–4.

28. Hindle 1982, pp. 13–16, 24–6 and Fig. 21; Platt 1973, pp. 159–62 and Fig. 9.

29. PRO E101/5/7, m. 1; E101/571/3, *passim*; E101/501/23, m. 1; Anderson 1928, pp. 229 and 231–2; E101/42/39, m. 5; E101/43/6, m. 5.

30. PRO E101/571/3, m. 3; E36/11, ff. 71–109, *passim*.

31. PRO E372/147, m. 2v; E101/5/21; E364/54 D, m. 2v.
32. PRO E101/44/17, m. 8; E364/59 F, m. 2 and G. m. 2; Mayhew 1987, p. 34; Oppenheim 1926, p. 271.
33. PRO E101/42/39, mm. 3–6; Becker 1930, p. 95; RBT Ac. no. 50, m. 2.
34. PRO E101/36/6, m. 6; Burwash 1969, pp. 143–4.
35. Anderson 1928, p. 225; E101/19/31, m. 1; Oppenheim 1896a, p. 324; Whitwell and Johnson 1926, p. 162.
36. Farr 1977, p. v; Hearnshaw 1905, p. 92 and Hearnshaw 1906, pp. 251, 411.
37. Carus-Wilson 1937, pp. 139–40.
38. PRO E101/501/21, m. 1; Anderson 1928, pp. 222–3; Whitwell and Johnson 1926, p. 163; E101/5/8, m. 2; E101/19/31, m. 1; E101/53/5, f. 9.
39. Runyan 1974, pp. 325–7; PRO E101/29/4 (1 m.); E101/38/13 (1 m.); E364/61 G, m. 2v; E364/69 S, m. 2.
40. Anderson 1928, p. 226; PRO E101/11/28, m. 3v.
41. PRO E101/5/7, m. 1; E101/571/3, m. 16; E101/5/21, m. 3; Whitwell and Johnson 1926, p. 233; E101/5/8, mm. 9–11; E101/19/31, m. 3.
42. PRO E101/20/27, m. 1v.
43. PRO E101/25/32, m. 2; E101/33/30 (1 m.).
44. PRO E101/43/6, E364/54, Rose 1982, pp. 72–7, E364/59, E364/57 and E364/61, passim.
45. Oppenheim 1896a, pp. xxxvii–ix, 143–59; PRO E36/11, f. 84.
46. Banbury 1971, p. 26.
47. PRO E101/5/8, mm. 2, 3, 5, 7, 9; Carpenter-Turner 1954, p. 64; E101/53/5, f. 8v; Goodman 1964, pp. 165–7; Calendar of Chancery Rolls (Various) 1277–1328, p. 251.
48. PRO E101/29/4 (1 m.); Salaman 1975, p. 89; Goodman 1964, pp. 29, 32; Chazelas 1977, p. 88.
49. Whitwell and Johnson 1926, pp. 162, 165, 167; PRO E101/5/8, mm. 3 and 9; E101/43/6, m. 4; Rose 1982, p. 72; Anderson 1928, p. 230; E101/42/39, m. 5; E101/571/3, m. 16; E364/61 L, m. 2v.
50. PRO E101/43/6, m. 1; E364/59 F, m. 2v; E101/53/5, f. 7v.
51. Whitwell and Johnson 1926, pp. 162–3; PRO E101/5/21, m. 2; E364/59 F, m. 2; Carpenter-Turner 1954, p. 62; Oppenheim 1896a, p. 175.
52. Whitwell and Johnson 1926, pp. 163, 181; PRO E101/43/6, m. 2; Oppenheim 1896a, p. 324.
53. Whitwell and Johnson 1926, pp. 174–5, 184–6; PRO E101/11/28; E101/19/31; E36/11, ff. 77–109.
54. PRO E101/5/8, m. 1; E36/11, ff. 77–109.
55. Greenhill 1976, pp. 241–4; PRO E101/5/21, m. 2; Anderson 1928, pp. 228, 230; Oppenheim 1896a, p. 313.
56. PRO E101/5/21, mm. 2–3v; E364/73 O, mm. 1–2.
57. PRO E101/19/31, m. 1; E101/25/32, m. 2; E101/29/4 (1 m.); E101/43/6, m. 7; E364/54 and E364/59, passim.
58. PRO E101/5/7, m. 1; E101/5/21, m. 3; Whitwell and Johnson 1926, pp. 173, 177; E101/42/39; E101/43/6.
59. PRO E101/25/32, m. 2; E364/59 G, m. 2; E101/44/11, roll 1, m. 8.
60. PRO E364/54 D, m. 2; Rule 1983, pp. 107–9.
61. PRO E101/19/31, m. 5; Whitwell and Johnson 1926, p. 180.
62. Dyer 1989, Fig. 1 and Chapter 8.
63. Unger 1980, pp. 37–42.
64. PRO E36/11, E36/5, passim.

4 Hulls and castles

1. Greenhill 1976, p. 27.
2. PRO E101/5/7, Anderson 1928, E101/571/3, E101/43/6, E101/25/32, E36/12, pp. 74–92. Mary Rose Trust 1986, p. 8.
3. For discussions of this, see Chapters 3 and 9.
4. Greenhill 1976, pp. 60–88.
5. Greenhill 1976, pp. 221–6 and Fig. 151; Anderson 1934; McKee 1972, p. 228; McGrail 1974 pp. 42–3; Sandahl 1951, pp. 33–113, passim; Goell 1970, p. 17.
6. Greenhill 1976, p. 74.
7. 14 lb ref.: Oppenheim 1896a, pp. 152, 228; McGrail 1993, pp. 45–8; costs: Friel 1990, p. 99; trenails in skeleton construction: Smith 1993, pp. 78–9.
8. Keels and oar numbers: Friel 1990, Tables 2.2 and 4.2.; Anderson 1976, p. 44.
9. Sandahl 1951, 1958 and 1982.
10. Sandahl 1951, pp. 40, 51, 56, 57, 60, 62, 80–1, 90–1, 97–8, 101, 130, 109–10; PRO E101/5/7, m. 1, Whitwell and Johnson 1926, pp. 162–3.
11. PRO E101/38/24, m. 2; Sandahl 1951, pp. 56–9, 114–15.
12. PRO E101/25/32, m. 5; E101/20/27, m. 1.
13. Sandahl 1951, pp. 173–84; for the use of canvas in caulking, see n. 12, and PRO E101/44/11, roll 1, mm. 7–9; OED, under 'pitch', 'turpentine' and 'tallow'; Zins 1972, pp. 8–10 and 24; McGrail 1993, p. 48.
14. Whitwell and Johnson 1926, pp. 179, 180, 181, 182, 189–93; Rose 1982, pp. 34–5; PRO E36/11, f. 108v.
15. Sandahl, pp. 190–3; Calendar of Documents Relating to Ireland, 1171–1251, pp. 71–2, 82, 84, 88–9; Crumlin Pedersen 1972, pp. 183–6; Cederlund 1980, pp. 80–1; Pryor 1988, p. 30; PRO E364/54 D, m. 2v.
16. PRO E101/6/22 (1 m.); E101/43/7, mm. 2–3; E101/20/29, m. 1; E101/20/27, m. 1v; E36/11, f. 109, 110.
17. Rule 1983, pp. 120–2; Anderson 1926, pp. 92–5.
18. The sample is based on images in: Ewe 1972, passim; National Museum of Wales 1982, p. 8; van Nerom-de Bue 1985; Bremen cog: Ellmers 1979.
19. Sandahl 1951, pp. 185, 195–6; Whitwell and Johnson 1926, pp. 177, 180, 182, 184; PRO E101/5/7, m. 1; Rule 1983, pp. 123, 125.
20. Rose 1982, pp. 214–16, 219–21, 259; Mallett 1967, pp. 256–60; Oppenheim 1896a, pp. 174–5.
21. Horrox 1983, pp. 99–100; Oppenheim 1896a, pp. 202, 272; Villain-Gandossi 1978; Sandahl 1951, pp. 116–31.
22. Tinniswood 1949, pp. 279; Anderson 1926, pp. 85–9; van der Merwe 1983, pp. 124–5; Sandahl 1951, pp. 128–9.

5 MOTIVE POWER

1. Modern distance for the London–Bordeaux route: Lloyd's 1981; Veale 1971, pp. 119–26; 1413–16 voyages: PRO E364/54; *Margaret Cely* voyage is in Veale 1971, p. 123.
2. Runyan 1974, p. 316; Sandahl 1951, p. 140; PRO E101/42/39, m. 7; E101/43/6, m. 6; E101/44/9, m. 3.
3. Salisbury 1961, pp. 85, 88, Figs 1, 2; Sandahl 1958, p. 102; PRO E364/59, G, m. 2.
4. PRO E364/69, S m. 2. Sandahl 1951, pp. 74–7, 1958, pp. 48–9, 129–30; E101/20/27, m. 1; E101/44/9, m. 5 and E101/44/11, roll 2, m. 2; Rose 1982, pp. 214–5.
5. PRO E372/147; E101/43/6, m. 4.
6. PRO E101/14/14 (1 m.); E101/19/31, mm. 4–6; E101/20/22 (1 m.); Prynne 1977 (see n. 6); E101/692/42; Howard 1987, p. 29.
7. Friel 1990, p. 164.
8. Oppenheim 1896a, p. 241; PRO E315/317, f. 12; Sandahl 1951, p. 91; Bramwell 1979, pp. 231, 254, 263, 264; PRO E122/40/21; E36/11, f. 10; Rose 1982, p. 212.
9. PRO E101/20/27, m. 1; E101/42/39, m. 2; E101/44/17, m. 7; Oppenheim 1896a, pp. 39–40.
10. Sandahl 1958, pp. 61–5, 84–6.
11. Ewe 1972, pp. 122, 139, 196, 210. Muckleroy 1980, p. 80.
12. Bunney 1985, p. 94; Latham 1965, s.v. *cannabus*; Godwin 1967, pp. 44–47; Hallam 1981, pp. 41, 136.
13. Crick 1908, pp. 344–6; PRO E101/25/37, mm. 1–3.
14. Rowe 1906, p. 385; Watkin 1935, pp. 31, 46, 55, 71; *OED*; PRO E364/54, *passim*.
15. Sandahl 1958, p. 66; PRO E101/29/4 (1 m.); *OED*, s. vv. 'Top', 'Whelp'; Kemp 1979, pp. 721–2.
16. Kemp 1979, pp. 125, 380, 721–2; Table: PRO E364/43, E101/44/11, E101/44/12, E364/54 and E364/59, *passim*.
17. PRO E364/54 and E364/59, *passim*; Oppenheim 1896b, pp. 123–5.
18. Warner 1926, pp. x, xxxviii; Platt 1973, pp. 157, 159; PRO E364/59 and E364/61, *passim*; Kerridge 1985, pp. 65, 123–4, 138; Oppenheim 1896b, pp. 98, 103, 182; Hewitt 1966, p. 70 and n. 6; PRO E101/31/7 (1 m.); E364/54 D, m. 2.
19. PRO E101/11/28, m. 3; E372/140, m. 19v; E101/42/39, mm. 3 and 6; E101/43/6, m. 6; E101/53/5, ff. 9r–v; Oppenheim 1896a, pp. 299, 324; E101/19/31, m. 5; *OED*, s.v. 'Pack-needle'.
20. Friel 1990, pp. 292–7.
21. Kemp 1979, pp. 93, 737–9; Lees 1984, pp. 134–45; Sandahl 1958, 20–4, 31–2, 115–17; PRO E101/31/7 (1 m.).
22. Sandahl 1958, pp. 28–9, 42–4, 51–2, 67–8, 72–3, 89–92, 104–6, 123–8; Sandahl 1982, pp. 115–16.
23. PRO E101/43/6, m. 3; E101/19/31, m. 5; Laughton 1929, p. 76; Anderson 1976, pp. 47–50; Zupko 1968, pp. 21, 53–4; *OED*, s.v. 'Bolt'; E364/59 G m. 1v.
24. PRO E364/59, G m. 2; E364/54 D, m. 1v and E364/59 F, m. 1v; E364/59 G, m. 1 and m. 2; E364/61 I, m. 2;

25. E101/31/7 (1 m.); E364/54. E364/59 and E364/61, *passim*.
26. Tabular information is from the following sources. *passim*: E372/147; Whitwell and Johnson 1926; E101/14/14; E101/19/31; E101/20/22; Sandahl 1958; E101/26/14; Runyan 1974; Riley 1868; E101/38/24; E101/42/39; E101/44/9; E101/43/7; E101/44/17; *CIM* Vol. 8; E364/54; E364/59; E364/61; E101/53/5; Oppenheim 1896a. Other information: Lees 1984, pp. 40–42; Howard 1987, pp. 31–3.
27. Sandahl 1982, pp. 19–131, *passim*.
28. Sandahl 1982, *passim*; Christensen 1979, p. 191; Neerso 1985, pp. 33–6; Lees 1984, pp. ix–xi.
29. Sandahl 1982, pp. 48–50, 123–5; Lees 1984, p. 64; Howard 1987, p. 34; PRO E364/54 F, m. 2–m. 1v; E364/61 *passim*; E364/59 *passim*; E101/44/9, m. 3.
30. Rose 1982, p. 215; PRO E364/61; Oppenheim 1896a, pp. 189, 255, 266.
31. Sandahl 1958, pp. 9–14, 71, 82, 87–88, 100–2, 117–23 and 1982, pp. 9–10; Rule 1983, pp. 18–19, 141, 143, 145; PRO E364/57 I, m. 2; Oppenheim 1896a, p. 268; E101/44/17, m. 9; Friel 1990, Table 6.16.
32. Sandahl 1982, pp. 16–17, 102–6, 128–31; Friel 1990, pp. 256–8 and pp. 268–9.
33. PRO E364/54 D, m. 2; E364/59 F, m. 1v and G, m. 2v.
34. PRO E101/19/31; Riley 1868, p. 368.
35. PRO E101/42/39, m. 7; E101/43/6, m. 4; Oppenheim 1896a, p. 247; Bramwell 1979, pp. 110–1, 158, 206; E36/13, ff. 58–9.
36. PRO E101/43/6, m. 4; E101/44/17, m. 11v; Oppenheim 1896a, pp. 36–7 and nn. 8, 9; Rule 1983, pp. 136–48.
37. Evans 1980 in Muckleroy 1980, pp. 68–74; Christensen 1972 in Bass 1972, pp. 162–7.
38. Brooks 1933, pp. 77–8.
39. Brooks 1933, p. 41; Latham 1965, s.v. *'galea'*; Pryor 1988, p. 76.
40. Riley 1868, pp. 368, 374; Whitwell and Johnson 1926, pp. 171, 177–8, 185; PRO E101/43/6, *passim*; E364/43 D, m. 2v – E m. 1; Anderson 1976, pp. 44–6.
41. PRO E364/59 F, m. 1 and G, m. 2.
42. PRO E364/43, *loc. cit.*; E364/54 F, m. 1; E101/11/28, m. 3.
43. Runyan 1974, p. 324; Sandahl 1975, p. 192; PRO E101/25/32, m. 4; E101/53/5, ff. 8v, 9.
44. Friel 1990, Table 4.2; Oppenheim 1896a, pp. 185, 246–7, 298, 322.
45. Anderson 1920, pp. 274–5 and Anderson 1976, pp. 61–7; PRO E36/11, f. 80v; Guilmartin 1974, p. 70.

6 LIFE, WORK AND EQUIPMENT ON BOARD

1. Burwash 1969, pp. 72–6; PRO 101/25/7, m. 1; Crawford 1992, I, p. 345; Rule 1983, pp. 196–7.
2. Christensen 1972, p. 166; PRO E372/147, m. 2v;

E101/5/7, m. 1; E372/140, m. 19v; Whitwell and Johnson 1926, p. 185.

3. Pryor 1988, pp. 75–86.
4. PRO E101/20/27, m. 1v; E101/25/13, m. 1; E101/44/9, mm. 3–6; Crawford 1992, p. 209; Oppenheim 1896a, pp. 230–31; E364/61; Rule 1983, pp. 107–9; Mary Rose Trust 1986, p. 20; Crumlin Pedersen 1979 (Kollerup and Vejby wrecks).
5. PRO C176/163, m. 6; E364/54, E364/59 and E364/61, *passim*; E101/44/17, m. 7; Oppenheim 1896a, pp. 67–74, 165–8, 195–6, 245–61.
6. Crawford 1992, II, pp. 3, 39; PRO E101/44/17, mm. 7 and 11v; Oppenheim 1896a, pp. 67–70, 258.
7. Crawford 1992, I, pp. 208, 410.
8. PRO E101/5/21, m. 3; Anderson 1928, p. 229; E101/20/27, m. 1; E372/140, m. 19v; E372/182, m. 39v; Whitwell and Johnson 1926, pp. 178, 179, 181, 182, 186; Latham 1965, s. vv. *'capitatio'*, *'truncus'* and *'wyndasius'*; Sandahl 1951, pp. 91–3; E364/43, m. 1v and *OED*, s.v. 'Winch'.
9. Howard 1987, pp. 15, 24, 113–14; *OED*, s.v. 'Capstan'.
10. PRO E101/44/17, m. 7; E364/59 F mm. 1v–2v and J m. 1v; E364/54 D, m. 2; E101/42/39, mm. 6 and 8; *OED*, s.v. 'Ferrule'; E101/44.9, m. 5; Oppenheim 1896a, pp. 37, 48, 55, 191–2, 259.
11. Kemp 1979, pp. 21–2, 120, 138, 358, 942; Howard 1987, pp. 21, 41.
12. PRO E101/5/7, m. 1; E101/5/21, m. 3; E372/147, m. 2v; E364/54 G, mm. 1 and 2; E364/59 I, m. 1.
13. PRO E101/20.20 (1 m.); E101/20/22 (1 m.); E101/19/31, m. 5; E364/59 G, m. 2.
14. PRO E364/86 G, mm. 1v–2; E364/57 I, m. 1v; E101/44/17, m. 2; E364/59 K, m. 2; Latham 1965, s.v. *'virga'* (for reasons explained in the text, Latham's explanation that *virga* = shank is disputed).
15. PRO E101/612/31, m. 2; E101/42/39, m. 6; E101/43/6, mm 6 and 7; E101/43/7, m. 2; E101/44/9, roll 1, m. 6; Oppenheim 1896a, p. 323.
16. PRO E101/19/31, m. 5; E364/61 I, m. 2; Oppenheim 1896a, pp. 184, 193, 245–6, 260, 262–4, 320–1, Kemp 1979, pp. 102, 442–3, 778, 924–5; *OED*, s.v. 'Kedge'.
17. PRO E364/54 D, m. 2; E364/61 I m. 1v and 2v, and L, m. 2v; *OED*, s.vv., 'Paint', 'Painter'.
18. Oppenheim 1896a, pp. 38, 49, 245–6; *OED*, s. vv. 'Cat', 'Fish'.
19. PRO E101/5/21, m. 3; Riley 1868; Rose 1982, pp. 191–2; E364/59 I, m. 2; Oppenheim 1896a, p. 50.
20. *OED*, s.vv. 'Bast', 'Junk'; PRO E364/61 H, m. 2v.
21. PRO E101/20/27, mm. 1–1v; *OED*, s.vv, 'Bail', 'Scoop'; E372/147, m. 2v; E101/5/7, m. 1; E101/5/21, m. 3; E101/5/8, m. 13; E101/176/3 (1 m.); E101/25/32, m. 4; E101/38/13 (1 m.); E101/38/24, m. 2; E364/54, G, m. 1.
22. PRO E101/20/27, mm. 1–1v; Manwaring and Perrin 1921, p. 171.
23. Oertling 1982.
24. PRO E101/19/31, m. 5; E372/147, m. 2v; Riley 1868;

E101/38/13 (1 m.); *CCR 1369–1374*, pp. 213–14 and E101/31/21.

25. Oertling 1982.
26. *OED*, s.vv. 'Pumpe', 'Vyrre'; Howard 1987, p. 25; PRO E101/44/11, roll 3, m. 2; E364/54, E364/57, E364/59 and E364/61, *passim*.
27. Oppenheim 1896a, p. 272; Rule 1983, p. 116.
28. Oppenheim 1896a, pp. 229, 259; Rose 1982, pp. 100, 186–7; PRO E36/12, p. 92.
29. Anderson 1926, p. 93.

7 SHIPS FOR TRADE

1. Bolton 1980, pp. 274–5, 287–319.
2. Bolton 1980, pp. 305–06; Burwash 1969, pl. v, p. 147.
3. *CPR 1266–1272*, pp. 177, 192, 308, 720.
4. PRO E101/158/10, E101/163/4, E101/174/4, E101/183/11 and E101/188/12; I owe this information to the kindness of Dr Wendy Childs; Bolton 1980, p. 290.
5. Blake 1967, pp. 11–13, 17–21; Burwash 1969, p. 140–1; *OED*, s.vv., 'Chalder', 'Chaldron', 'Keel'.
6. Bridbury 1955, pp. 16–21, 23–4, 26, 31–2, 38–46, 56–68, 76–84, 89–90, 110–38.
7. PRO E101/612/31, m. 1; *OED*, s.vv. 'Cortine', 'Curtain', 'Garner', 'Litter'.
8. PRO E101/585/15, mm. 4–6; for horses as cargo, see e.g., Gardiner 1976, no. 46a.
9. Pryor 1982 (horse transports); PRO E101/585/15, mm. 1–3 and 7–15; E101/575/9 (1 m.); E101/24/18 (1 m.); Hewitt 1966, p. 79.
10. Burwash 1969, pp. 123, 158; Childs 1992, pp. 82–4.

8 SHIPS FOR WAR

1. Sanderson 1975, pp. 7, 36, 59, 65, 71, 88, 103, 165, 170.
2. Richmond 1971, p. 103; Sherborne 1969.
3. Dobson 1970, pp. 126–7; Richmond 1971, pp. 98, 106; Platt 1973, pp. 107–18.
4. Gardiner 1976, nos. 45a–45d.
5. Corbett 1905, pp. 14–17.
6. Garmonsway 1975, p. 90; Warren 1966, pp. 137–42; Tinniswood 1949.
7. PRO E101/19/31; E101/44/17, m. 2; Sherborne 1977; *OED*, s.v. 'Balinger'; E364/54; E101/43/6; Rose 1982, pp. 42, 250; Burwash 1969, pp. 103–17; Richmond 1971, pp. 101–2, 109; Anderson 1974, pp. 5–8.
8. Friel 1990, pp. 129–34; Crumlin Pedersen 1972, pp. 190–1.
9. Chazelas 1977, II, pp. 33–54; Rose 1982, pp. 48–9; Taylor and Roskell 1975, pp. 160–7.
10. PRO E364/59 I, m. 1; Taylor and Roskell 1975, pp. 144–9; Rule 1983, pp. 168–83; Mary Rose Trust 1986, pp. 28–33.
11. Contamine 1984, pp. 138–41; PRO E101/20/27, *passim*.
12. PRO E364/54, E364/59 and E364/61, *passim*.

13. PRO C76/163, m. 6; Oppenheim 1896a, pp. 38–9, 50, 69, 73, 194–5, 261; Oppenheim 1896b, pp. 379–380; PRO E36/13, f. 60; *OED*, s.v. 'Miche' – quotes the origin of the word, but mistakenly then interprets it as a sighting-device for a gun; Laughton 1960, pp. 266–9, 272.

14. Jal 1840, s.v. 'Sabord'; Rule 1983, pp. 149–56; Laughton 1960, pp. 250–2; Laughton 1961; Anderson 1960; Howard 1987, pp. 48, 78–9, 82, 161–3; Smith 1993, pp. 71–3.

15. PRO State Papers, SP1/204, f. 154.

16. Martin 1988 and Lyon 1988.

9 INVENTIONS OR ACCIDENTS?

1. Gimpel 1976; Braudel 1979, p. 302.

2. Cipolla 1965.

3. Unger 1983, pp. 183–8; van der Merwe 1983; Pryor 1984.

4. Pryor 1988, pp. 25–44; van der Merwe 1983, pp. 124–6.

5. Rose 1982, p. 33; *CCR 1409–1413*, pp. 10–11, 35; PRO E101/44/17, m. 2.

6. Rose 1982, pp. 222–8, 251; Friel 1993.

7. PRO E364/57, E364/59 and E364/61, *passim*.

8. Cederlund 1980, p. 79; Sandahl 1958, pp. 30–1, 73–8.

9. Pryor 1988, pp. 31, 43; PRO E364/57 and E10, E364/61, *passim*; E101/53/5, f. 9 and E101/53/11, m. 1; Sandahl 1958, pp. 38–71; Friel 1990, p. 390, m. 9.

10. Bautier 1971, pp. 237–9.

11. Sanz 1977, p. 61.

12. Salisbury and Anderson 1958, p. 47.

13. Sandahl 1951, pp. 137–9; Hasslof *et al.* 1972, pp. 42–7; Greenhill 1976, pp. 65–6; Unger 1980, p. 37; McGrail 1981, pp. 30–3; Fenwick 1978; Anderson 1934; Pedersen 1979; Reinders 1979; Veen *et al.* 1980, pp. 47–50.

14. Unger 1980, pp. 37, 104–5; Morrison 1980, pp. 55–8; van Doorninck 1972; Bass and van Doorninck 1978.

15. Bonino 1978; Unger 1980, p. 129; Ruddock 1951, p. 19.

16. De la Roncière 1899, pp. 406–7 and n. 1.

17. PRO E101/31/21; Rose 1982, pp. 30, 33, 252 and n. 106; E101/44/12, document no. 5; *CCR 1409–1413*, pp. 10–11, 35; E101/44/17, mm. 2 and 9; Anderson 1976, p. 51; E364/54 F, m. 2v and G, m. 2v; *Nouveau Jal 1978*, s.v. 'Comiter'.

18. PRO E364/54 G, mm. 1v and 2v; *CPR 1408–1413*, p. 476; Sandahl 1958, p. 149; *Nouveau Jal 1978*,

pp. 359–60; Anderson 1925, pp. 138–9; Lane 1934, pp. 32–3.

19. Rose 1982, pp. 12, 20–55, 248, 268, n. 153; PRO E28/38; E364/59, *passim*.

20. PRO E364/59 and E364/61, *passim*.

21. PRO E364/59 and E364/61, *passim*; Rose 1982, pp. 214, 242; E364/59 G, m. 1v and H, m. 1v; E364/61 G, m. 2 and H, m. 2; *OED*, s.vv., 'Careen', 'Raft'; Kemp 1979, pp. 139–40.

22. Salisbury 1961; Rule 1983, pp. 22–3, 103–16; Anderson 1920.

23. Jal 1848, p. 417; Niermeyer 1976, s.v. 'Carabo'; Hussey 1967, p. 46; Unger 1980, p. 212; Smith 1993, pp. 34–46.

24. Unger 1973; van Beylen 1970, pp. 7–8; PRO C76/130, m. 7; Gardiner 1976, no. 60; *CPR 1441–1446, p.* 421; *CPR 1446–1452*, pp. 140, 188–90, 432; E364/92, M.

25. PRO C1/17/102a; C1/19/122 and C1/24/211; C1/28/472; C1/28/476; C1/30/60; *CPR 1452–1461*, pp. 17–8, 60–1, 212–13, 253, 254, 258, 281–2, 453–8; *CPR 1461–1467,̓* p. 559; Burwash 1969, p. 198; Crawford 1992, I, *passim*.

26. *Exchequer Rolls of Scotland 1437–1454*, pp. 384, 387, and *Exchequer Rolls of Scotland 1455–1460*, p. 3.

27. Crawford 1992, I, *passim*.

28. Sandahl 1951, pp. 136–7; Bernard 1968, II, pp. 841–4.

29. Scammell 1961, p. 332; Braudel 1986, I, pp. 300–1.

30. PRO SP1/204, f. 154; Oppenheim 1896b, p. 54.

10 AT THE EDGE OF THE OCEAN

1. Marcus 1980, pp. 63–78, 91–8.

2. National Maritime Museum 1988, pp. 151–84, 233–70.

3. Bernard 1968, vol. III, *passim*; Marcus 1980, pp. 39–43; Dietz 1991; Oppenheim 1896b, pp. 174–5.

4. Reddaway and Ruddock 1969, *passim*, National Maritime Museum 1988, p. 257.

5. Reddaway and Ruddock 1969, pp. 11–14; Andrews 1984, pp. 43–63; Marcus 1980, pp. 163–73; Williamson 1962, pp. 187–8, 206, 209, 213; Cell 1969, 3–4, 130, 132; Quinn 1974, pp. 127, 174–81.

6. Information from PRO HCA24/50 to HCA24/57, *passim*.

7. PRO HCA24/52, f. 62; Oppenheim 1896b, p. 54; Greenhill 1976, p. 292; HCA24/51, f. 96; HCA24/53, ff. 60–62.

8. PRO E364/54 D, m. 1v; E364/59, f, m. 1v; E364/61 H, m. 2; Rose 1982, pp. 72–7; Friel 1993, pp. 4, 10–11.

Brief glossary of nautical terms

Aft: the rearwards direction in a ship

Bilge: the lowest part of a hull interior

Bonaventure mast: fourth mast in a four-masted ship, set on the stern

Bow: front part of a vessel, the stem

Bowlines: ropes attached to the middle parts of both vertical edges or leeches of a square sail; when a ship is sailing to windward, one of the bowlines is pulled tight in order to keep the weather leech of the sail taut

Bowsprit: spar protruding from the bow of a vessel, used as an attachment point for the bowlines

Braces: ropes attached to the ends of a yard, and led aft; bracing the yard involves pulling a brace on one side of the ship taut, so that that end of the yard swings across to that side of the ship

Caulking: material used to fill and waterproof the seams between planks in a hull

Close-hauled: a ship is said to be sailing close-hauled when it is sailing as close as possible into the direction of the wind

Foremast: mast set in the fore part of a ship

Forward: in a nautical sense, the forwards or fore direction in a ship

Frames/framing: internal hull timbers, used to give shape and additional strength to the hull

Leech: vertical edge of a sail

Lifts: ropes attached to the ends of a yard, and used to help raise or lower it

Keel: the lowest and most important timber in a hull, the 'backbone' of a vessel; the frames and keelson are normally attached to the keel

Keelson: internal longitudinal strengthening timber, fixed to the top of the keel

Made mast: mast composed of several pieces of timber fitted together

Mainmast: the largest and most important mast in a ship

Mast: vertical timber carrying a yard and sail; masts are denoted by their position: thus even though a mainmast may have a main topmast and main topgallant mast set above it, the whole assemblage is known as the 'mainmast'

Mast step: point in a hull in which the lower end of a mast is set or 'stepped'

Mizzenmast: mast set behind the mainmast

Parral: rope and/or rope and wood device used to help hold a yard against a mast, and to allow it to move up and down

Pole mast: mast made from a single timber

Rig: general term for the masts and sails of a ship

Running rigging: rigging used to move and control the yards and sails

Sheets: ropes attached to the lower corners of a sail, and led aft

Spritsail: in the sense used in this book, a sail carried on the sprit yard, which was slung underneath the bowsprit

Square rig/square sail: rectangular or square-shaped sail, carried on a yard normally set at right-angles to the mast

Standing rigging: rigging used to support the mast

Stem: this can mean the fore part of a ship, in a general sense, or the foremost timber, the stempost

Stempost: see Stem

Stern: this can mean the rear part of a ship, in a general sense, or the rearmost timber, the sternpost

Sternpost: see stern

Tacks: ropes attached to the lower corners of a sail, and led forward

Tie/tye/uptie: rope or ropes attached to the centre of a yard and used to raise or lower it

Topmast: mast attached to the top of a larger lower mast (e.g., fore topmast)

Topgallant mast: mast attached to the top of a topmast (e.g., mizzen topgallant)

Uptie: see tie

Weather-leech: vertical edge of a sail closest to the wind direction when a ship is sailing to windward: 'weather' in this sense means 'to windward'

Yard: spar to which a sail is attached; qualified according to which mast, etc

Bibliography

Albion 1926. R. G. Albion, *Forests and Sea Power: The Timber Problem of the Royal Navy 1652–1863*, Cambridge, Mass.

Allmand 1992, C. Allmand, *Henry I*, London.

Anderson 1919, R. C. Anderson, 'The *Grace de Dieu* of 1446–86', *EHR*, 34, pp. 584–6.

——1920, 'Henry VIII's "Great Galley"', *MM*, 6, pp. 274–81.

——1925, 'Italian naval architecture about 1445', *MM*, 11, pp. 135–63.

——1928, 'English galleys in 1295', *MM*, 14, pp. 220–41.

——1934, 'The Bursledon Ship', *MM*, 20, pp. 158–70.

——1960, 'The Mary Gonson', *MM*, 46, pp. 199–204.

——1974, *List of English Men-of-War 1509–1645*, Greenwich.

——1976. *Oared Fighting Ships from Classical Times to the Coming of Steam*, Kings Langley.

Anderson 1926. R. and R. C. Anderson. *The Sailing Ship. Six Thousand Years of History*, London.

Andrews 1984. *Trade. Plunder and Settlement: Maritime Enterprise and the Genesis of the British Empire 1480–1630*, Cambridge.

Bailey 1992. M. Bailey (ed.), *The Bailiff's Minute Book of Dunwich 1402–1430*, Suffolk Records Society, 34, Ipswich.

Bautier 1971. R.-H. Bautier. *The Economic Development of Medieval Europe*, London.

Banbury 1971. P. Banbury. *Shipbuilders of the Thames and Medway*. Newton Abbot.

Bass 1972. G. Bass. *A History of Seafaring Based on Underwater Archaeology*, London.

Bass and van Doorninck 1978. G. Bass and F. van Doorninck. 'An 11th century shipwreck at Serçe Limani. Turkey'. *IJNA*, 7. pp. 119–32.

Becker 1930. M. J. Becker. *Rochester Bridge: A History of its Early Years*, London.

Beresford 1968. M. Beresford. *New Towns of the Middle Ages: Town Plantation in England, Wales and Gascony*, London.

Bernard 1968. J. Bernard. *Navires et gens de mer a Bordeaux. vers 1400–vers 1550*, 3 vols, Paris.

van Beylen 1970. J. van Beylen. *Schepen van de Nederlanden*, Amsterdam.

Blake 1967. J. B. Blake. 'The medieval coal trade of North East England: some fourteenth-century evidence'. *Northern History*, 2. pp. 1–26.

Bolton 1980. J. L. Bolton, *The Medieval English Economy 1150–1500*, London.

Bonino 1978. M. Bonino, 'Lateen-rigged medieval ships: New evidence from wrecks in the Po Delta (Italy) and notes on pictorial and other documents', *IJNA*, 7, pp. 9–28.

Bramwell 1979. M. Bramwell (ed.), *The International Book of Wood*, London.

Braudel 1979. F. Braudel, *Capitalism and Material Life 1400–1800*, London

——1986. F. Braudel, *The Mediterranean and the Mediterranean World in the Age of Philip II*, vol. 1, London.

Brereton 1978. G. Brereton (ed.), *Froissart: Chronicles*, London.

Bridbury 1955. A. R. Bridbury, *England and the Salt Trade in the Later Middle Ages*, Oxford.

Brooks 1933. F. W. Brooks, *The English Naval Forces 1199–1272*, London.

Brown 1894. W. Brown (ed.), *Yorkshire Lay Subsidy: Being a Ninth Collected in 25 Edward I (1297)*, Yorkshire, Archaeological Society Record Series, 16.

Bunney 1975. S. Bunney (ed.), *The Illustrated Book of Herbs: Their Medicinal and Culinary Uses*, London.

Burwash 1969. D. Burwash, *English Merchant Shipping 1460–1540*, Newton Abbot.

Calendar of Chancery Rolls, Various.

Calendar of Close Rolls (passim).

Calendar of Inquisitions Miscellaneous (passim).

Calendar of Memoranda Rolls, 1326–7.

Calendar of Patent Rolls (passim).

Carpenter-Turner 1954. W. G. Carpenter-Turner, 'The building of the *Gracedieu*, *Valentine* and *Falconer* at Southampton, 1416–20', *MM*, 40, pp. 55–72.

Carus-Wilson 1937. E. M. Carus-Wilson (ed.), *The Overseas Trade of Bristol in the later Middle Ages*, Bristol Record Society, 7, Bristol.

Cederlund 1980. C. O. Cederlund, 'Background to the Baltic', in Muckleroy 1980, pp. 78–81.

Cell 1969. G. T. Cell, *English Enterprise in Newfoundland 1577–1660*, Toronto and Buffalo.

Chazelas 1977. A. Merlin-Chazelas (ed.), *Documents relatifs au Clos du Galées de Rouen*, 2 vols, Paris.

Childs 1981. W. Childs, 'England's iron trade in the fifteenth century', *EcHR*, second series, 34, pp. 25–47.

——1992. 'Devon's overseas trade in the late Middle Ages', in Duffy *et al.*, pp. 79–89.

Christensen 1972. A. E. Christensen, 'Scandinavian ships from the earliest times to the Vikings', in Bass 1972, pp. 160–80.

——1979. 'Viking age rigging', in McGrail 1979, pp. 183–94.

Cipolla 1965. C. M. Cipolla, *Guns, Sails and Empires: Technological Innovation and the Early Phases of European Expansion*, New York.

Cleere and Crossley 1985. H. Cleere and D. Crossley, *The Iron Industry of the Weald*, Leicester.

Clowes 1897. W. Laird Clowes, *The Royal Navy: A History*, vol. 1, London.

Contamine. P. Contamine, *War in the Middle Ages*, Oxford.

Corbett 1905. J. S. Corbett (ed.), *Fighting Instructions 1530–1816*, Navy Records Society, 29, London.

Crawford 1992. A. Crawford (ed. and introduction), *The Household Books of John Howard, Duke of Norfolk, 1462–1471, 1481–1483*, Stroud.

Crumlin Pedersen 1967. O. Crumlin Pedersen, 'The Skuldelev Ships', *Acta Archaeologica*, 48, pp. 73–174.

——1965. 'Cog-Kogge-Kaag: Track af en frisisk skibstypes historie, *Handels og Sofartsmuseet pa Kronborg Arbog*, pp. 81–144 (English summary pp. 140–44).

——1972. 'The Vikings and the Hanseatic Merchants', in Bass 1972, pp. 181–204.

——1979. 'Danish cog finds' in McGrail 1979, pp. 17–34.

Davies 1965. C. S. L. Davies, 'The administration of the Royal Navy under Henry VIII: the origins of the Navy Board', *EHR*, 80, pp. 268–88.

Dobson 1970. R. B. Dobson, *The Peasants' Revolt of 1381*, London.

Duffy *et al.*, 1992. M. Duffy, S. Fisher, B. Greenhill, D.J. Starkey and J Youings (eds), *The New Maritime History of Devon*, London.

Dunning and Tremlett 1971. R. W. Dunning and T. D. Tremlett, *Bridgwater Borough Archives V. 1468–1485*, Somerset Record Society, 70, Frome.

Dyer 1989. C. Dyer, *Standards of Living in the Late Middle Ages: Social Change in England 1200–1520*, Cambridge.

Ellmers 1979. D. Ellmers, 'The Cog of Bremen and related boats', in McGrail 1979, pp. 1–16.

Evans 1980. 'Keels, sails and the coming of the Vikings', in Muckleroy 1980, pp. 72–7.

Ewe 1972. H. Ewe, *Schiffe auf Siegeln*, Berlin.

Exchequer Rolls of Scotland 1437–1454, Exchequer Rolls of Scotland 1455–60, Edinburgh.

Farmer 1979. D. H. Farmer (ed.), *The Oxford Dictionary of Saints*, Oxford.

Farr 1977. G. Farr, *Shipbuilding in the Port of Bristol*, National Maritime Museum Monographs, 27, Greenwich.

Fenwick 1978. V. Fenwick, *The Graveney Boat*, British Archaeological Reports, 53, National Maritime Museum Archaeological Series, 3, Oxford.

Finn 1911. A. Finn (ed.), *Records of Lydd*, Ashford.

Ford 1978. C. J. Ford, 'Piracy or policy: the crisis in the Channel 1400–1403', *TRHS*, fifth series, 29, pp. 63–77.

Fowler 1971. K. Fowler (ed.), *The Hundred Years War*, London.

——1980. *The Age of Plantagenet and Valois*, London.

Friel 1983. I. Friel, 'Documentary sources and the medieval ship: some aspects of the evidence', *IJNA*, 12, pp. 41–62.

——1986. 'The building of the Lyme galley, 1294–1296', *Proceedings of the Dorset Natural History and Archaeological Society*, 108, pp. 41–4.

——1990. *The Documentary Evidence for Maritime Technology in Later Medieval England and Wales*, Ph.D. diss., University of Keele.

——1993. 'Henry V's *Grace Dieu* and the wreck in the R. Hamble near Bursledon, Hampshire', *IJNA*, 22, pp. 3–19.

——1994. 'Spanish and English shipping in the Middle Ages', in C. M. Gerrard (ed.), *Spanish Medieval Ceramics*, Oxford.

Gardiner 1976. D. M. Gardiner (ed.), *A Calendar of Early Chancery Proceedings Relating to West Country Shipping*, Devon and Cornwall Record Society, 21, Torquay.

Garmonsway 1975. G. N. Garmonsway (ed.), *The Anglo-Saxon Chronicle*, London.

Gidden 1919. H. W. Gidden (ed.), *The Letters Patent of Southampton (1415–1612)*, Southampton Record Society, 2, Southampton.

Gimpel 1976. J. Gimpel, *The Medieval Machine*, London.

Godwin 1967. H. Godwin, 'The ancient cultivation of hemp', *Antiquity*, 41, pp. 44–7.

Goell 1970. K. Goell (ed.), *A Sea Grammar ... Written by Captain John Smith*, London.

Goodman 1964. W. L. Goodman, *The History of Woodworking Tools*, London.

Greenhill 1976. B. Greenhill, *Archaeology of the Boat*, London.

Guilmartin 1974. J. F. Guilmartin, *Gunpowder and Galleys: Changing Technology and Mediterranean Warfare at Sea in the Sixteenth Century*, Cambridge.

Hallam 1981. H. E. Hallam, *Rural England 1066–1348*, London.

Hasslof *et al.* 1972. O. Hasslof, H. Hennigen and A. E. Christensen (eds), *Ships and Shipyards, Sailors and Fishermen*, Copenhagen.

Hearnshaw 1905 and 1906. F. J. C. Hearnshaw and D. M. Hearnshaw (eds), *Southampton Court Leet Records*, Southampton Record Society, vol. 1, part 2, Southampton 1905 and vol. 1, part 2, Southampton 1906.

Hewitt 1966. H. J. Hewitt, *The Organisation of War under Edward III 1338–62*, Manchester.

Hickmore 1937. M. A. S. Hickmore, *The Shipbuilding Industry of the East and South Coasts of England in the Fifteenth Century*, M.A. diss., University of London.

Hindle 1982. B. P. Hindle, *Medieval Roads*, Princes Risborough.

Hollister 1975. C. W. Hollister, *The Military Organisation of Norman England*, Oxford.

Horrox 1983. R. Horrox (ed.), *Selected Rentals and Accounts of Medieval Hull 1293–1528*, Yorkshire Archaeological Record Series, vol. 141, Leeds.

Howard 1987. F. Howard, *Sailing Ships of War 1400–1860*, London.

Hussey 1967. J. M. Hussey (ed.), *The Byzantine Empire*, vol. 4, part 2 of *The Cambridge Medieval History*, Cambridge.

Jal 1848. A. Jal, *Glossaire nautique*, Paris.

Kemp 1979. P. Kemp, *The Oxford Companion to Ships and the Sea*, Oxford.

Kerridge 1985. E. Kerridge, *Textile Manufactures in Early Modern England*, Manchester.

Kowaleski 1992. M. Kowaleski, 'The port towns of fourteenth-century Devon', in Duffy *et al.* 1992, pp. 62–72.

Lancashire 1984. I. Lancashire, *Dramatic Texts and Records of Britain: A Chronological Topography to 1558*, Cambridge.

Landstrom 1976. B. Landstrom, *The Ship*, London.

Lane 1934. F. C. Lane, *Venetian Ships and Shipbuilders of the Renaissance*, Baltimore.

Latham 1965. R. E. Latham (ed.), *Revised Medieval Latin Word-List*, London.

Laughton 1923. L. G. Carr Laughton, 'The Bayonne ship', *MM*, 9, pp. 83 ff.

——1929. 'La Phelipe', *MM*, 15, p. 76.

——1960. 'Early Tudor ship-guns', *MM*, 46, pp. 242–85.

——1961. 'The square tuck and the gun deck', *MM*, 47, pp. 100–5.

Lees 1984. J. Lees, *The Masting and Rigging of English Ships of War 1625–1860*, second edition, London.

L'Hour and Veyrat 1989. M. L'Hour and E. Veyrat, 'A mid-15th century clinker boat off the north coast of France: the Aber Wrac'h I wreck: a preliminary report', *IJNA*, 18, pp. 285–98.

Lloyd's 1981. *Lloyd's Maritime Atlas*, London.

Loades 1992. D. Loades, *The Tudor Navy: An Administrative, Political and Military History*, Aldershot.

Lyon 1988. D. Lyon, 'English guns and gunnery', in National Maritime Museum 1988, pp. 175–6.

McDonnell 1978. K. G. T. McDonnell, *Medieval London Suburbs*, London and Chichester.

McGowan 1981. A. McGowan, *Tiller and Whipstaff: The Development of the Sailing Ship 1400–1700*, London.

McGrail 1974. S. McGrail, *The Building and Trials of the Replica of an Ancient Boat: The Gokstad Faering*, National Maritime Museum Monograph, 11, 2 parts.

——1979. (ed.), *Medieval Ships and Harbours of Northern Europe*, British Archaeological Reports, International Series, 66, National Maritime Museum Archaeological Series, 5, Oxford.

——1981. *Rafts, Boats and Ships from Prehistoric Times to the Medieval Era*, London.

——1982 (ed.). *Woodworking Techniques before A.D. 1500*, British Archaeological Reports, International Series, 129, National Maritime Museum Archaeological Series, 5, Oxford.

——1993. 'The future of the designated wreck site in the R. Hamble', *IJNA*, 22, pp. 45–51.

McGrath 1985. P. McGrath (ed.), *A Bristol Miscellany*, Bristol Records Society, 37, Gloucester.

McKee 1976. E. McKee, *Clenched Lap or Clinker*, London.

Mallett 1967. M. E. Mallett, *The Florentine Galleys in the Fifteenth Century*, London.

Manwaring and Perrin 1921. G. E. Manwaring and W. G. Perrin (eds), *The Life and Works of Sir Henry Mainwaring*, vol. 2, Navy Records Society, 56, London.

Marcus 1980. G. J. Marcus, *The Conquest of the North Atlantic*, Woodbridge.

Marsden 1979. P. R. V. Marsden, 'The medieval ships of London', in McGrail 1979, pp. 83–92.

Martin 1988. C. Martin, 'Armada guns and gunnery', in National Maritime Museum 1988, pp. 173–5.

Mary Rose Trust 1986. *Guide*, Portsmouth.

Mayhew 1987. G. Mayhew, *Tudor Rye*, Falmer.

Merwe, van der 1983. P. van der Merwe, 'Towards a three-masted ship', *International Congress of Maritime Museums 4th Conference Proceedings 1981*, Paris, pp. 121–9.

Mollat 1977. M. Mollat, 'Constructions navales à Dieppe au XVe siècle', in his *Etudes d'histoire maritime (1938–75)*, Turin, pp. 417–27.

Morrison 1980. J. Morrison, *Longships and Roundships: Warfare and Trade in the Mediterranean 300 BC to 500 AD*, London.

Muckleroy 1980. K. Muckleroy, *Archaeology under Water: An Atlas of the World's Submerged Sites*, London.

Nance 1955. R. M. Nance, 'The ship of the Renaissance', *MM*, 41, pp. 180–92, 281–95.

National Maritime Museum 1988. National Maritime Museum, *Armada 1588–1988*, London.

National Museum of Wales 1982. National Museum of Wales, *Welsh History through Seals*, Cardiff.

Neerso 1985. *A Viking Ship: Roar Ege: A reconstruction of a Trading Vessel from the Viking Age*, Denmark.

Nerom -de Bue, van 1985. C. van Nerom-de Bue, 'Deuxième sceau de Richard Coeur de Lion et sceaux inédits des Cinque Ports dans les archives de l'Abbaye des Dunes', *Citeaux*, 3–4, pp. 204–10 and Figs 3–7.

Nicolas 1847. N. H. Nicolas, *History of the Royal Navy*, 2 vols, London.

Niermeyer 1976. J. F. Niermeyer (ed.), *Mediae Latinitatis Lexicon Minus*, Leiden.

Nouveau Jal 1978. *Nouveau Glossaire Nautique d'Augustin Jal*, Paris.

Oertling 1982. T. J. Oertling, 'The chain pump: an 18th-century example', *IJNA*, 11, pp. 113–24.

Oppenheim 1896a. M. M. Oppenheim (ed.), *Naval accounts and Inventories of the Reign of Henry VII 1485–98 and 1495–7*, Navy Records Society, 8, London.

——1896b. *A History of the Administration of the Royal Navy 1509–1660*, London.

——1926. 'The maritime history of Kent', in Page 1926, pp. 243–88.

Page 1908. W. Page (ed.), *Victoria History of Dorset*, London.

——1926. *Victoria History of Kent*, vol. 2, London.

Platt 1973. C. Platt, *Medieval Southampton: The Port and Trading Community*, A.D. 1000–1600, London and Boston.

Prynne 1977. M. W. Prynne, 'The dimensions of the *Grace Dieu* (1418)', *MM*, 63, pp. 6–7.

Pryor 1982. J. H. Pryor, 'The transportation of horses by sea during the era of the Crusades: eighth century to 1285 A.D.', *MM*, 68, pp. 9–27, 103–25.

——1984. 'The naval architecture of Crusader transport ships: a reconstruction of some archetypes for round-hulled sailing ships', *MM*, 70, pp. 171–219, 275–92, 363–86.

——1988. *Geography, Technology and War: Studies in the Maritime History of the Mediterranean 649–1571*, Cambridge.

Quinn 1974. D. B. Quinn, *England and the Discovery of America 1481–1620*, London.

Rackham 1976. O. Rackham, *Trees and Woodland in the British Landscape*, London.

——1982. 'The growing and transport of timber and underwood', in McGrail 1982.

Reddaway and Ruddock 1969. T. F. Reddaway and A. A. Ruddock (eds), 'The accounts of John Balsall, purser of the *Trinity* of Bristol, 1480–1', *Camden Miscellany*, 23, pp. 1–27.

Rees Davies 1942. H. Rees Davies, *A Review of the Records of the Conway and Menai Ferries*, Board of Celtic Studies, University of Wales, History and Law Series, 8, Cardiff.

Reeves 1983. A. C. Reeves, *Purveyors and Purveyance*, Notre Dame, Indiana.

Reinders 1979. R. Reinders, 'Medieval ships: recent finds in the Netherlands', in McGrail 1979, pp. 35–44.

Reinders *et al.* 1980. R. Reinders, H. van Veen, K. Vlierman and P. B. Swiers, *Drie Schepen ut de Late Middeleeuen*, Flevobreicht, 166, Lelystad.

Richmond 1971. C. F. Richmond, 'The war at sea', in Fowler 1971, pp. 96–121.

Ridge 1939. C. H. Ridge, *1428–1780*, vol. 1 of *Records of the Worshipful Company of Shipwrights*, London.

Riley 1868. H. T. Riley (ed.), *Memorials of London and London Life in the XIIIth, XIVth and XVth*, Rolls series, London.

Roncière, de la 1899. C. de la Roncière, *Histoire de la marine francaise*, vol. 1, Paris.

Rose 1977. S. P. Rose, 'Henry V's *Gracedieu* and mutiny at sea: some new evidence', *MM*, 63, pp. 3–6.

——1982 (ed.). *The Navy of the Lancastrian Kings, Accounts and Inventories of William Soper, Keeper of the King's Ships 1422–1427*, Navy Records Society, 123, London.

Row 1906. J. B. Rowe, *A History of the Borough of Plympton Erle*, Exeter.

Ruddock 1951. A. A. Ruddock, *Italian Merchants and Shipping in Southampton 1290–1600*, Southampton Record Series, Southampton.

Rotuli Normanniae, ed. T.D. Hardy, London 1835.

Rule 1983. M. Rule, *The Mary Rose: The Excavation and Raising of Henry VIII's Flagship*, London.

Runyan 1974. T. J. Runyan, 'A fourteenth century cordage account', *MM*, 60, pp. 311–28.

Salaman 1975. R. A. Salaman, *Dictionary of Tools Used in the Woodworking Trades*, London.

Salisbury 1961. W. Salisbury, 'The Woolwich ship', *MM*, 47, pp. 81–90.

——1964. 'Early tonnage measurement in England', *MM*, 50, pp. 41–9.

Salisbury and Anderson 1958. W. Salisbury and R. C. Anderson (eds), *A Treatise on Shipbuilding and a Treatise on Rigging Written about 1620–1625*, London.

Salzman 1952. L. F. Salzman, *Building in England to 1540*, Cambridge.

Sandahl 1951, 1958 and 1982. B. Sandahl, *Middle English Sea Terms*, 3 vols, Uppsala.

——1975. 'Notes on Runyan 1974', *MM*, 61, pp. 192–3.

Sanderson 1974. M. Sanderson, *Sea Battles: A Reference Guide*, Newton Abbot.

Sanz 1977. A. Garcia Sanz, *Historia de la marina catalana*, Barcelona.

Scammell 1961. G. V. Scammell, 'English merchant shipping at the end of the Middle Ages: some east coast evidence', *EcHR*, second series, 13, pp. 327–41.

——1962. 'Shipowning in England, c. 1450–1550', *TRHS*, fifth series, 12, pp. 105–22.

Sharpe 1911. R. R. Sharpe (ed.), *Calendar of Letter-books of the City of London*, London.

Sherborne 1969. J. W. Sherborne, 'The Battle of La Rochelle and the war at sea', *Bulletin of the Institute of Historical Research*, 42.

——1977. 'English barges and balingers of the later fourteenth century', *MM*, 63, pp. 109–14.

Sleeswyk 1990. A. W. Sleeswyk, 'The engraver Willem à Cruce and the development of the chain-wale', *MM*, 76, pp. 345–61.

Smith 1993. R. C. Smith, *Vanguard of Empire: Ships of Exploration in the Age of Columbus*, New York.

Spencer 1980. B. Spencer, *Medieval Pilgrim Badges from Norwich*, Norwich.

Sweetman 1875. H. S. Sweetman (ed.), *Calendar of Documents Relating to Ireland 1170–1251*, London.

Taylor 1974. A.J. Taylor, *The King's Works in Wales 1277–1330*, London.

Taylor and Roskell 1975. F. Taylor and J. S. Roskell (eds), *Gesta Henrici Quinti/The Deeds of Henry V*, Oxford.

Thrupp 1977. S. Thrupp, *The Merchant Class of Medieval London 1300–1500*, Ann Arbor, Michigan.

Tinniswood 1949. J. T. Tinniswood, 'English galleys 1272–1377', *MM*, 35, pp. 276–315.

Unger 1973. R. W. Unger, 'Dutch ship design in the fifteenth and sixteenth centuries', *Viator*, 4, pp. 387–411.

——1980. *The Ship in the Medieval Economy 600–1600*, London and Montreal.

Veale 1971. E. M. Veale, (ed.), *Studies in the Medieval Wine Trade*, Oxford (studies by M. K. James).

Villain-Gandossi 1978. C. Villain-Gandossi, 'Terminologie de l'appareil de gouverne (IXe–XVIIIe siècles)', *Archaeonautica*, 2, pp. 281–310.

Warner 1926. G. Warner (ed.), *The Libelle of Englyshe Polycye*, Oxford.

Warren 1966. W. L. Warren, *King John*, London.

——1977. *Henry II*, London.

Watkin 1935. H. R. Watkin, *Pre-Reformation*, vol. 1 of *Dartmouth*, Devonshire Association Parochial Histories of Devonshire, 5.

Whitwell and Johnson 1926. R. Whitewell and C. Johnson, 'The Newcastle Galley', *Archaeologia Aeliana*, fourth series, 2, pp. 142–96.

Williamson 1962. J. A. Williamson (ed.), *The Cabot Voyages and Bristol Discovery under Henry VII*, Hakluyt Society, second series, 120, Cambridge.

Woodruff 1895. C. E. Woodruff, *A History of the Town and Port of Fordwich*, Canterbury.

Zins 1972. H. Zins, *England and the Baltic in the Elizabethan Era*, Manchester.

Zupko 1968. R. E. Zupko, *A Dictionary of English Weights and Measures from Anglo-Saxon Times to the Nineteenth Century*, Madison, Milwaukee and London.

Illustration Acknowledgements

The author and publishers would like to thank the following for their kind permission to publish illustrations.

Abbreviations:

BM By courtesy of the Trustees of the British Museum
BL By permission of the British Library
NMM © National Maritime Museum, Greenwich
IF Photograph by the author
LF Drawing by Lynne Friel

Front jacket: Reproduction by permission of the Syndics of the Fitzwilliam Museum, Cambridge. MS Marley Add. I, f. 86.
Back jacket: BL MS Cotton Julius EIV, art VI, f. 25

1.1 LF after Warren 1977, fig. 21 i.
1.2 LF after Ewe 1972.
1.3 Dyfed Museum Service.
1.4 King's Lynn Museum.
1.5 Musée de Cluny, Paris, inv. CL 14335. Photo © Reunion des musées nationaux.
1.6 IF.
1.7 Deutsches Shiffahrtsmuseum, Bremerhaven, Photo: E. Laska/DSM.
1.8 Mary Rose Trust.
2.1 BL MS Roy 2B VII, f. 73.
2.2 IF.
2.3 NMM.
2.4 Corpus Christi College, Oxford. Photo: John Gibbons.
2.5 NMM.
2.6 NMM.
3.1 IF.
3.2 LF.
3.3 Stedelijke Musea te Gouda, inv. 55.106.
3.4 LF.
3.5 LF.
3.6 LF.
3.7 LF.
3.8 LF.
3.9 IF.
3.10 LF.
3.11 St John's College Library, Cambridge, MS. 231.
3.12 BL MS Add. 18850, f. 15v.
3.13 BL MS Roy 15D, f. 12.
3.14 LF after BL Roy 15 EIV, f. 57v.
3.15 © National Gallery of Art, Washington. From Samuel Kress Collection. Detail of *The Martyrdom of Saint Catherine*, possibly by Matthys Cock.
4.1 LF after Haslof.
4.2 LF.
4.3 LF after Ewe 1972, p. 74.
4.4 LF after Ewe 1972, p. 85.
4.5 Ashmolean Museum, Oxford, inv. PA 1310.
5.1 LF after Howard 1987, p. 19.
5.2 LF after Salisbury 1961.
5.3 BL MS Add. 47682, f. 24.
5.4 Bodleian Library, Oxford. MS Auct. D. 4.17, f. 2v detail.
5.5 LF.
5.6 LF.
5.7 LF.
5.8 LF after Ewe 1972, p. 90.
5.9 BL MS Add. 10290, f. 77v.
5.10 Victoria and Albert Museum.
5.11 LF.
6.1 Deutsches Schiffahrtsmuseum. Photo: E. Laska.
6.2 BL MS Roy 2B VII (Queen Mary's Psalter), f. 6v.
6.3 LF.
7.1 LF.
7.2 BL MS Cotton Tib. AVII, f. 81.
7.3 BL MS Roy. 16GI, f. 9.
7.4 Bodleian Library, Oxford. MS Bodley 401, f. 55v.
8.1 Reproduction by permission of the Syndics of the Fitzwilliam Museum, Cambridge. MS Marley Add. I, f. 86.
8.2 BL MS Cotton Julius EIV, art. VI, f. 18v.
8.3 BL MS Roy 10 EIV, f. 19.
8.4 © cliché Bibliothèque Nationale, Paris. MS Fr 2643, f. 393.
8.5 BL MS Add 10290, f. 118.
8.6 Christchurch College, Oxford, MS 92, f. 70v.
8.7 BL MS Cotton Julius EIV, art VI, f. 25.
9.1 LF.
9.2 Victoria and Albert Museum, W. 16-1921.
9.3 Bench end in Hotel Jacques, Bourges. Caisse nationale des monuments historiques et des sites. Longchampt Delehaye/© C.N.M.H.S./S.P.A.D.E.M.
9.4 LF after Liebgott 1973.
9.5 Bibliothèque Nationale, Paris. MS Lat 5565A, f. 101.
9.6 Archives Générales du Royaume et Archives de L'Etat dans les Provinces, Brussels. From *Inventaire des Cartes et Plans, Manuscrits et Graves, qui sont Conservés aux Archives Generaux du Royaume*, Brussels 1848, p. 46, no. 351.
9.7 NMM.
9.8 Alte Pinakothek, Munich, WAF 452.
9.9 Collections artistiques de L'Université de Liège. Inv. 10.414.
10.1 LF.
10.2 LF. After Marcus 1980, p. 138.
10.3 Städelsches Kunstinstitut Frankfurt am Main. Photo Ursula Edelmann.

Appendix: Tables

Table 1: Small merchant fleets, 1450–51:

Owner	No. of Ships	Tonnages
John Clerk, Dartmouth	3	200/100/400
Jenyn Troivuse, Plymouth [sic]	3	160/200
Robert Aylward, Southampton	2	100/110
Henry, Duke of Exeter	2	75/220

Source: see p. 189, Ch. 2, note 8.

Table 2: Ships in fleets and other groups

Date	No. of Ships	Total tons	Average Tonnage
1327	206	20,434	99.7
1346	c. 690	n/a	n/a
1359	151	5498	36.4
1385–6	153	14,365.5	93.9
1409–10	173	11,378.5	65.8
1417	118	n/a	n/a
1448–9	124	12,991	104.8
1450	100	10,032	100.3
1451	61*	8873	145.5
1512–14	113	6586	58.3

* two tonnages not listed. Sources: see p. 190, Ch. 2, note 13 and Table 3.

Table 3: Tonnage ranges, English ships 1327–1451

Date	Total tons	<50	Tons 50–99	100–199	200–299	300+
1327	206	13	87	101	5	
	100%	6%	42.2%	49%	2.4%	–
1355–6*	90	12	43	35	–	–
	100%	13.3%	47.8%	38.9%		
1359	151	115	19	16	1	–
	100%	76.2%	12.6%	10.6%	0.6%	
1372–3*	99	19	49	30	1	
	100%	19.2%	49.5%	30.3%	1%	–
1385–6*	153	30	56	61	6	–
	100%	19.6%	36.6%	39.9%	3.9%	
1400–12	75	32	27	13	3	–
	100%	42.7%	36%	17.3%	4%	
1409–10*	173	62	87	24		
	100%	35.8%	50.3%	13.9%	–	–
1412–13*	137	57	54	26	–	–
	100%	41.6%	39.4%	19%		
1435–6*	131	41	46	36	8	–
	100%	31.3%	35.1%	27.5%	6.1%	
1444–5*	110	29	35	38	7	1
	100%	26.4%	31.8%	34.5%	6.4%	0.9%
1448–9*	124	34	40	32	15	1
	100%	27.4%	32.3%	25.8%	12.1%	0.8%
1450	98#	22	40	23	15	1
	100%	22.4%	40.8%	23.5%	15.3%	1%
1451	61	1	21	21	12	6
	100%	1.6%	34.4%	34.4%	19.6%	9.8%
1512–14	113	49	51	12	1	–
	100%	43.4%	45.1%	10.6%	0.9%	

Sources: see p. 190, Ch. 2, note 19.
* Bordeaux customs accounts, figures based on cargoes actually laded
# Two tonnages not listed

Table 4: Average percentage costs of some ship-building materials and wages, 1295–1514

Item	1295–1348 %	1400–1514 %
Materials		
Site costs*	1.44	0.86
Timber	14.08	5.58
Boards	15.49	11.51
Iron nails	7.39	14.04
Waterproofing materials	4.44	4.24
Rig	12.01	14.17
Wages		
Shipwrights' wages	23.33	36.99
Totals		
Total materials (1)	65.48	55.63
Total wages (2)	35.52	44.36

* buildings, fences, tools etc.
(1) miscellaneous ironwork, gear and items listed above
(2) all workers, including shipwrights

Table 6: Mast sizes

Date	Ship	Tons/oars	Mast length: ft (m)
1307–8	*Marie*, barge	48 oars	72 ft (22 m)
1337	*Philippe*, galley	80 oars	75 ft+ (22.9 m+)
1337–38	Winchelsea galley	?	84 ft? (25.6 m?)
c. 1418	*Grace Dieu*, great ship	1400 tons	190 ft? (57.9 m?)
1466	John Howard's spynas	?	24 ft+ (7.3 m+)
c. 1512	*Regent*, ship	1000 tons	specified: Mainmast: 114 ft (34.8 m) Mizzenmast: 93 ft (28.4 m) actual: Mainmast: 107.25 ft (32.7 m) Mizzenmast: 105 ft (32.0 m)

Sources: see p. 192, Ch. 5, note 6

Table 5: The sequence of shell construction, Southampton 1295

Time	Named parts of hull structure
Before construction	Keel, stems, 323 boards
Week 1	–
'' 2	–
'' 3	*Kivillis*
'' 4	72 boards
'' 5	*Wrangnayles* (trenails for the floor-timbers), 100 boards
'' 6	–
'' 7	100 boards, 500 nuhud (?)
'' 8	Boards
'' 9	17 *wrangis* (floor-timbers), 2 beams
'' 10	Futtocks, 1 koron (?)
'' 11	Spiking nails, wrang-nails, small boards
'' 12	6 elm beams, spars and boards for making *hachis* (decks) and hurdis (breastworks), making of *porte-loff* (tacking-boom for sail), wrang-nails
'' 13	Rudder, 2 skegs, floor-timbers, futtocks and halse-knees, nails ?for decks, large nails for *rivesinges* (frame elements?), making of the *coule*, small planks to make decks, 50 small planks, windlass and windlass stocks
'' 14	2 rivesinges, 1 sawn beam, 6 barrels to fasten the breastworks, 6 fenders, 4 knees and futtocks, 1 futtock, 1 halse-knee, floor timbers and *fotinges* (?)
'' 15	–
'' 16	Barrels and planks for decks and breastworks, 50 planks, nails for the castle(s), hasps and staples for the breastworks, mast, yard and sail, spikes for the castle, hinges and spikes for the castle
'' 17	Davit(?), iron *kyvill*, small timbers for the 3 castles, 2 posts for the great castle, 50 small boards for the castle and its breastworks, second rudder, 60 oars, 2 anchors, digging of launching-ditch

Note: seam-nails (clench-nails) made from week 2 to week 7
Source: Anderson 1928.

Table 7: Weight ranges of cordage, 1399–1420

Weight in cwts*	Numbers of items		
	Rope	Hawser	Cable
0–1	243 (75.5%)	24 (14.1%)	2 (1.8%)
2–5	79 (24.5%)	123 (72.4%)	62 (55.9%)
6–10		13 (7.6%)	43 (38.7%)
11–20		10 (5.9%)	2 (1.8%)
21–41			2 (1.8%)
Totals	322 (100.0%)	170 (100.0%)	111 (100.0%)

1 cwt = 112 lb = 50.9 kg
Sources: see p. 192, Ch. 5, note 16

Table 8

Dates	No. of inventories	Forestays listed			
		Single	Double	Triple	Quad.
1295–1378	19	4	3	6	2
1400–1436	52	40	4	3	–
1485–1495	11	10	–	–	–

Source: see p. 192, Ch. 5, note 25

Table 9

Tonnage range	No. of tons per couple of headropes:	Number of examples
0–49	6.3	6
50–99	14.0	3
100–99	17.9	10
200–99	23.9	4
300–499	36.5	4
500–1000	56.5	6

Source: see p. 192, Ch. 5, note 25

Table 10: Actual and proportional rigging weights (in pounds) of the galley *Philippe* and its barge, 1337, and the balinger *Nicholas*, 1417–20

	Philippe	Barge	*Nicholas*
Forestay	420	—	388
	= 1.00		= 1.00
Headropes	1680	224	1166
	4.00	= 1.00	3.01
Backstays	280	28	469
	1.50	8.00	1.21
Upties	560	42	676*
	0.75	5.33	1.74
Stetings	210	—	188†
	2.00		0.48
Yardropes	112	14	96
	3.75	16.00	0.25
Trusses	280	—	—
	1.50		

* another rope bought for this purpose weighed 1150 lb (2.96)
† another rope bought for this purpose weighed 1150 lb (2.96)
170 lb (0.45)
Sources: see p. 192, Ch. 5, note 26

Table 11: Guns on large royal ships, 1485–1514

Ship and date	Tons	Guns (exc. handguns)	Chambers
1485			
Mary of the Tower	?	48	110
Martin Garsia	?	30	86
Governor	?	70	265
1497			
Sovereign	600	141	419
Regent	1000	181	453
1514			
Henri Grâce à Dieu	1000	184	313
Mary Rose	600	78	200

Sources: see p. 194, Ch. 8, note 13

Index

English and Welsh counties cited are pre-1974. Page numbers in *italics* denote illustrations.